HEROES of HORTICULTURE

HEROES *of* HORTICULTURE

Americans Who Transformed the Landscape

Barbara Paul Robinson

DAVID R. GODINE · PUBLISHER
BOSTON

First published in 2018 by
DAVID R. GODINE · *Publisher*
Post Office Box 450
Jaffrey, New Hampshire 03452
www.godine.com

A CIP CATALOGUE RECORD FOR THIS BOOK
IS AVAILABLE FROM THE LIBRARY OF CONGRESS

ISBN 978-1-56792-614-9

LCCN 2017040111

FIRST EDITION
Printed in China

ADDITIONAL PHOTOGRAPHS

P. 1, The Cherry Esplanade at the Brooklyn Botanic Garden;
P. 2, The Pigeonnier at Les Quatre Vents; P. 6 Ruth Bancroft Garden; P. 11, Gardens at Hooverness; P. 51, Bethesda
Fountain in Central Park; P. 83, Longwood Gardens Main
Fountain Garden in summer; P. 155, Plant Delights Nursery border featuring color; shape and contrast; P. 229,
White tulips and myosotis in the parterre at Hollister
House; P. 258, The front entrance to Hooverness.

PHOTOGRAPH CREDITS

P. 1, by Rebecca Bullene, courtesy of Brooklyn Botanic
Garden; PP. 2, 11, 35, 40, 112, 128, 155, 156, 162, 165,
167, 168, 258, by the author; PP. 6, 12, 19, 22–25, 30,
33, 37, 38, 44, 49, courtesy of the Garden Conservancy;
PP. 16, 26, courtesy of Stonecrop Gardens; P. 27, by
Marina Schinz, courtesy of The Garden Conservancy;
PP. 51, 52, 55, 60, 62, 63, 66, by Sara Cedar Miller,
courtesy of The Central Park Conservancy; PP. 72, 73,
courtesy of The New York Botanical Garden; PP. 77, 81,
courtesy of Lynden Miller; P. 79, by Howard Korn; P. 83,
courtesy of Longwood Gardens; PP. 84, 87, by Robert
Bensen, courtesy of New York Botanical Garden; PP. 90,
91, 100, 103, courtesy of New York Botanical Garden;
PP. 106, 109, by Antonio Rosario, courtesy of Brooklyn
Botanic Garden; P. 111 by Alga Doubravova, courtesy of
Brooklyn Botanic Garden; PP. 116, 117, 122, 123, 126,
129, courtesy of Wave Hill; PP. 134, 135, 139, by Jessica
Norman, courtesy of Stephen Byrns and Untermyer Gardens; P. 140, courtesy of Stephen Byrns and Untermyer
Gardens; P. 142, courtesy of Dick Lighty; PP. 145, 146,
147, 150, 151, courtesy of Longwood Gardens; P. 153,
courtesy of Mt. Cuba Center; PP. 154, 155, courtesy of
Tony Avent and Plant Delights Nursery; P. 161, by
Andrew Bunting; PP. 171, 174, 175, 178, 179, 181, courtesy of Pierre Bennerup and Sunny Border Nurseries;
P. 182, by Darrell Probst; P. 185, by Karen Perkins, courtesy of Darrell Probst; P. 187, courtesy of Darrell Probst;
P. 190, by John Casertano, courtesy of Darrell Probst;
PP. 195, 198, 200, 201, 202, courtesy of Andrew Bunting; PP. 204, 207, 211, 214, 216, courtesy of Tony
Avent and Plant Delights Nursery; PP. 218, 220, 221,
225, 227, 228, courtesy of Barry Yinger; PP. 229, 230,
233, 234, 238, 239, 241, 242, 243, courtesy of George
Schoellkopf; PP. 244, 249, 253, 255, 256, courtesy of
John Fairey.

Contents

Introduction

A HERO IS DEFINED as someone noted for great or brave acts, for nobility of character, a person whose special abilities, achievements, and personal qualities serve as a role model or ideal. The eighteen people profiled in this book are my own pantheon of heroes of horticulture – all Americans who have had a major impact on the landscape around us. I hope you will find their stories as inspiring as I do. I have had the great privilege and pleasure of getting to know and admire each of them, to consider them friends. I would like to share with you a sense of their vibrant personalities and tell you how they have enriched all our lives, whether you garden or not. Here are institution builders, plant explorers, and garden creators. While each chapter profiles an individual hero, their stories connect in countless ways; they have worked together and helped and encouraged each other. Concurring in the view that gardens are a form of art, I was not surprised to find art to be a recurring theme in many of their lives. These stories also include other horticultural heroes, as success often depends upon the support of others. In turn, these eighteen have mentored their juniors, promoted and encouraged new talent and fresh work.

Although I have divided the chapters into sections, these multifaceted people defy labels – they operate in many different spheres – so most of these heroes do not fit neatly into any single category. Nevertheless, I have grouped them according to the part of each story I most want to emphasize. The sections are: The Garden Conservancy; Public Parks and Public Spaces; Public Garden Institutions; Plantsmen, Plant Finders, Nurserymen; and Garden Creators.

Frank Cabot's idea to create the Garden Conservancy to preserve exceptional American gardens was a brilliant and innovative concept. But like many great ideas, it might never have come to fruition. Thanks to Frank Cabot's fortunate move to enlist Antonia Adezio and Tom Armstrong to the cause, this trio built a vibrant national organization.

The Garden Conservancy has helped preserve many exceptional

American gardens, including the two described in the last chapters, George Shoellkopf's Hollister House in Washington, Connecticut, just two miles down the road from my own gardens at Brush Hill, and John Fairey's Peckerwood Garden in Hempstead, Texas. Almost everyone profiled in this book has also been a garden creator, but these two will endure as public gardens in the future.

Others have restored and revived vital public parks and spaces. Betsy Barlow Rogers deserves her well-earned credit for saving Central Park from devastation when others shunned it. In her work, Betsy asked Lynden Miller to pitch in to revive the Conservatory Garden at the park's northeast end, opening Lynden's path to working in many other public parks and public spaces, where she set new standards for aesthetics and wider public use.

Botanical gardens and other major public garden institutions are centers of scientific research and education, as well as ornamental display gardens. The New York Botanical Garden, located in the Bronx, one of the poorest urban counties in the country, was an historic treasure but in the 1970s had fallen on hard times. Gregory Long came to the rescue more than twenty-five years ago. Under his impressive leadership, NYBG rebuilt its infrastructure, restored its scientific reputation in the United States and abroad while enhancing and expanding its gardens, improving education, and increasing visitation. Coming from South Africa, it was not to be predicted that Betty Scholtz would become President of the Brooklyn Botanic Garden, a smaller but now vibrant institution thanks to her and her successors.

Other public gardens are more recent and much smaller institutions but have outsized impact. The three described here all began as private estates that transitioned to public institutions. Marco Polo Stufano, as the first head of horticulture at Wave Hill in Riverdale, New York, was a pioneer in creating gardens that have become a showcase for exciting and artistic planting combinations. In turn, he has been an important advisor to Stephen Byrns who fell in love with the ruin of Untermyer Gardens, in Yonkers, New York, once one of the greatest gardens in the country. Stephen is now devoting his talents full time to Untermyer's resurrection. Dick Lighty, scientist, plant finder, builder of institutions, educator, and more, became the first director of the Mt. Cuba Center on the outskirts of Wilmington, Delaware, featuring native plants and the protection of habitats that sustain them.

Then there are the intrepid adventurers, those plant explorers who endure unspeakable conditions in impossible terrains to find and bring back plants to enhance American gardens. Each cares passionately about the hunt for new plants and for insuring their broad dissemination to the public. Most have also established nurseries (some large, others boutiques, all personal, but sadly many no longer in operation) offering special plants not otherwise available. Dan Hinkley opened Heronswood Nursery in Kingston, Washington. His catalog was a treasure of amazing plants written in his uniquely witty style. When Heronswood eventually closed, there were gardeners in mourning across the land. Dan continues to write and set out on plant-finding expeditions, often accompanied by others profiled in this book.

Pierre Bennerup inherited a small nursery, Sunny Border, that he built into a wholesale business and a major force for the greater use of perennials at a time when most homeowners restricted themselves to lawns and foundation shrubs. Darrell Probst, a protégé of Dick Lighty, focused intensely on a single genus, *Epimedium*, while traveling to find and bring back plants unknown to the West. Now he is breeding and patenting *Coreopsis* in colors once thought impossible.

Andrew Bunting spent most of his professional life as curator at the Scott Arboretum, of Swarthmore College; he is now assistant director and director of plant collections at the Chicago Botanic Garden, where his new and exciting challenge is to develop a ten-year plant-finding plan to work in collaboration with other public institutions. Tony Avent established Plant Delights Nursery, in Raleigh, North Carolina with its hilariously funny catalog as the go-to place for the most garden-worthy plants. Tony uses revenue from his nursery to support Juniper Level Botanic Garden, which he established on the same site, but he plans to close the nursery as soon as Juniper Level becomes self-sustaining. Barry Yinger's nursery, Asiatica, has also sadly gone the way of too many specialty nurseries, although he now has a nursery in Thailand. His fluency in several Asian languages gave Barry special access on his many plant-finding trips to places otherwise closed to outsiders, enabling him to bring back plant treasures.

Plants and garden ideas from all of these heroes of horticulture continue to grace my own gardens. Every time I rejoice in these signs of their presence, I renew my admiration and affection for those who have been the source of such pleasure and beauty in my life. And in the lives of all who garden, admire gardens, or appreciate the landscape – we all benefit from their passion and their work.

BARBARA PAUL ROBINSON
January 2018

THE GARDEN CONSERVANCY

Frank Cabot

Men build stately before they build finely. Anyone can build a house,
but to create a great garden is a lifetime of work.

LENDER AND TALL, graceful and elegant, Frank Cabot was in every respect the quintessential patrician gentleman, even when caught in what came to be his happiest and signature pose: on his knees, trowel in hand, working in his garden. In all, he created three extraordinary gardens in three different countries, but his greatest legacy was the creation of the Garden Conservancy. Thanks to his vision, the Garden Conservancy preserves exceptional American gardens while encouraging the public to create their own. Frank had a grand vision and was blessed with the intelligence and financial resources to bring it to life. And his enthusiasm was boundless. Thomas Jefferson wrote: "No occupation is so delightful to me as the culture of the earth, and no culture comparable to that of the garden . . . But though an old man, I am but a young gardener." Frank personified that view. It was classic Frank to buy land and begin a third garden late in his life on the southern tip of New Zealand. He planted a two-kilometer-long allée of young sequoias knowing he would not live long enough to see them grow to maturity but nevertheless planning for them to be eventually thinned sixty feet apart. He was sure that someday "they should be reassuringly visible from outer space."

His first garden at Stonecrop in Cold Spring, New York, sixty miles north of New York City along the Hudson River, is now a public garden. It is one of many exceptional gardens preserved and open to the public thanks to Frank and the Garden Conservancy. The creation of his second garden at La Malbaie, Canada, which I consider the Taj Mahal of gardens, is described in his book, *The Greater Perfection: The Story of the Gardens at Les Quatre Vents.* Les Quatre Vents is truly a modern masterpiece on a grand scale.

Water feature at Les Quatre Vents

Frank did not start out in life with an interest in gardening. To the contrary, he followed a predictable path. Born on August 6, 1925, to Francis Higginson Cabot and Currie D. Matthews Cabot in New York City, he belonged to the famous Boston Cabot clan. As the well-known poem goes:

> *This is good old Boston,*
> *The home of the bean and the cod,*
> *Where the Lowells talk to the Cabots*
> *And the Cabots talk only to God.*

Gardening was a wild card that didn't fit neatly into the deck Frank had been dealt, but it managed to creep up on him and eventually defined his life. His full name was Francis Higginson Cabot although he was always later known as Frank Cabot – or at his most formal Francis H. Cabot. He attended the elite private day school at St. Bernard's in New York City, then went on to boarding school at Groton in Massachusetts, and finally to Boston and Harvard. But first World War II intervened, and Frank served in the Army Signal Corps, which took him to Japan as part of the occupying forces as the war ended.

At Harvard after the war, Frank's sense of humor and fun, along with his social credentials, brought him into the selective ranks of the Hasty Pudding Club, which claims to be the oldest social club in the United States. Former U.S. presidents along with countless others of distinguished ancestry and later achievements have been members. The Pudding, as it is known, produces theatrical performances known for clever wit and satire. Frank was also a founder of an a cappella group called the Krokodiloes, a name that strongly suggests that he was the one who invented it. It is definitely his kind of humor. The Krokodiloes continue to be part of the Hasty Pudding Club, now called the Hasty Pudding Institute of 1770; the group of twelve men sing a cappella and are always handsomely tuxedo-clad.

After graduating from Harvard in 1949, Frank made the smartest move of his life – he married Anne Perkins. The young newlyweds returned to Frank's New York City roots when he joined his father's investment firm of Stone & Webster. While there his path crossed with the young Thomas Armstrong's. That early friendship would unite the two again many years later for the birth of the Garden Conservancy.

Frank was a success in the financial world, first at Stone & Webster, and then as a partner in the firm of Train, Cabot & Associates, but the work didn't speak to his heart. He described himself as being "a good promoter. But I was a good promoter of ventures that didn't always work out. So I threw myself into gardening."

He and Anne lived in Manhattan and began raising their young family of three children there, and as many New Yorkers still do, began spending their weekends and holidays with their children in the countryside north of the city, just outside the town of Cold Spring along the Hudson River on property that belonged to Anne's family. After they had stayed for some years in Anne's parents' house, Anne's grandmother, Evelina Ball Perkins, gave them forty acres out of the family's three-thousand-acre property called Glynwood Farm. Frank and Anne built a French-style house in 1957 on a bare hilltop, and their first improvement was planting some trees to shade the house.

True to character, Frank didn't begin with an easy challenge. He was excited about growing alpines, those finicky rock garden plants that appeal to the most dedicated and serious cognoscenti of the horticultural world. As Frank observed, "Who knows why a certain type of plant turns out to have such irresistible appeal to an individual. In my case alpine plants were the hook that dragged me from a normal existence into a lifelong involvement with, and attachment to, plants."

Alpines require very precise growing conditions that mimic their native haunts in high elevations above the tree line. Tiny treasures, they often produce outsized blooms but only when provided their demanding requirements, usually raised beds and perfect drainage. It was actually Anne who first started gardening, growing a few alpines during a brief stint in Boston before they returned to New York. As they began developing their garden around their new country house, Frank turned to the New York Botanical Garden for information and help. There he met the famous Miss Elizabeth Hall, the librarian who introduced Frank to the newly formed American Rock Garden Society.

Frank was soon an active member of the American Rock Garden Society, eventually becoming its Treasurer. When the Society celebrated its fiftieth anniversary in 1984, Frank composed a song called "The ARGS Hymn – (or the Alpine Gardeners Lament)." Perhaps harking back to his days on the Krokodiloes at Harvard, he sang its witty refrain with great gusto:

> *Does your horticultural life fail to sustain you?...*
> *Have you tried gardening with alpine plants?*
> *For they are so full of romance.*
> *They are sessile and sweet,*
> *they're procumbent and neat.*
> *And conveniently located down by your feet.*
> *And their blossoms are visions of beauty –*
> *lighting up all the screes and moraines.*
> *Give them grit, give them rain,*

give them snow, make sure they drain.
Why wait? Propagate – alpine plants!

And he added his wry motto – "Alpine plantsmen never die, they de-compose."

Frank began concentrating on alpines, growing many small rarities in stone troughs and building stone walls to feature them. Appropriately, he finally named the property Stonecrop, for the low growing, rock garden plants of the genus *Sedum*. But like any devoted gardener, his garden kept getting bigger, expanding from the small scale of his collection of rock garden plants to something much grander in scope. The gardens at Stonecrop kept growing, first to herbaceous borders planted around the house, then farther out to an extensive woodland walk and beyond. An ambitious series of large artificial cascading pools and waterfalls was created around carefully installed large rock outcroppings. Of course, each new project required more plants, so he built greenhouses in addition to the first sunken one that featured his alpines, allowing him even more growing space and the chance to propagate other plants for his ever-larger garden.

Because it was difficult to find the alpine plants Frank coveted, he turned to English nurseries to import them. With so few specialty nurseries available in America, in 1960 he started his own small nursery to propagate and sell alpines. The nursery carried on for six years, and during this time Frank also began traveling to remote parts of the world on plant exploration trips, often under challenging and difficult conditions. His interest in alpines took him to the mountains of Asia with like-minded souls seeking to collect seeds from species not otherwise known in the West.

By 1973, Frank had become such a force in horticultural circles that he was elected chairman of the board of the New York Botanical Garden and he served a three-year term. When he stepped down as chairman in 1976, he was ready to retire from Train, Cabot and turn to his gardening full time.

He also helped found the Friends of Horticulture at Wave Hill, the exciting public garden that was developing in Riverdale, New York. Wave Hill had belonged to Anne's family; the Perkins gave the estate to the City of New York in 1960. Like many other New York City cultural institutions, the property is owned by the city but managed by its own independent governing board that raises funds from private sources. Situated on twenty-eight acres, Wave Hill overlooks the Hudson River with stunning views across the river to the magnificent Palisades escarpment on the west. Anne's father, George Perkins, was the founding chairman of the Interstate Parks Commission, which worked with the Rockefellers to help preserve the Palisades. The property came with two major houses and an existing greenhouse that wasn't in very good shape. While there were some beautiful trees, the gardens were eventually added with the encouragement and advice of Frank's Friends of Horticulture and the brilliant work of Marco Polo Stufano, its first head of horticulture.

While Stonecrop increasingly demanded his time and attention, Frank also had responsibility for extensive land holdings that belonged to his family in the Charlevoix region of Quebec Province, Canada. The property was near the town of La Malbaie, located on the north banks of the Saint Lawrence River, a two-hour drive east of the city of Quebec. His great-grandfather, George T. Bonner, had purchased the Seigneurie de Mont-Murray in 1902, primarily to pursue salmon fishing. He gave his former house, Mount Murray Manor, to his daughter Maud, who married Francis Higginson Cabot, Frank's grandfather. Frank's grandmother's summer home and the land holdings cover several square miles of land – plenty of room for Frank's growing garden ambitions.

Although he took over the management of the property in the 1960s, it wasn't until 1970 that Frank began to seriously develop the garden there that eventually became known as Les Quatre Vents ("the Four Winds"). Here Frank had the opportunity to work on a truly heroic scale, designing extensive formal herbaceous borders, small lakes, cascading water features, winding woodland walks, and astonishing garden structures. It was a work in progress for more than twenty-five years, and he never really stopped improving it.

His book, *The Greater Perfection: The Story of the Gardens at Les Quatre Vents,* describes it all in wonderful detail enhanced by exquisite photographs. He took the title from a quote he admired from Francis Bacon:

> *God Almighty first planted a garden. And indeed it is the purest of human pleasures. It is the greatest refreshment to the spirits of man; without which buildings and palaces are but gross handiworks; and a man shall ever see that when ages grow to civility and elegancy, men come to build stately sooner than to garden finely; as if gardening were the greater perfection.*

Frank loved taking visitors through the gardens at Les Quatre Vents, but he insisted on his own special sequence of proceeding. When I stayed there one weekend with my friend Penelope Bardel, Frank insisted that we remain indoors in our bedroom with no peeking allowed until he was ready to collect us and lead us through the gardens. We were like kids on Christmas morning, confined to our room, not allowed to go downstairs to see what Santa had brought until the grown-ups (in this case Frank) allowed us.

Frank's goal was to enchant and delight us by following the sequence of paths and leading us through one enclosed garden area after another, each revelation carefully staged to provide maximum astonishment. Familiar with the famous quote of Alexander Pope to "consult the genius of the place," Frank respected the natural landscape but, like a director staging a play, he had his own script for revealing the plot with the appropriate crescendos and drama.

He admitted, "Whenever possible I choose to prolong the suspense." To quote Pope in that same poem, Frank believed that he should

> *Let not each beauty ev'ry where be spied,*
> *Where half the skill is decently to hide.*
> *He gains all points who pleasingly confounds*
> *Surprises, varies, and conceals the bounds.*

Surprise, vary, and conceal he certainly did. He took us out to hedge-enclosed areas to experience formal rooms with rich herbaceous borders, each on different levels with a major water cascade descending between the hedges to a charming small lake graced by the perfect red Chinese bridge, built ingeniously and deliberately with a railing on only one side, which created the perfect picture in a small space but made the walk over the bridge quite scary. In a more distant part of the woodland, a more substantial Chinese moon bridge was kinder.

Then on to a wilder part of the garden where a strong stream ran through a ravine, creating a gap that had to be crossed by way of an Asian rope bridge, a heart-stopping experience. Compared to the precarious rope bridges of Nepal, Frank thought his "new bridge looked like a piece of cake" when he first ventured to cross it. But he recalled "by the time I was halfway across, however, I was convinced that I had made a terrible mistake. The bridge swung in *three* directions at once – at least two more than I'd bargained for. It not only swayed from side to side but the floorboards undulated along the axis of the bridge as well as wobbling alarmingly. It was terrifying." Frank loved it. He thought that in "the best romantic tradition, terror might as well be included in the range of emotions to be evoked by a journey through the elements in the garden."

By the time we arrived to cross the bridge, Frank had long since

Les Quatre Vents
Above: The Rope Bridge
Above right: The Chinese Bridge
Right: The Chinese Moon Bridge

mastered the technique and the terror. He seemed to skip across the bridge and then turned back to watch us struggle to follow. I know he relished watching the panic in my eyes as I shakily tottered across, each step causing the flimsy rope bridge to shake, threatening to tip me over the side into the abyss. Frank said that a garden is "all about the senses. You are surprised and amused, and even scared at one point. All your emotions should be involved and after two or three hours you should come up and embrace me." *Embrace* wasn't the sentiment I was feeling as I finally stepped off that bridge.

Below and farther along the ravine, after an impressive waterfall that fell over huge boulders from heights above to the stream below (all artificially created by a superb stonemason Frank kept busily employed), we came to a Japanese teahouse in an enclosed Japanese garden of stone, gravel, and appropriate plantings. The teahouse had been built by hand (in the classic style, cutting and drying the wood for the construction and installing the paper screens) in the authentic way by a master craftsman and took seven years to complete.

A tall sculpted arch interrupted the long row of hedges to frame the view across wide meadows to the magnificent mountains beyond. Precisely at the hour for cocktails each night a huge, shaggy Highland bull would appear in the meadow perfectly framed by the arch. Leaving nothing to chance, Frank had trained this beast with treats given exactly at the right time each day to give his guests a thrill – a characteristic Frank Cabot touch.

And then at last to the iconic three-story Pigeonnier that is pictured on the cover of his book, a replica of a French dovecote. Like the Taj Mahal, it is reflected in a long, narrow rectangular pool. Although the architecture reflects the local country French vernacular, the design was clearly influenced by the Pin Mill at the famous gardens of Bodnant, in Wales. Frank was not insulted when anyone suggested he "copied" ideas: "Plagiarism is the lifeblood and principal impetus in the creation of gardens. There is no more agreeable challenge than adapting someone else's good idea to one's own surroundings. When I'm told that others are doing just that with ideas they have gleaned from Les Quatre Vents, considering myself a lifelong practitioner, I am indeed sincerely flattered."

Visible on the other side of the Pigeonnier, through the arch of its foundation, is a small lake populated by picturesque white swans. To gain entry, Frank told me I would have to guess the magic word that opened the door. I had earlier experienced walking through a hedged enclosure only to see a large group of life-sized bronze frog figures burst into operatic song while in another enclosure a different frog assemblage played loud jazz, so a magic password to open the door to the Pigeonnier seemed entirely appropriate. After several false starts, I finally got it. "Open sesame," I said, and the door flew open!

Inside was his secret sanctum. Beautifully hand-painted murals adorned the walls. There was a tiny boudoir on the top floor, its curtained bed looking out at views across the valley to the mountains beyond. As we departed, I could see public visitors had begun to arrive and gather below, so I whispered the secret words to open the door to depart so no one outside could hear and learn the secret of entering this magical place. But the door remained firmly shut. Frank kept encouraging me to speak louder and louder. Frustrated, I finally shouted, "Open sesame!" and the door flew open, allowing us to get out. When I recounted this saga at lunch, I noted Anne had an amused expression on her face. Then Frank, with a sly smile, pulled the electric door opener out of his pocket! Gullible me!

As his reputation became increasingly well known in horticultural circles across the country, Frank was invited to visit wonderful private as well as public gardens wherever he went. On one trip to California in the late 1980s, he and Anne went to visit Ruth Bancroft to see her highly original dry garden in Walnut Creek on the outskirts of San Francisco. Her plant compositions struck a chord with Frank. Here were plants such as agaves and cactus not common in the moist climate of northern California, and normally seen only in desert conditions. There was a memorable variety of plants, all presented in wonderful combinations almost sculptural in nature, whose texture, color, and shapes were evidence of Ruth Bancroft's great plantsmanship and artistry.

Born in 1908, Ruth Bancroft had begun to study architecture at the University of California, Berkeley, but after the stock market crash of 1929, she feared she would never get a job as an architect. She became a teacher instead, married, and moved to her husband's family farm of four hundred acres that grew walnuts and pears. She began gardening right away, but over time the land was divided and sold off to developers. In 1971, her husband gave her the last three acres for her garden. She was fascinated by succulents and other water-conserving plants that she collected and grew in lath and greenhouses. Then she began experimenting, successfully growing them unprotected, outdoors in the ground. Her architectural background served her well. Her strong artistic combinations of color, texture, and shape created a stunning visual experience.

A woman of moderate means with a simple house, Ruth confessed her concerns to Frank as they toured her garden together. Then eighty years old, she told him she worried terribly about the future of the garden after her death – a concern that turned out to be a bit premature, as she outlived Frank and is still around at age 108 in 2017.

Frank was overwhelmed by the experience, as he later recounted: "Much to my great surprise, I remember actually shivering at the beauty of it. As we drove away, I said to my wife, 'We have to find some way to help this woman.' And she said, 'Why don't you start a garden conservancy?' And of course, that rang all sorts of bells."

Les Quatre Vents: The Pigeonnier viewed across the small lake

Frank always credits this conversation with Anne as the inspiration for the Garden Conservancy, his "ah-ha!" moment. But from inspiration to execution is quite a leap. Frank was wise enough to consult others he respected to see what they thought. One was Dr. Richard W. Lighty. The two chanced on each other at a meeting of the American Association of Botanical Gardens and Arboreta at the Missouri Botanical Garden, each well aware of the other's impressive credentials. They hit it off immediately. Later, Frank wrote a letter to Dr. Lighty outlining his idea for an organization to preserve exceptional American gardens and asking him for a critique. Dr. Lighty thought it had no chance of success, that it would be very hard to create an organization that was truly national in scope focusing on gardens across the vast United States. Undeterred, Frank's response was to enlist Lighty to insure that his conclusion was wrong. He invited him to join the first advisory committee and Lighty agreed.

The Bancroft Garden: Agave punctuating the plantings

The Garden Conservancy officially claims to have been born in 1989, but it really began earlier with Frank's initial vision and with Anne's encouragement. His network in both the gardening world and of prominent social leaders was essential. Even before officially incorporating, he talked the famous actress Angela Lansbury into serving as honorary chair, with Betty Corning, a force in the Garden Club of America, as vice chair. He attracted a group of another fifty people from twenty-four states and several others from Canada to constitute the first advisory committee of his nascent organization. Although Frank was never happy asking other people for money, preferring to use his own, here he attracted a long list of founding angels, benefactors, and friends to support the cause.

Best of all, he enlisted the talents of others to broaden the leadership team in ways that complemented his own role. Tom Armstrong, his friend from their early banking days together at Stone & Webster, where they had both been equally unhappy, was tapped at a fortunate time in Tom's life. Marco Polo Stufano, whom Frank knew as head of horticulture at Wave Hill, agreed to chair the screening committee that would be charged with identifying gardens worthy of preservation. Most important, he hired Antonia Adezio to be the executive director.

Wisely, Frank did not set out to have the Garden Conservancy identify and then take on the ownership of exceptional American gardens. Unlike the model of the National Trust in England, which becomes the owner-manager of significant gardens on the condition that each comes with its own sufficient endowment, Frank's vision was to have a distinguished team of heavies in the horticultural world, headed by Marco Polo Stufano, propose gardens to become projects of the Garden Conservancy. Rather like the "Good Housekeeping Seal of Approval," this identifier would serve as an important credential to each garden chosen. Then, with its oversight and encouragement, the Garden Conservancy would provide the technical support and advice necessary for each garden to organize its own leadership and financial support.

Frank said, "The original conception was to try to save the private works of art created by people like Ruth Bancroft. We would not only be an advocate for the preservation of that kind of garden but a catalyst that would actually make it happen. We would set up an organization that would facilitate the transition from private to public ownership for posterity."

In the case of Ruth Bancroft's garden, it was clear she was a woman of modest means who, although in no position to endow her garden, was eager to have it continue for public enjoyment after her life. Rather than taking it over,

The Bancroft Garden: Colorful combinations of succulents

the Garden Conservancy helped her and her garden's existing fans organize their own charitable organization, begin to raise funds, and plan for its future preservation. The Ruth Bancroft Garden was officially declared to be the first Garden Conservancy preservation project and became the model for all the other gardens that followed. Many were eventually well enough on track to be let loose and fly on their own. In the interim, the Garden Conservancy also could provide and confer favorable tax-exempt status for these early project gardens. The Garden Conservancy was incorporated in 1990 with modest offices in Cold Spring, New York, not surprisingly handy to Frank's home at Stonecrop.

Leading by example, Frank and Anne turned their home and garden at Stonecrop into a charitable organization linked to the Garden Conservancy and first opened it to the public in 1992. The gardens there had been much improved under the hand of Caroline Burgess, who arrived in 1983 after having worked for

Rosemary Verey, the renowned English garden writer and designer who recommended her to Frank. Caroline first came for a brief stint, but returned to take charge of Stonecrop's gardens after she completed the prestigious English horticultural study program at Kew. With an endowment provided by the Cabots, Stonecrop is now one of the many exceptional American gardens being preserved for the public, as well as serving as a superb training ground for young, promising gardeners. By 2014, the Stonecrop intern program had had more than seventy-three interns go through an intensive educational experience of living and working there.

Once he got going, Frank did not limit his interest in garden preservation to North America. When he saw the historic sixteenth-century garden at Aberglasney, located in Carmarthenshire, Wales, he was entranced. He could see what it might become if funds were raised to support its restoration and revival. But Frank also knew how much hard work would be required. When he arrived to help, those who welcomed him were taken a bit aback to see him ready to pitch in, not decked out in his normally elegant garb, but equipped with his favorite kneepads and trowel, wearing his wellies, set to get to work. Frank was a hands-on gardener, and he most admired and enjoyed the company of others like him: real gardeners. The house and its ten acres of garden were transferred to the Aberglasney Restoration Trust in 1995.

The Garden Conservancy has grown into a national organization with offices on both coasts. Celebrating its twenty-fifth anniversary in 2014 under new leadership, it articulated its mission:

Stonecrop: View of Lake and Hillside Garden

To save and share outstanding American gardens for the education and inspiration of the public.

In recognition of his extraordinary contribution to the world of horticulture, Frank received the highest honors possible, including the Gold Veitch Memorial Medal in 2002, the highest honor given by the Royal Horticultural Society and one almost never awarded to an American. He was also made a Chevalier of National Order of Quebec (2001), and an Honorary Member of the Order of Canada (2005), as well as receiving awards from Winterthur, the Scott Arboretum, the Pennsylvania Horticultural Society, the Massachusetts Horticultural Society, and countless others.

Frank died at La Malbaie on November 19, 2011, at the age of 86, but his greatest legacy of all, the Garden Conservancy, is alive and strong, as are the two extraordinarily artistic gardens he created at Stonecrop and Les Quatre Vents. That these, his own garden creations, will carry on to inspire and move others would please him most. As he said, "The greatest of all compliments is when a visitor responds to the beauty encompassing the garden and its settings by shedding a tear. Now there is a soul mate!"

Frank Cabot

Tom Armstrong

For more than sixty years I have either made art, collected art, or presented art to the public. This book is about the joy of seeing – of having a particular visual response to art and design within a house and its adjacent landscape.

Tom Armstrong proved to be the perfect partner for Frank Cabot in turning Frank's vision of the Garden Conservancy into a thriving enterprise. In 1989 when Frank Cabot asked him to be the first president of the Garden Conservancy, the timing was perfect. A major figure in American art circles for almost all his adult life, Tom had just stepped down as director of the Whitney Museum of American Art. He was free to devote the full force of his energies and talents to this project. Along the way, Tom would come to appreciate gardens as another form of art, one that would become an important part of his life. He knew from experience how to run a successful organization, how to build a board, how to raise funds, and how to draw appreciative audiences. And Tom's exuberant spirit ensured that the entire journey would be enormous fun.

When Tom and Frank first met, they were both young men working in the investment firm of Stone & Webster. If Frank Cabot didn't complain out loud about his life in the world of finance, Tom made no secret of the fact that he "absolutely hated it!" Even though Frank was older by seven years, they were friends from the start. No doubt they were drawn together because they had so much in common – down to elegant style, a mutual devotion to bow ties, and a wicked sense of humor. Although their working lives later diverged when they both left finance, they remained good friends and came to share a passion for gardens, which is how they became the leading players in the success of the Garden Conservancy.

Unlike Frank, Tom was not born to a family of wealth and privilege. He arrived on July 30, 1932, in Portsmouth, Virginia, in the depths of the Great

Depression, the older of two children. His father was fortunate to have a job with the International Nickel Company, but it soon meant the family had to leave Virginia and move north to Summit, New Jersey, where Tom attended public schools. His mother also went to work as a schoolteacher. Tom was artistic at an early age, but as he later observed, "This was when art news appeared on the women's pages in the newspaper and, among my peer group, artists were generally considered 'different' or suspect. As I got older, I developed an affable personality and a facility with humor to overcome rejection by my athletic schoolmates."

Although Tom's father had a job, he also had a problem with alcohol. By the time Tom was a teenager, his father joined Alcoholics Anonymous, and Tom's mother wanted Tom out of the way during the school's long summer vacation. Since she couldn't afford to send him to summer camp, she found a program that sent students away to work on farms. Tom went to work for a farmer in Montague, New Jersey, and did that for six summers. By the second summer, Tom asked the farmer if he could have his own row where he could raise flowers after he finished work, and it wasn't long before he was winning prizes for horticulture and flower arranging at the county fairs.

With his artistic bent, he told his parents he wanted to study to become an artist, but his parents' response was "We go into business." Tom realized that for his parents, who had endured the Great Depression after growing up in the South just one generation away from the searing devastation of the Civil War, his having "a career in art was not an option." But architecture seemed a "legitimate serious outlet" instead. He applied to Cornell and Princeton and was accepted by both, but before making his final choice, he took an aptitude test and was told, among other things, that he would never be a farmer. After his six summers working on a farm, that got his back up, so Tom chose Cornell and in 1950, enrolled in its highly regarded Agricultural School. How unlikely that goal seems in light of the rest of Tom's life in the arts. By his sophomore year, Tom realized farming was not a realistic option either. Unlike most of the other students, he didn't have a farm to which to return, and, in fact, couldn't even afford to buy a cow. He switched his major to Fine Arts and that, but for his brief stint in finance, defined his life.

Like Frank Cabot, Tom too served in the army but only after graduating from Cornell with a BFA. He had been in the ROTC program at Cornell that required him to serve in the army after he graduated. As was often true in Tom's life, he was the beneficiary of luck and timing. The Korean War had just ended, sparing him from engaging in active combat, and he landed in a sweet spot in the army in Hawaii. He was assigned to be the chauffeur for a general; driving a jeep was hardly an onerous assignment. After serving the required amount of

time, Tom left the military with the rank of lieutenant and returned to New York to join Stone & Webster.

Although his nine years at Stone & Webster were not to Tom's taste, he was successful and, best of all, met his future wife there. One of the name partners and chairman of the board, Whitney Stone, chose Tom to become his closest assistant. Whitney Stone also happened to be the uncle of his namesake, Virginia Whitney Brewster, known to all as Bunty. Tom had been engaged to marry another woman when he met Bunty, but just two weeks before the wedding, the bride-to-be changed her mind, and Tom, recovering quickly from that rejection, proposed to Bunty. With the approval of Bunty's mother, he went to her bedroom, woke her up, and informed her that "both her mother and I thought we should be married." In her typical no-nonsense, blunt style, Bunty's only reply was, "See me in the morning." Despite her retort, Tom and Bunty did marry on May 18, 1963, a few years after they met.

While at Stone & Webster Tom kept his artistic inclinations alive by taking on the job of redecorating the firm's offices. Finally, shortly before he and Bunty were married, he left the firm and returned to his interest in art by enrolling in the museum administration program at the NYU Institute of Fine Arts. Although he never earned his master's degree – Bunty says he flunked the German requirement – he undertook a research project for the Abby Aldrich Rockefeller Folk Art Collection in Williamsburg, Virginia. That work led to his appointment as the curator there in 1967. Not long afterward, he became the director. He moved his young family to Williamsburg, back to his Virginia roots, and into the start of his life's work in museum administration.

No doubt Tom's excellent work as the director of the Rockefeller Folk Art Collection earned him well-deserved respect, for his reputation reached beyond Virginia and he was asked to become the head of the Pennsylvania Academy of Fine Arts. In 1971, the young Armstrong family moved to the suburbs of Philadelphia to Upper Roxborough, near Chestnut Hill.

The Pennsylvania Academy of Fines Arts is an important, historic art institution, and it was a distinct honor for Tom to be selected to lead it while still in his thirties. Founded in Philadelphia in 1805, the academy is the oldest museum and art school in the country. Modelled on the academies of Europe, it was started by American artists and other leading citizens to serve as a locus in which to exhibit art and train aspiring artists and sculptors in the classical tradition, using live models. The original building suffered a great fire, and eventually the academy moved to a new location in the center of the city and commissioned a new building. Begun by the architects Frank Furness and George Hewitt Jr. in 1871, the marvelous building opened in 1876 as part of the Philadelphia Exposition of the same year. The great American artist Thomas Eakins taught there, among others. By the time Tom arrived, the structure had been badly neglected, patched here and there with inappropriate modern "improvements." In light of his own early interest in architecture, Tom was quick to realize the building was a treasure that demanded restoration. But this was the early days of the oil crisis of the 1970s, and the academy was already in financial straits.

Tom's greatest legacy at the academy is the tasteful and sensitive restoration he orchestrated of the building under the direction of Hyman Meyers in the 1970s. It is now a National Historic Landmark and continues to be a wonderful museum. Part of the joy of the brilliant original galleries, after restoration, is the display of paintings graced by natural light that pours in through the glass ceilings. Certainly Tom's leadership helped save what is a superb historic structure and revive interest in it, its history, and its collection of leading American artists.

Tom's success in Philadelphia soon drew attention from other quarters. In 1974, Tom was lured away to return to New York City to lead the Whitney Museum of Modern Art. A very different institution from the historic academy, the Whitney Museum was only forty-three years old when Tom arrived. It had been founded by Gertrude Vanderbilt Whitney, who began collecting works of living American artists early in the twentieth century, especially artists not recognized by the establishment. It was still very much a parochial family-dominated institution. By 1926, Gertrude had amassed a significant collection and offered five hundred works along with a generous endowment to the Metropolitan Museum of Art. She was promptly turned down. Instead, she started her own museum in 1931 in Greenwich Village. Several years after her death in 1942, the museum moved uptown first to West 54th Street and then, after acquiring land at 75th Street and Madison Avenue, to a new building the museum leaders had commissioned from Marcel Breuer and Hamilton Smith. Opening in 1966, it was totally unlike the elegantly traditional academy building Tom had worked to restore in Philadelphia. The new Whitney building was brutalist and stark, a massive, looming cement presence.

Given his prior experience with more traditional art, Tom seemed an unlikely choice to become director. He confessed to the press, "I'm not exactly the kind of person who can now be considered as an active participant on the contemporary scene." But he added, "I go to galleries all the time and I used to be a painter myself." He was just forty-two years old, and his energy and enthusiasm proved to be exactly what the Whitney needed.

Once the family returned and settled back in New York with the four kids in school, Tom and Bunty began to rent property on Fishers Island, both for weekend retreats and a place to spend their summers. Fishers Island is officially part of New York State, but is located just off the southern coast of Connecticut in Long Island Sound, reachable by ferry from New London. The island is only three thousand acres, with varying widths over its seven-mile length, surrounded by marvelous views of water everywhere. There are only 240 full-time residents but the number swells to more than two thousand when weekenders and summer residents are included. When Bunty brought Tom to see the house she had rented, she said, "Don't look!" She knew it wouldn't please his demanding eye, but it served their needs until 1985, when they finally bought a property on the eastern end of the island, a handsome though derelict colonial revival style house with beautiful views across the water to the Connecticut shore.

While they were still renting, Tom had gone to a dinner party on Fishers Island and despite his usual lively, conversational abilities, ran out of things to discuss with what must have been a very dull dinner partner. He recalls resorting to discussing the merits of different brands of vacuum cleaners, debating Hoover versus Electrolux. Another guest overheard this conversation and later produced a costume for him to wear at his forty-fifth birthday party, complete with satin cape, T-shirt with an appliquéd Hoover vacuum on the front, and black tights with a cord that wrapped around to Tom's rear end; a black baseball cap completed the composition with the words in red felt, super vac. Tom showed up in the outfit for that year's golf tournament. Cape flying in the breeze, he proceeded to "hoover" up golf balls on the greens.

Naturally, the only name suitable for their new home was Hoover Hall. A proper coat of arms was designed with two crossed Hoovers on a shield below a crown and a banner with the Latin motto, *"Verro Ergo Cogito"* which translates, "I clean, therefore I think." It took over three years to restore, but, by 1989, Hoover Hall had been restored and furnished to Tom and Bunty's delight, and Tom could begin to garden again.

The eastern end of Fishers Island had been designed for limited development and open space by Frederick Law Olmsted Jr. in the 1920s. The climate of the island, which is surrounded by the waters of Long Island Sound, is benign and the soil suitable for growing a wide range of plants. As part of making Hoover Hall their own, Tom turned his attentions to the landscape, linking the existing traditional architecture of the house to the dramatic views of Long Island Sound outside and adding plantings of unusual trees to those already there. "As the garden evolved, I realized for the first time in my life that in looking at nature I was contemplating the same concepts that I celebrate in art. The landscape I finally developed is my ultimate creative endeavor, filled with relationships to art. I am intrigued with the variety of flower forms, colors and textures, and am gratified when forming collections of various plants, shrubs, and trees."

In New York City, Tom threw himself into his new role at the Whitney Museum with his usual style and flair, featuring many artists who were not well

Hooverness on Daffodil Days

known at the time but who have since become household names, such as Frank Stella and Jasper Johns, and many others. Over time, he more than quadrupled the size of the collection, raising money when needed and cajoling gifts of important art from collectors and artists. He also mentored young curators who went on to become leaders of other great institutions, including the Guggenheim Museum and the Metropolitan Museum of Art.

With his jaunty bow ties and sense of fun, he often surprised members of the Board of Trustees. He loved to produce wind-up toys and run them over the tables at formal board dinners, adding a touch of whimsy and levity to what might otherwise have been stuffy occasions. He even grew tomatoes on the terrace outside his fifth-floor office and opened what he called the All-American Vegetable Stand in front of the museum where each year he sold tomatoes attractively housed in baskets. The profits went to benefit the museum's annual fund. Tom had hopes of raising enough so that the All-American Vegetable Stand would be listed among the museum's donors. In time, that did happen, but many of the museum's trustees thought this whole endeavor "undignified." On occasion he was known to sport surprising adornments; one Christmas holiday board dinner an astonished trustee arrived to see "somebody who had furry hoofs and antlers coming out of his head, and it was Tom Armstrong!"

But Tom was no lightweight. He knew that a major part of his job was to keep the museum relevant and also financially sound. Fund-raising was essential, along with the cultivation of the public and the press. He expanded the board beyond the original family members, increased the museum's membership, and broadened audiences and attendance. He built a national network of patrons and supporters and instituted what became a major art event, the Whitney Biennial, featuring provocative contemporary works. One of the seminal Biennial exhibitions, presented in 1976, was "200 Years of American Sculpture," and other major surveys followed. He organized retrospectives of the likes of Jasper Johns, Andy Warhol, Cy Twombly, Marsden Hartley, and others, along with mounting large exhibitions of enormous sculpture by artists such as Mark di Suvero.

Alexander Calder's famous *Circus,* with its assemblage of more than fifty miniature performers and animals, was about to be sold in Europe after having been on long-term loan to the Whitney; Tom found a way to raise more than $1.25 million to buy it (an enormous sum in 1982) at a time when the museum had very modest acquisition funds. In classic Tom style, he arranged to celebrate this success by "borrowing" an elephant from the Ringling Bros. Circus. Tom and Flora Biddle, a descendant of Gertrude Whitney and president of the board during most of Tom's tenure, joined the merriment, parading as clowns.

In due course, Tom concluded that the expanding collection and the need for exhibition space, particularly for large works on canvas and huge

Pool Garden with The Birth of Venus fountain
by Robert Laurent

sculptures, required more space. He set to work developing plans for a ten-story building as an addition to the main museum at an estimated cost of $37.5 million. He selected Michael Graves as the architect, but, once announced, the plans drew an immediate uproar from the surrounding community. NIMBY – "Not in My Backyard" – voices were raised and many architects voiced concern about the integrity of the existing Breuer building. Eventually, the plans were dropped, and Tom became the scapegoat. The board dismissed him as director in 1989 after a fifteen-year tenure.

To recover, Tom took time off, just at the time when Frank Cabot conceived of establishing the Garden Conservancy. Frank wisely reached out and asked Tom to join the first board. Tom's experience as director of major nonprofit institutions had given him important experience dealing with building strong and supportive boards and, most important, in developing financial support. Although Frank had also served on nonprofit boards and well understood the importance of fund-raising, he hated asking people for money. He much preferred to use his own capital for the causes he cared about, leading by example. That very generosity often worked against him when trying to raise money from others. Tom, much as he loved arranging art exhibitions and working with artists, fully understood that his main job was to raise funds and schmooze with everyone important.

Frank asked Tom to become president of the Garden Conservancy; Tom agreed but asked Frank to be sure to "never leave me alone in the presence of seasoned gardeners." When Tom first joined the board in those early days, he observed, "This is not a rich board." He set out to remedy that, knowing that financial support had to start with support from the board beyond Frank, whose delight in the company of hands-on gardeners had led him to invite many like-minded, hands-in-the-dirt souls to join the board. They were devoted to the aims of the Garden Conservancy but were not always individuals who could write the requisite checks.

Having transformed what had been a parochial family board at the Whitney into one composed of the rich and powerful, Tom knew how to reel patrons in. The Conservancy's original board was quite small but quickly rounded out to around fifteen, including Patti Bush (wife of William H. T. Bush, brother of President George H. W. Bush and uncle of President George W. Bush), Joe McCann (a senior vice president at PepsiCo), Dr. Richard W. Lighty, and other high-profile people. He also created the Society of Fellows for donors above a certain level and then developed a popular study tour program for the Fellows, taking them on elegant trips to private gardens open just for them. It wasn't long before Tom pressed for the launch of the first drive to raise an endowment to ensure the Conservancy's permanent support.

Having built an outstanding curatorial and administrative team at the Whitney Museum, Tom appreciated the importance of establishing a strong professional staff. He was an immediate ally of Antonia Adezio, the executive director, as she hired superb people and expanded the Garden Conservancy's agenda beyond its initial preservation of exceptional American gardens to include educational programs, symposia, and assistance to existing public gardens facing challenges. If something was worth doing, Tom was sure that first it must be done well and then somehow the money would follow.

With his success in growing audiences for the Whitney, Tom cheered for the beginning of the Conservancy's Open Days Program in 1995 and shortly became a participant, opening his own gardens at Hoover Hall. Unlike some of the more intellectuals of his art world colleagues, Tom had always viewed art as more than a sober and solitary endeavor – he believed it should be a celebration, shared with the public as much as possible. In the same spirit, he immediately understood and supported the appeal of the Open Days. Hoover Hall opened not only for Open Days but later for Fishers Island community groups as well. What he dubbed his Daffodil Days drew large, appreciative crowds who came to *ooh* and *ahh* over the thousands of daffodils he had planted in his usual exuberant style.

After leaving the Whitney, Tom, in addition to his work at the Conservancy, was not idle professionally. A champion of Andy Warhol's work while director of the Whitney, he became involved in the plans to establish a Warhol museum in Pittsburgh after the artist's death. As early as 1979, Tom had organized a Whitney exhibition of Warhol's portraits, so he was a natural candidate to be chosen as director of the new museum when it opened in 1994. But running the new Andy Warhol Museum was another matter. The Carnegie Institute owned the museum and managed it. Tom was the director, but it was quite different from being the leader of an independent institution with its own governing board. He found it more like being head of a department in a large university and competing internally for institutional funds. After a brief stint of not quite two years, Tom concluded he was the Warhol's director in name only, and so he quit.

He then wrote *An American Odyssey,* a book commissioned by Sotheby's about Jack Warner, a businessman, philanthropist, and art collector, and the art collection he created in Tuscaloosa. Tom's book came out in 2002 and was well reviewed. After the book was published, Tom kept an office at Sotheby's and occasionally consulted for the firm. But neither the Warhol Museum nor his role at Sotheby's precluded him from working with Frank in building the Garden Conservancy.

Tom quickly came to share Frank's view that great gardens were works of art. His exposure to the many other gardens he saw thanks to his role at the Conservancy reinforced that view. He had gardened on a farm in his youth and hoped to be a painter. His own garden at Hoover Hall was Tom's three-dimensional creation, reflecting his artistic sensibilities. He recognized that "strategies I continually see in art, and have employed in my garden, are repetition in form; variation in form; contrast of straight lines and curves; relationship of solids and voids; flat, perspective, and ambiguous space; and emphasis of edges."

Tom was justifiably proud of his own garden and the landscape that he had created at Hoover Hall with the help of many professional advisers and nurserymen. He wrote a book about its evolution that was accepted for publication in 2003. Then on December 16, just before Christmas that year, Tom received a call from his caretaker who said grimly, "It's gone." Tom knew immediately what the words meant – a total loss. He cried. A contractor, working with a heat gun to remove old paint, had accidently started a fire. The fire hoses couldn't reach the hydrants so water was pumped out of Long Island Sound into the house for more than eight hours. Meanwhile, the local residents got word of the disaster and, despite the cold, quickly arrived to form an assembly line to help rescue the house's valuable paintings, glassware, and other antiques before all were gone.

Eighteen years had passed since the original purchase of Hoover Hall and Tom was seventy-one years old. It hardly seemed time to start building another house but that is precisely what he did. He did not want to simply recreate the colonial-style house that had burned to the ground. It was time to try something modern, in line with his tenure at the Whitney. There was no other modernist house on Fishers Island; there had been one years earlier, but it had

View of Hooverness from the garden

Hooverness

been dismantled. After finding the right architect in Thomas Phifer, Tom set out to build a glass-and-steel one-bedroom house. His plan to later build a separate four-bedroom guesthouse never materialized. For the next five years, Tom was out on Fishers Island every ten days or so collaborating with Phifer on the design and construction. Because the new structure was so completely different from Hoover Hall, yet stood on the same footprint, Tom named it Hooverness – "ness" is Celtic for "point," and the house sits on a point of land jutting into the sea.

With the insurance money for the many treasures that hadn't been salvaged, Tom established a special art fund and commenced to build a collection of modern works of art appropriate to the style of the house. Each work was chosen and hung with Tom's eye for marrying the colors and shapes to the architecture and to the landscape just beyond the glass walls. Handsome pieces of sculpture added their touch.

The Garden Conservancy continued to go from strength to strength. In 2003, Tom paid tribute to Antonia Adezio's important role in its success by surrendering his title of president to her. He became vice chairman until 2007, when Frank Cabot, the founder and visionary, stepped down and asked Tom to take over his role as chairman of the board. (Frank remained on the board until his death in 2011).

Tom told the story of Hooverness in marvelous detail in *A Singular Vision: Architecture, Art, Landscape,* describing its creation, with its marvelous art collection inside and brilliant garden outside. Published by the Quantuck Lane Press, the book appeared shortly after Tom's untimely death on June 20, 2011, just a few short months before Frank Cabot's.

In *A Singular Vision,* Tom wrote, "For more than sixty years I have either made art, collected art or presented art to the public. This book is about the joy of seeing – of having a particular visual response to art and design within a house and its adjacent landscape."

I had the great pleasure of having Tom give me his curator's tour of the interior of Hooverness, with garden views from every room, after first visiting the extraordinary gardens he had developed as its complement. Every room in the house was surrounded by exterior walls of glass, and a corridor linking each room to that glass exterior was the uninterrupted perimeter. Bunty did point out that she insisted on having some opaque walls, at least in her bathroom! Sensitive to how incredibly opaque and black glass walls can become at night from the interior, Tom carefully placed exterior lighting in the garden to draw the eye through the glass to the spaces beyond.

Sadly, Tom died too young; he was only seventy-eight and a vibrant seventy-eight at that. As he would have chosen, the end came suddenly and dramatically, sparing him prolonged disability and suffering. At a memorial celebration of his life, Bunty displayed all his colorful bow ties and encouraged the guests to select one or two to wear in joyful remembrance. My husband, Charlie, proudly wears them to this day. Tom's larger-than-life smile, and his joy in sharing his passion for art and for gardens as art, had attracted essential support for the Garden Conservancy, securing its strong future. And at Hooverness, Tom had achieved his "lifelong dream to live in a garden with art."

Tom said, "Gardeners are artists, and great gardens like paintings and sculpture, must be preserved. Our cultural heritage must include, forever, gardens."

Looking north out from the house over the reflecting pool to Long Island Sound

Antonia Adezio

*Just viewing gardens is therapeutic. That connection with creativity
and beauty is something we all need.*

NTONIA ADEZIO was the critically important third member of the triumvirate that made the Garden Conservancy. This extraordinary trio's individual strengths and talents complemented and reinforced one another's. Unifying them was a shared view of gardens as works of art, worthy of attention and preservation.

When she received the Place Keeper Award from the Foundation for Landscape Studies in 2013, she paid tribute to both Tom Armstrong and Frank Cabot. She first recognized Tom, calling him "a garden creator, long-time boss, and coconspirator with me at the Garden Conservancy, whose dedication and imagination made the Conservancy what it is today." She then added, "And, of course, Frank Cabot, was the visionary founder of the Conservancy and creator of two stupendous gardens, Stonecrop in Cold Spring, New York, and Les Quatre Vents in La Malbaie, Quebec."

While art is a common thread in all their backgrounds, Antonia began with music. The visual arts and gardening as art came later in her life story, which would ultimately propel her to join Frank and Tom to become the full-time force that launched the Garden Conservancy and built it into a major organization.

From the moment she was born, Antonia was surrounded by music, which could have defined her life but for serendipity. She was born in 1954 to an Italian father and an Irish mother and lived on the outskirts of Philadelphia. Her Father, Louis Adezio, grew up in an Italian immigrant community on the rough South Side of Chicago. He learned music at Hull House, an early settlement house started by Jane Addams and Ellen Gates Starr to offer social and educational services to the working class, principally new immigrants, in the surrounding neighborhoods. Hull House is now a museum, where there is still a picture of Louis Adezio performing with his sisters and mother. He went on to study violin at the prestigious Peabody Conservatory in Baltimore, Maryland, until World War II intervened to take him off to the army. On his return, he sought a "real job," got a degree in engineering from Johns Hopkins, and went to work in Perth Amboy, New Jersey, selling RCA components to support his family. But music never left his life, or his daughter's after she arrived. She first began playing the piano at age three.

Antonia's mother, Madeline Fagan, came from "lace curtain" Irish Catholic stock; her father strongly disapproved of Louis, viewing all Italians as lazy, "not good workers in the vineyard." Determined to win Madeline and her father's blessing, Louis confronted him and said, "Who is your boss?" Without waiting for a reply, Louis provided the answer – it was the Pope and the Pope was Italian. With that kind of nerve, Louis prevailed. Madeline was an impressive person who both stood up for Louis to her father and had joined the Coast Guard during the war as a SPAR. Later, after bearing three children, Madeline went to night school to earn her master's in social work, going on to work in social service agencies when her children were teenagers. She always thought of herself as a professional woman and was an important role model for Antonia, the oldest of the three Adezio children.

After her early childhood years in Pennsylvania, Antonia moved with her family to Moorestown, in southern New Jersey near Philadelphia. After graduating from a Catholic high school, she went on to the intensely academic Bryn Mawr College, a prestigious women's liberal arts college in the suburbs of Philadelphia, where she juggled her studies with her music. Before deciding to attend Bryn Mawr, Antonia had an audition at the tuition-free Curtis Institute of Music with the renowned Rudolf Serkin, an experience she remembers as terrifying. Serkin told the high school teacher who had sent her that although he thought Antonia was very talented, "It's too bad that she studies so hard," meaning that her record of straight A's surely meant that she hadn't spent enough time practicing the piano. At Bryn Mawr, Antonia majored in Greek and English, having developed an interest in the classics from her high school Latin, while continuing to work on the piano. In 1975, she graduated with the highest possible honors, summa cum laude, in her double major, an astonishing achievement.

After graduation, she moved in with a roommate in Germantown in Philadelphia and continued working on the piano before auditioning for New York's highly competitive Juilliard School. Once accepted, she spent three years earning her master's of music degree in performance. Antonia taught piano and accompanied singers. In her musical circles, she met and then married Philip Setzer, a violinist, who was among the founding members of the

Emerson String Quartet, which quickly became very successful. They divorced, and Antonia left her career in music to find other work to support herself.

A product of the late 1970s and early 1980s, Antonia, like so many of her generation, was interested in the environment and working for the public interest. New Yorkers were girding up for a prolonged battle over the proposed Westway project, which would have replaced a portion of the old West Side Elevated Highway with a new underground highway to reconnect lower Manhattan to the Hudson River waterfront; atop the highway would be 220 new acres of landfill planned for development. Environmentalists were bitterly opposed, concerned about corruption, adding more traffic to the West Side, and damaging the environment, pushing instead for funds to be allocated to providing more mass transit. Antonia worked briefly for a wealthy individual who was fighting Westway – for her, a match not made in heaven. Just six months later, Antonia was unemployed.

Back at the drawing board, Antonia searched for ads from the Sierra Club, Amnesty International, and other nonprofit organizations. Word of mouth from a friend of a friend informed her of a job opening at Wave Hill, where she was fated to meet Frank Cabot, as well as Marco Polo Stufano, who was then head of horticulture. She was hired to work for the development director in 1983, which was surprising, given her lack of any prior fund-raising experience. As luck would have it, the development director left shortly thereafter for a job in city government, and Antonia, the only other person in the office, was promoted to become the director just six months after her arrival. Those were early days for Wave Hill when its very small staff worked to transform what had been the private estate of Anne Perkins Cabot's family into an important public garden. Although the property is owned by New York City, Wave Hill is a separate nonprofit corporation with its own endowment and governing board. It was quickly to become the most exciting and innovative public garden in America, thanks to the horticultural brilliance of Marco Polo Stufano, head of horticulture.

It was while at Wave Hill that Antonia met Peter Clark, the man she would next marry. He was one of the gardeners under Marco. Before coming to Wave Hill, Peter had started out in publishing, but he decided he preferred working with his hands. He went to San Francisco to study woodworking and returned to New York, driving a taxi to support himself while he pursued his talent as a sculptor. A mutual friend of his and Marco's suggested he try to get a job at Wave Hill because, although he had never been a professional gardener, he loved using his hands in an artistic endeavor, and this was regular work. Antonia and Peter married in 1985 before a justice of the peace with only Marco and his partner, John Nally, as the witnesses.

While at Wave Hill, Peter employed his woodworking skills to construct

and market what became the signature Wave Hill chairs, based on a 1918 design by a Dutch architect, Gerrit Rietveld. After a year or so constructing the chairs, Peter felt burnt out and quit Wave Hill. He began to pick through flea markets outside the city, to salvage things he found to fix and then to sell.

Antonia wanted to live outside the city as well, so the couple moved north to Bedford, New York, where they rented a tiny converted chicken coop, heated only by wood. Antonia continued to work at Wave Hill, despite her new long commute, and Peter opened an antiques store in Cold Spring, New York, and he soon blossomed into a full-time artist and sculptor. By 1987, Antonia and Peter decided that her long commute from Bedford to Wave Hill and his to Cold Spring was too hard, so they moved to Cold Spring near Peter's store, and Antonia left Wave Hill to become an independent development consultant.

Their move to Cold Spring would change Antonia's life. As they were moving furniture into their new home, Peter and Antonia were struggling to carry a heavy couch across the road when Frank Cabot spotted them. Their home happened to be right across the street from Frank's office. Frank recognized Antonia from their work together at Wave Hill. He quickly stopped her, sofa in hand, to hand her a one-page proposal he had drafted and was circulating widely, outlining his idea for the creation of the Garden Conservancy. Antonia admits she thought the whole concept "quixotic."

Though she thought the idea far-fetched, it was very hard to say no to Frank. Even after he told her he would hire her on a trial basis since "he only had enough money to pay me for thirty days," she said yes. "But I felt if Frank believed in it, it would be very exciting and successful. I was willing to take that risk and see what happened." He also told her that they would only have enough money to establish the Conservancy if, with his help and extensive contacts and her hard work, she could raise at least a hundred thousand dollars in three months' time. If not, he would call the whole thing off.

After successfully surviving the ninety-day trial period by raising more than enough funds, Antonia was appointed the executive director, and the Garden Conservancy was on its way. Frank recalled later that "she moved into the back of my messy little office in Cold Spring, New York, and within six months she had her own building, her own staff, and the thing up and running!"

Frank front-loaded the funds needed to get the work off the ground and treated the money as an advance, a loan to an organization that wasn't even born. By 1989, Frank had cajoled the Tides Foundation into adopting his proposal as one of its projects. An established charitable organization, Tides exists to act as an incubator for incipient nonprofits with promise. That sponsorship provides donors with an immediate tax-deduction for contributions made to Tides, even though the funds are designated for the benefit of a particular program. Contributions to the Tides Foundation on behalf of the Garden Conservancy qualified as charitable gifts even though the Conservancy itself had not yet been legally incorporated or received tax exemption recognition from the Internal Revenue Service. The foundation also provided administrative backup for this sponsorship and charged a basic fee, as well as a fee based on a percentage of funds raised.

In addition to choosing the Conservancy's initial board and an advisory committee of sixty-five people from twenty-three states, Frank and Antonia created a screening committee to set the standards and select the gardens to take on as preservation projects. The chair was Marco Polo Stufano, who Antonia views as "the greatest contribution to American horticulture ever." She thought his willingness to chair this screening committee was "epic!" He was at the table with Frank and Antonia from the beginning, and his early choices set the criteria and style for the future. Antonia relied on him and the screening committee to provide guidelines for the Conservancy's preservation priorities.

The eight other members of the Screening Committee were all distinguished people in the horticulture community, including Elizabeth Scholtz (Brooklyn Botanic Garden, the only woman), John Trexler (Tower Hill Botanic

Garden), Kris Fenderson (the New Hampshire chapter of the American Rock Garden Society), George Waters (*Pacific Horticulture* magazine), John Fitzpatrick (Monticello), and others of like qualifications. Not surprisingly, Ruth Bancroft's garden was designated the first preservation project. After all, hers was the garden that had inspired Frank Cabot to create the Garden Conservancy.

Frank wanted to avoid paying fees to the Tides Foundation as soon as he could. Once he decided that sufficient funds were being raised and that their early efforts were successful, he and Antonia moved ahead to establish the Garden Conservancy as an independent legal entity and qualified charitable organization in 1990. The Tides Foundation continued to provide administrative services for a fixed fee until the Garden Conservancy could stand on its own. The experience with the Tides Foundation as the nurturing entity would serve as an important future model for the Garden Conservancy as it undertook to identify, and then assist in, the preservation of exceptional American gardens.

With Tom Armstrong's encouragement, the Society of Fellows was created in 1991 to include donors contributing at least a thousand dollars, forming a cadre of financial supporters and important advocates. Drawing from her development experience at Wave Hill, Antonia realized that the fellows had to be offered some form of thanks for their support. So she developed a program of garden study tours to offer them an opportunity to visit special private gardens, enhanced by elegant receptions and meals hosted by the garden owners. The fellows signing up paid for the costs of their trips and, over time, were asked to make a significant additional donation for the privilege. Other categories of membership at lower levels were also established. Antonia, with the support of the excellent staff she hired, expanded the organization's activities beyond garden preservation projects to include public education, lectures, educational conferences, and symposia.

Frank, Tom, and Antonia made an inspired team. Frank was the visionary, but he did not particularly enjoy the quotidian work of hiring staff and running an office. And he never liked asking anyone for money. He was the founding father, the charming and elegant spokesman, able to attract others to his cause. Tom, having run major nonprofit organizations, knew how to help build a board of rich donors and how to raise money.

And although this was her first time running an organization, Antonia proved to be a superb leader, with the right combination of skills to do it all. She astutely built an outstanding staff and, most important of all, hired Bill Noble as Director of Preservation. When she turned to developing a strategic plan and implementing it, he could not help but admire "her skill in being able to explain why something is important and then to galvanize people's hopes and mobilize their energy to work together in a collegial way toward very special concrete goals." Tom was sure that the partnerships Antonia created with other organizations, such as public gardens and preservation groups, would prove invaluable.

Articulate in both written and oral communications, she helped Frank, Tom, and the board formulate a mission statement for the Conservancy that was understandable to broader audiences and attracted their support. She understood that "the whole activity of gardening speaks to a very important human need to connect with the earth, and being creative with plants is a piece of that – the way people have taken their own vision and put it into a garden." In her tactful way, she could work with everyone, from hands-on gardeners to grand dames to business leaders. John Trexler, the distinguished director of the Tower Hill Botanic Garden, later characterized Antonia when paying tribute to her contribution: "She's a smart, smart, smart woman. She might have been a corporate executive, but instead she has given us this gift."

The mission evolved and expanded over time. Beyond its garden preservation projects, the Conservancy also provides help to existing important public gardens in times of need. An early example was the help it provided to revive the McKee Botanical Garden in Vero Beach, Florida, and develop a master plan. Another was the effort to reclaim Dumbarton Oaks Park in Washington, D.C., designed by Beatrix Farrand, the great American landscape architect of the first half of the twentieth century. Later, when Hurricane Katrina devastated New Orleans, the Conservancy and others assisted Longue Vue Gardens and the New Orleans Botanical Garden as they struggled to recover.

Perhaps the most surprising example of expanding the Conservancy's focus was the program at Alcatraz, the high-security prison on the rocky island in San Francisco Bay to celebrate and preserve the gardens the prisoners had created there.

In its first ten years of its existence, the Garden Conservancy took on a total of ten garden preservation projects, each requiring different levels of assistance, in states ranging from Maine to Florida, Washington, California, and Texas. It also began to accept conservation easements on existing gardens to insure their future protection. By the time of its twenty-fifth anniversary in 2015, the Garden Conservancy had helped preserve a hundred private gardens around the country, with five named as National Historic Landmarks and seventeen listed on the National Register of Historic Places. It is the only national organization dedicated to garden preservation in the United States.

Frank was never shy about copying ideas in his own gardens, so why not do the same for the Conservancy? England has long maintained what is called the National Garden Scheme, a program in which owners of private gardens voluntarily open their gardens to the public on certain days during the year. Each open garden collects admission fees to support charity. The dates and locations of the participating open gardens are listed with driving directions in *The Garden Visitor's Handbook* published each year, and commonly called simply *The Yellow Book*.

In 1995, two enthusiastic Conservancy members, Page Dickey and Penelope "Pepe" Maynard, suggested and helped launch the Open Days program, copying the English idea so closely that the book listing the gardens was, in fact, yellow. That first year, 110 gardens in Connecticut and New York were opened to the public and listed in the first yellow book, *The Garden Conservancy Open Days Directory* 1995.The plan was to expand nationally.

Modest admission fees were charged to benefit the Garden Conservancy; garden owners had the option of having their fees split between the Conservancy and a charity of their choice. This was a very smart idea and avoided raising the competitive hackles of local garden clubs and charities that might feel threatened by a new program. In 2015, twenty years after Open Days launched, 320 private gardens were open on specified dates throughout the growing season in twenty-two states across the country; the program now attracts more than seventy-five thousand visitors to participating gardens every year.

I remember when my own garden, Brush Hill, in Washington, Connecticut, opened for the first time in June 1995. Like all the other garden owners, I was nervous and worked like mad to be sure everything was as tidy and fresh as possible. There was what one wag called a lot of "fluffing up the sofa pillows" before the company arrived. And although the logistics of having someone at the gate to take tickets and collect admission was a challenge, it was all very exciting. More than two hundred visitors came to my garden that day. The garden owners learned from the many knowledgeable people who came, and the visitors discovered which plants could work well in their area. Both entertaining and educational, Open Days also attract new members to the Garden Conservancy since members are entitled to a discount on the admission fees.

The end of the Conservancy's first decade in 1999 was marked by a major celebration in Charleston, South Carolina, with more than three hundred participants from thirty-four states attending an event entitled "The Exceptional American Garden: Past, Present and Future." The Garden Conservancy was becoming a national organization. People came from near and far to visit private gardens in Charleston and to attend lectures by distinguished speakers. I accompanied Rosemary Verey, who flew in from London to lend her imprimatur. In a relatively short time, the Garden Conservancy had become a major presence on the horticultural scene.

In recognition of the importance of her role in its achievements over the first decade, Antonia was given Tom Armstrong's title as president of the Conservancy while Tom became vice chair of the board.

Antonia Adezio in Sonoma, California

When Antonia felt the Conservancy's goal of serving as a truly national organization required a West coast presence, Tom agreed and supported her plans. In 2003, it opened a West Coast office in San Francisco to expand its regional activities.

That same year, Antonia's husband, Peter Clark, died. With Peter gone, Antonia no longer had a compelling reason to continue living in Cold Spring, and a few years later, in 2005, she moved to San Francisco. If her early commute from Bedford, New York, to Wave Hill had proved challenging, her bicoastal life managing two offices in New York and California was punishing.

Tom had observed early on that the Garden Conservancy did not have a "rich board," but Frank, Tom, and Antonia had worked hard to remedy that. When the first endowment campaign launched in 2010, it successfully concluded by raising $15 million.

The Conservancy's original trio was still in place, though with different titles, but things were changing. Frank's health continued to deteriorate. Suddenly, the younger Tom Armstrong died at age seventy-eight in June 2011. By

November of that year, Frank was also gone at eighty-six. With new leadership at the board level, Antonia was the only one of the original three remaining. The new board leadership was eager to set its own agenda and strike out in new directions. The grueling coast-to-coast commute was also taking its toll on Antonia. She stepped down in 2012 after twenty-three years.

She left at a time when the Garden Conservancy was vibrant and strong, and as usual, she gave credit to others, saying, "The Garden Conservancy was founded to find and save the best American gardens, and we were successful thanks to the many professionals, allied organizations, and individual gardeners who believed in the importance of gardens as works of art and personal expression." She also observed, "Gardens are more important than ever as centers for community engagement and stewardship of our natural heritage and resources. Knowledge of our garden history, skilled horticulture, and creative design are the necessary components for carrying forward our gardening traditions in a changing environment and inspiring the love of plants and gardens in a new generation."

Dick Lighty paid tribute to Antonia and her role, saying, "Working closely with Antonia on the Garden Conservancy's mission over almost a quarter century has been one of the high points of my career. It has been a privilege to interact professionally with a leader of her imposing competence and high character, and I will continue to value the friendship that has come about."

After leaving, Antonia started her own consulting firm, Be Vision Driven, and after a few years agreed to accept a new leadership role as executive director of the Marin Art & Garden Center. Its logo is MAGC, pronounced "Magic." Founded in the 1940s to be a self-sustaining colony of artists and craftspeople in a parklike setting, MAGC's present mission is to promote appreciation and education of the arts, horticultural and environmental conservation. No doubt Antonia will work her own magic at this place, bringing her rich background in art, horticulture and conservation to an organization that is lucky to have her.

PUBLIC PARKS AND PUBLIC SPACES

Elizabeth Barlow Rogers

The three Ps of successful partnerships are passion, patience, and persistence. You also need a strong vision.

New York was fortunate that Elizabeth Barlow Rogers abandoned her Texas roots to become an easterner. She was determined not to be like those other Texans who came east but didn't really want to be there. She described them as "professional Texans. The east was not where their heart was." Once she came to New York as a young married woman, she resolved to give it her heart. She gave it so much more.

Blessed with a keen mind and a determined spirit, Betsy has been justifiably called "the savior of Central Park." Beautiful as Central Park has now become, it is hard to remember how it looked when she first became involved in the late 1960s and early 1970s. Covering 843 acres in the center of Manhattan, Central Park has had its ups and downs over its 160-year history. Those decades were definitely among the most severe downs. New Yorkers shunned the park; it was seen as far too dangerous to enter. Cars buzzed through its roads where the once impressive landscape and all its structures were in ruinous condition. Garbage was everywhere; the soil was so compacted that grass refused to grow; there were no lawns; the benches and lighting fixtures were nearly all broken; graffiti covered virtually every hard surface. Crime was rampant; drug pushers and muggers ruled the place.

Handsome, elegant John Lindsay had served as mayor from 1966 through 1973, leaving office with the city deeply in debt as the worst of the oil embargo rocked the economy. Lindsay was followed by Abraham Beame, who inherited the fiscal crisis facing both the city and the state. Beame served only one term – from 1974 through 1977 – and was ill-equipped to solve the dire financial problems. Both the city and New York State threatened to default on

53

Aerial view of Central Park

their bonds and were desperate for a bailout to avoid bankruptcy. On October 30, 1975, the front page of the *Daily News* trumpeted FORD TO CITY: DROP DEAD after President Ford vowed to veto any possible federal bailout for New York. In the midst of the challenges facing the city, there were no funds to spend on improving the public parks.

When Betsy was born in Texas in 1936, it was highly unpredictable that she would end up living in the center of Manhattan and saving Central Park. She lived in a comfortable home in San Antonio with her father, Caleb Leonidas Browning (known always as C.L.), a native Texan, and her mother, Elizabeth, an Oklahoman who went to the University of Texas, or UT as it is known. Betsy's life seemed destined to follow the pattern set by her mother. Many of the girls she grew up with went to Sweetbriar College in Virginia, but Betsy, who was a very bright student, graduated from St. Mary's Hall, an Episcopal day school, and decided to go to Wellesley College. Since a few earlier graduates of St. Mary's had made the move to Massachusetts, her parents agreed, but only because they expected her to attend for two years and then return to finish at UT, join a sorority, get married, and become a member of the Junior League. But when Betsy got over her freshman-year homesickness and realized how much she enjoyed her walks back and forth to class through the sublime Wellesley campus, she made up her mind to remain.

She majored in art history, focusing on painting, sculpture, and architecture. No doubt to her parents' relief, one month after her graduation in 1957 she did get married, to Ed Barlow. They met on a spring break in Bermuda while he was at Yale. When he joined the navy after Yale and went to work in the Pentagon, the newlyweds moved to Washington, D.C., where their child, Lisa, was born a year later. After Ed left the navy, Betsy's father, C.L., who hadn't given up on his hope for Betsy's return to Texas, invited Ed to join him in his construction business. Ed gave it a brief try but wasn't happy. Betsy couldn't see herself living her mother's socially conservative life, so she encouraged Ed to apply to Yale Law School, and he was accepted. They moved to New Haven.

Since her daughter was in nursery school and headed to kindergarten, Betsy thought she could pursue further studies. While she was interested in architecture and Yale had a fine school, it was a four-year course – too long. There was no program in landscape architecture, and she didn't see herself with a Ph.D. in art history, so she signed up for courses in city planning. Her interest was in urban design, particularly open space preservation, and she was lucky enough to study with the great Vincent Scully, one of Yale's shining lights.

When Ed graduated from Yale Law School in 1964, she had earned her master's in city planning. He had a job with a New York law firm as a beginning associate. When they moved to New York City, Betsy wanted to be involved with

the parks, and she volunteered for what was then the Park Association (later to become the Parks Council and then New Yorkers for Parks).

At the time, the city did not assign a lot of priority to even maintaining its parks, much less improving or restoring them. Betsy ended up writing a lot of reports that went nowhere. When Mayor Lindsay took office in 1966, he appointed Thomas Hoving, like himself an elegant patrician, to serve as parks commissioner. Hoving's idea was to sponsor big extravaganzas, "bread and circuses" as Betsy recalls them, to bring people into the parks. He organized Happenings, Be-ins and Love-ins, consistent with the mood of the times but punishing to Central Park. He also persuaded Mayor Lindsay to create a super-agency combining the administration of the parks with the city's cultural institutions, although it should have been clear that the parks and the cultural institutions had very different needs and demanded very different solutions. Hoving stayed in office only a little more than a year, then left to become director of the Metropolitan Museum of Art, a position far more suited to his talents.

He was succeeded by the scholarly (and equally patrician) August Heckscher, whose real heart was also in the cultural institutions, rather than the parks.

What was needed was a commissioner who knew how to manage the park workers and their unions. At the time, the managers and the workers belonged to the same unions, and union rules added heavily to the parks' financial woes. Under the rules, it took three workers to prune one tree – one to climb it, one to hold the tools, and one to drive the requisite motor vehicle. No wonder the trees, along with everything else, were in terrible shape.

When Abe Beame became mayor in 1973 at the height of the oil embargo, he appointed Edwin Weisl Jr. as parks commissioner, but the job was considered simply a political plum. Weisl served almost two years and was followed by three other short-term commissioners, two of whom served for only a matter of months. Not much changed.

Adele Auchincloss was a civic-minded citizen and not a politician. When at a dinner party she happened to meet Ed Weisl, he asked her to become one of his deputy parks commissioners. The title was intended to be purely honorific, but she decided to step in and take charge. With private funding, a master plan to restore Central Park had been prepared, and Adele was determined to find a way to convert the plan to a reality. She had already begun to enlist her friends for support – women like herself who were civic leaders and others who were major philanthropists such as Brooke Astor (widow of Vincent Astor and head of his foundation), Iphigene Ochs Sulzberger (whose family published the *New York Times*), and Lucy Moses (major benefactor of hospitals, schools, and parks). Adele knew Betsy from her work as a volunteer and was familiar with Betsy's intelligent written reports, her testimony on park budget issues before government officials, and her knowledge and commitment to improving park management.

By then, Betsy had also written two books. The first was *The Forests and Wetlands of New York City*, published by Little, Brown and Co. in 1971, which won the prestigious John Burroughs Medal and was nominated for the National Book Award. Even more important, she had also written a book about Frederick Law Olmsted, the famous designer of Central Park. Olmsted was not then as widely recognized a name. In fact, he was almost forgotten as the park's primary architect. But Charles McLaughlin, who was working with Charles Beveridge to publish Olmsted's papers, generously loaned Betsy some of Olmsted's manuscripts and other materials essential to her second book, *Frederick Law Olmsted's New York* (Praeger, 1971), that showed how invaluable his Central Park design was to New York City and described his incredible vision for the overall landscape design.

Despite President Ford's view that New York could "drop dead," Adele

Auchincloss somehow managed to attract a bit of federal funding to pay for a program to employ city kids in the park. And although Adele knew that Betsy had no experience running any program – never mind one serving needy kids – she was smart enough to recognize that Betsy could most likely accomplish anything she undertook and do it brilliantly. She believed in Betsy, and Betsy repaid her trust by running a successful summer program for sixty kids. Once that ended, Adele made sure that Betsy stayed on at the park.

From her city planning background, Betsy quickly realized that the existing master plan for the park covered only management and restoration; it was not really a full strategic plan with an overarching and long-term vision. But it was a start. Now the small, privately funded Central Park Task Force was created to put it into action. It was early days, and Betsy recalls, "I wrote an article '33 Ways Your Time and Money Can Help Save Central Park,' which was like an L. L. Bean catalogue of opportunities. It was kind of a preliminary vision. The next week $25,000 came over the transom. It came in $5, $25, $50 contributions."

The task force relied on private seed money, contributions that were intentionally kept out of the city coffers and free of any city control. But the funds were focused on a public park, so the task force had to navigate uncharted waters and fight to retain control. The parks commissioners and their staff wanted to grab any grant moneys they caught scent of. Finally, the indomitable Brooke Astor got into an elegant dress and went to confront the commissioner. Once the commissioner fully understood what she was saying, he demanded incredulously, "You mean, Mrs. Astor, you want *her* [Betsy] to manage the money?!" At the time "the money" was about $65,000, a considerably more meaningful amount than it would be today. And yes, that is exactly what Mrs. Astor meant, with the result that these women simply opened a special bank account that Betsy controlled. She went into high gear. She hired a horticulturist, organized volunteers, ran education programs, and raised awareness. After holding a competition for plans to restore Belvedere Castle, the neo-gothic stone structure atop Vista Rock with views across the park, she hired the architects who won.

All this happened in 1974. There was then no model for a private philanthropy working to improve a government-run property, not only by giving money but also by managing the money and the work. There also began to be some federal money available under the federal Comprehensive Employment and Training Act (CETA). But the city controlled the funds that were intended for, and used to, hire back many of the park workers laid off in the fiscal crisis.

Betsy recalls this time as very "idealistic" – and also "intense," a word she also uses (appropriately) to describe herself. Beneath her engaging charm, there is a fierce devotion to anything she undertakes with passion – and Central Park indeed became her consuming passion. She was extraordinarily effective because she tempered that passion with incredible patience and unflagging persistence. But she was always driven by an overarching mission; she believed that Olmsted's vision for Central Park, the Greensward Plan, was a masterpiece, an ideal of scenic beauty that had to be the guiding light for any future plan. Studying the Greensward Plan, Betsy observed, "It becomes obvious that the park's design is holistic, rather than simply a 'to-do' list of unrelated projects: a brilliant, Romantic symphony in which the visitor moves through passages of turf, woods, and water by means of curvilinear carriage drives, pedestrian paths, and bridle trails."

However, as was true of the original Greensward Plan submitted by Olmsted and Calvert Vaux, that vision had to be balanced with making the park a place for people. To that end, Betsy wrote what became *The Central Park Book,* later published in 1985 by the Central Park Conservancy. It was a collection of essays on the park's natural history and organized to serve as an educational support for teachers and students on their class trips to the park.

In these early and difficult days still under the Beame Administration, Betsy also had to learn how to raise funds. Undaunted by the challenge, she learned how to write grant proposals. She elicited funds from corporations such as Exxon, received a $140,000 grant from the National Endowment for the Humanities, and even made a film. In connection with the restoration of Grand Army Plaza, she persuaded the wealthy residents with apartments overlooking the plaza to pay what she called a "window tax" to support the improvement of their view. The task force continued to strengthen and grow.

Finally, Ed Koch was elected mayor in 1978 (he served until 1989). He appointed as his first parks commissioner Gordon Davis, who went on to serve for more than five years, the first commissioner in more than a decade with any longevity. Davis, discovering Betsy working away in a small office inside the Parks Department, saw what she was accomplishing and, as she recalls, "plucked me out of my little space and made up a title for me, Park Administrator." She had accountability with her official title as part of city management but was without any authority to manage the park employees. Betsy enjoyed being a "public servant," a role she thought of as an important trust, but she was a hybrid; as the *New York Times* put it, she was "not the archetypical public servant." She reported to the commissioner but she took up none of the budget since she had herself raised all the funds to pay her own salary. But since there was apparently a surplus of available municipal drivers, she was awarded one! (A great asset in New York City.)

Betsy realized the Central Park Task Force had to grow into something bigger. She was determined "to make the people of New York City see the park in the same light as the Museum of Natural History, or the Bronx Zoo, or the Botanical Gardens – they must see it as a major cultural institution. Grace Glueck of the *New York Times* came to write a story, and asked, 'You mean you think of this park as a cultural institution; and those trees, those sculptures, as your collection?' And I said, 'You've got it.' That's really how the Conservancy was launched."

In 1980, the Central Park Conservancy was born, an independent legal entity with charitable tax-exempt status. This was the start of a public-private partnership to encourage citizen support for the restoration and renewed management of the park. Gordon Davis, endorsing the idea of the Conservancy from the start, joined with Betsy to ask Bill Beinecke to serve as the first chair. He was perfect – a wealthy businessman and philanthropist who committed himself fully to anything he undertook. He was smart, focused, and liked to get things done but always in his gracious, gentlemanly style. With free reign to build the first board, Beinecke and Betsy recruited other business leaders who gave generously to city causes, including Howard Clark of American Express; Richard Gilder of Gilder, Gagnon, Howe & Co.; Arthur Ross; and others, including of course some original members of the Central Park Task Force such as Adele Auchincloss.

Some of these same men had already formed a group called the Central Park Community Fund, which had commissioned a study of the park's needs. Ed Savas, a Columbia University professor, conducted that study, outlining the current state of the park, analyzing its management, and pointing out its serious problems. But no one on the Community Fund had yet begun to work productively on the cure.

The Central Park Task Force and the Central Park Community Fund merged to create the Central Park Conservancy, its board headed by Bill Beinecke with Betsy as president.

Everyone was excited and full of bold ideas. The city was slowly recovering from the fiscal crisis; the time was ripe for civic leadership and private philanthropy to save the day. The Conservancy's early leadership also tried to ensure that the board included members representing the ethnic diversity of the park users. The distinguished federal second circuit judge Barrington Daniels Parker Jr., an African American, was one example. Their first mission statement was simple and bold: "To Make Central Park clean, safe, and beautiful."

An obvious first task was to remove all the graffiti that covered more than fifty thousand square feet of park surfaces. Betsy elicited a $65,000 grant from Bankers Trust Company for graffiti removal, and it took three years to finish that job.

She completed other projects, raised funds, and hired additional crews

Central Park: Glen Span Arch

for tree, turf, planting, and landscape restoration. One of the earliest and largest gifts was $1.5 million from Alan Weiler and his sister Joan Arnow in memory of their mother. It was for restoration of the Conservatory Garden on Fifth Avenue, which has an entrance through the handsome Vanderbilt Gate between 104th and 105th Streets. This had once been a grand formal garden, complete with a beautiful glass house conservatory, elaborate fountains, and formal allées of flowering trees. Only a hint of its former glory was still evident in 1980, but the outlines of the garden remained.

Betsy reached out to her neighbor and friend, Lynden Miller, a painter who had become interested in gardening, and asked her to take this project on. Lynden, much like Betsy, proved a force to be reckoned with, although she had no prior experience in garden restoration or design. There were already garden club members who had been volunteering on the scene, but full restoration of the Conservatory Garden required a strong leader. Just as Adele had placed her confidence in Betsy early on, Betsy instinctively sensed that Lynden was cut from much the same cloth. The outcome was not only a spectacular success but the beginning of Lynden Miller's important professional career designing public gardens.

Success breeds success. Yoko Ono was the next important donor. She and her husband, John Lennon, lived in the historic Dakota apartment building on Central Park West overlooking the park. John Lennon was tragically shot down outside the Dakota in December 1980, when he was just forty years old, and Yoko Ono committed $1 million to create a special garden inside the park in his memory. She then paid for a huge ad asking the nations of the world to contribute trees for Strawberry Fields, named after one of the great John Lennon songs. That garden in Central Park continues to be a peaceful oasis and a beautiful tribute.

The work continued to be challenging, and always exciting. Central Park had been recognized as early as 1974 with the first Scenic Landmarks Designation, and Olmsted's design and overall vision continued to guide the Conservancy. Bruce Kelly, a landscape architect with a background in historic preservation, became part of Betsy's architectural team. She hired soil scientists, commissioned a user study, and prepared a circulation plan. From time to time, she also drew upon some of the people employed by the Parks Department. Always first consulting the Olmsted plan and considering the park in its entirety before making a decision, Betsy insisted that the "plan always had to grow out of the basic vision of overall scenic beauty." The result was the comprehensive plan to rebuild Central Park, later described by others as "both a fine planning tool and a masterful piece of fund-raising propaganda to promote the park to the corporations and residents whose premises look out over it." Her book, *Rebuilding Central Park: A Management and Restoration Plan,* was published by MIT in 1987.

Betsy's personal life was also enhanced. Her first marriage to Ed Barlow had ended in divorce in 1979, and in 1984 she married Ted Rogers and took time off for a wedding trip to Venice. Ted had been the CEO of NL Industries in Houston, so they shared Texas roots. When he came to New York he became interested in the Park because he was a long-distance runner, and the New York City Marathon always finishes in the park before cheering crowds. A highly cultured man, with a deep interest in the ballet, he eventually served as chair of

Central Park: The Mall and Literary Walk in fall

the New York City Ballet. Bill Beinecke knew Ted and recruited him to join the Conservancy board, but he told Ted he would first have to meet and pass muster with Betsy. Evidently, he did more than that, as they have been happily married ever since.

To this day, Betsy credits the generosity of New Yorkers for her success. For example, the Weilers and Joan and Bob Arnow were early supporters of Lynden Miller's work at the Conservatory Garden. They and other civic leaders like them raised the money required for the big projects to restore the park. Betsy also used direct mailings to solicit small gifts from the public so that everyone would feel involved in the effort. After all, this was the people's park, and as many people as possible had to feel engaged in and committed to it. Referring to the original Olmsted-Vaux plan for the park in her latest book, *Green Metropolis,* Betsy said, "They firmly believed that parks, as places accessible to all classes of society, were fundamental attributes of democracy."

Betsy decided to organize a benefit, which she thought should take place in the park. She planned an outdoor luncheon for the spring. Bill Beinecke, and others such as Paul Chase, Norma Dana, Maggie Purnell (Mrs. Richard Purnell), and Jean Clark (wife of Howard Clark of Amex) signed on. They recruited Phyllis Wagner, formerly the wife of Bennett Cerf and then of Robert Wagner, an earlier mayor of New York, to be their celebrity guest. The benefit was a huge success and still carries on each year. By now, the Olmsted Luncheon provides more than $3 million of the $7 million raised annually and is sold out by January. The women guests come wearing huge, glorious hats and are prominently featured in all the newspapers. Kitty Carlisle Hart observed, "We used to have the Easter Parade and now we have this luncheon!"

The Conservancy also raised funds by selling plaques to be affixed to park benches in the name of the donor or someone the donor wished to honor. Playgrounds were restored, a tree trust established. When Betsy was asked by board member Richard Gilder what it would take to complete all the desired projects outlined in the overall restoration plan if a second capital campaign were launched, Betsy told him $50 million. He immediately committed the first third ($17 million); he suggested she get the city to kick in a third and raise the rest. She eventually raised a total of $71 million! Today the Conservancy provides more than 75 percent of Central Park's total budget and has a contract with the city to manage the park.

Betsy put in place some essential principles for the park's management. First, she divided the park into zones; each had a head gardener assigned who "owned" that section and was fully accountable for its condition. The first head gardener took on Yoko Ono's three-acre Strawberry Fields. With this precedent set, there is now a head gardener for all fifty-three sections of the park.

When her mother died in 1992 (long after her father), Betsy took over the ownership and responsibility for the family ranch in the Texas Hill Country, not far from San Antonio, where she had spent many happy childhood summers. Her father, C. L., had bought the ranch in 1942; land was added over time, and Betsy now owns nearly a thousand acres, along with the barn and house her father built. Encouraged by the example of David Bamberger, owner of a much larger ranch nearby who called himself a "land steward," Betsy reflected on her responsibilities as a steward of the land she had inherited. Soon she was collaborating with the University of Texas, Texas A&M, and Texas State University, and with local, state, and federal agencies, and nonprofits such as the Lady Bird Johnson Wildflower Center. She has created a showcase of ecological landscape management on the ranch, celebrating the special aesthetic and environmental protection of that unique part of the world

As the C. L. Browning Ranch website puts it: "The Texas Hill Country is exceptionally beautiful. To own a property of great scenic value is a privilege. To preserve the natural landscape and promote biodiversity is a duty. To perpetuate a sense of place through conservation action is a way of enhancing one's personal identity." The ranch, going back to her original Texas roots, is in Betsy's heart.

By 1995, Betsy felt it was time to step down as president of the Central Park Conservancy. She had had a long and successful journey, from her early days as a volunteer to her work for the Central Park Task Force to her double title as Park Administrator and president of the Conservancy. Her leadership was clearly key to her triumphs, along with her mantra of patience, passion, and persistence – and vision. She had invented the template of a public-private partnership, and made it an extraordinarily productive reality, in restoring the park. And she had worked hard doing it.

After so many years at what Betsy calls the "best job in the world," she wisely believes there comes a time when the founder with the original vision and missionary zeal needs to step down. As a result of her success, the Central Park Conservancy had evolved into a large organization with its own substantial staff. Betsy says, "I am not temperamentally a big-organization administrator." And she wanted to return to what she saw as her original career – writing.

It is always hard for an organization to survive the departure of a strong, inspiring founder-leader. Anyone following in Betsy's shoes would have a hard time and that proved to be the case for several years. But Betsy left the Central Park Conservancy in superb shape with a strong staff. She believes it is now headed by the best parks administrator in America, Doug Blonsky, whom she had originally hired. Although no longer active on the Conservancy's board, Betsy remains a life trustee.

Once a civic reformer, always a civic reformer. Betsy couldn't quite quit. As she was stepping down as president, she established the Cityscape Institute to try to share good design beyond the borders of Central Park throughout the rest of the city. Thanks to the Conservancy, Central Park had redesigned lighting, signage, and litter bins. What if good design could be extended to all the city streets and all its parks? Despite her best efforts and to her regret, the Cityscape Institute came to an end, but Betsy's wish to have an impact beyond Central Park continues under the Conservancy's auspices as the Institute for Urban Parks, an educational arm that teaches other communities how to better design and manage their parks.

For some years, Betsy had been working on her next book, *Landscape Design: A Cultural and Architectural History,* a scholarly and comprehensive book that would serve as the definitive text for a course in landscape studies. Published by Harry N. Abrams in 2001, the book's more than five hundred pages are rich with content, illustrations, and designs. It continues to be an invaluable resource, covering the gamut from England's Stonehenge to Egypt, Greece, and Peru, and on to the present, seeking ambitiously to tell the history

Central Park: The Great Lawn

of "the relationship of human beings and their world, and of their attempts to invest nature with purposeful order and meaning and specific places with expressive form and heightened significance."

With the book as text, Betsy taught a course in landscape studies for three years at the Bard Graduate Center in New York. Along with teaching her classes, she began a journal called *Viewpoints,* raising the funds to cover the costs. Appropriately, the first issue came out in 2003 to celebrate the 150th Anniversary of Central Park. Betsy loved teaching and those years helped her build a network with other scholars.

In 2005 Betsy left Bard to create a new nonprofit organization, the Foundation for Landscape Studies to "foster an active understanding of the importance of place in human life." Building on her experience with *Viewpoints,* Betsy established the journal *SiteLines* as part of the foundation's mission. Full of thoughtful articles about landscape history and landscape design, theory, and practice, it comes out twice a year. The foundation also honors Place Makers and Place Keepers as well as authors at an annual benefit lunch in the boathouse in Central Park.

Besides publishing the writings of others, Betsy continues to write books herself. She still maintains the modest farmhouse in Wainscott, Long Island, she bought when she first moved to Manhattan, where she first learned to garden and where she met her neighbor, Lynden Miller. But as Wainscott, once surrounded by potato farms, became part of the crowded social power scene of the Hamptons, she and Ted began to spend time in the west. Since 1996, their retreat has been an adobe house in the historic district of Santa Fe where they spend Christmas and most of every summer, with a "mini wildflower meadow" along with a dry stream featuring handsome local rocks. At the southern end of the Rockies in the Sangre de Cristo mountains, with deep Spanish traditions and close to the Native American pueblos, it is a place with its own unique history and culture.

Despite these competing homes, Betsy's center of gravity remains in Manhattan, where she happily overlooks her beloved Central Park. She has been widely recognized with awards and honors for her critical role in its preservation. When she received the Pugsley Award from the American Academy for Park and Recreation Administration, she was "ranked with Olmsted, Vaux, and Moses for her impact on the park." Her pioneering success, in Central Park and elsewhere, has inspired and encouraged other communities to protect, revive, and reaffirm their own public spaces.

Betsy taught the world that "landscape design is as much a part of our heritage as painting and sculpture. The park should be treated like any other cultural institution, like any museum, botanical garden, or zoological society."

Lynden B. Miller

I was a painter who gardened and became a gardener who painted.

LYNDEN MILLER, the artist who gardened, evolved into a gardener who painted. Painted with plants, that is. Beginning in 1982, her artistry transformed the Conservatory Garden of Central Park and that began her distinguished career of designing and enhancing open spaces with plants. Applauded and recognized for her approach, she has transformed many public venues into beautiful and appealing areas that enrich the life of the surrounding community. After her work in the Conservatory Garden, she went on to other important projects, including the Central Park Zoo, Bryant Park, Madison Square Park, the New York Botanical Garden, Columbia University, and other places in and around New York City. Her approach serves as an important example and has had a major influence far beyond New York.

Artistic from an early age, Lynden was born in New York City on December 8, 1938, to Alan Ryder Breed and Rosilla Hornblower, both from well-established New York families. The Hornblowers included a judge of the Second Circuit Court of Appeals, and the Breeds founded the illustrious New York law firm now called Whitman Breed Abbott & Morgan. Tragically, Lynden's father developed MS shortly after she was born and died when she was only five years old. Because her father was so frail, her parents moved the family to Washington, D.C., to be near Rosilla's brother and to find a house that could accommodate a wheelchair. Lynden's mother remarried many years after her husband died, but there were no more children; Lynden had no siblings. She briefly attended the Chapin School in New York City, and, after the move to Washington, the Potomac School before heading off to boarding school at St. Timothy's, and then to Smith College, where she majored in art and graduated in 1960.

Several of Lynden's teachers encouraged her interest in art. Her maternal grandmother was also artistic; she had worked in Tiffany's studio. Lynden had drawn as a small child, and she thought she might teach art or possibly even survive as an artist. But after graduating from college, she realized that in those days the only job open to a young woman with a liberal arts education was as a secretary.

Rather than settle for being a typist, she returned to Washington to work on Capitol Hill for two different congressmen. She thinks of herself as a "political animal," a characteristic that would serve her well in her life's work. Eventually she went on to be an assistant to various editors at the *Washington Post*. Later, she enrolled at the University of Maryland for two years, studying studio art.

One evening in 1964, she attended a party hosted by her friend Mary Smith. Lynden felt quite brave in going since she was sure she wouldn't know anyone else there. When she arrived, Leigh Miller opened the door for her. Then working at USAID, Leigh was in the process of getting a divorce. Although it seemed an unlikely moment to begin a relationship, they married two years later, in 1966, and have celebrated fifty happy years together.

After Nixon's election in 1968, Leigh left his government job to join Schroders, a British asset management company, and later moved on to American Express Bank. They moved to New York City, where Lynden established her own small art studio. Nostalgic memories of her happy childhood summers spent in a white clapboard house in the country impelled Lynden to seek to replicate that experience for herself and her children. Like many New Yorkers, the Millers bought a lovely country house for weekends and summers in Ancram, New York. They soon discovered how hot Ancram was in the summer, so they began renting a house for the month of August in Wainscott, Long Island, to enjoy the beaches of the Hamptons.

While the family was away in August 1975, their house in Ancram was robbed. Devastated by the loss of precious things that had been in her family for generations, Lynden refused to return. They sold the house and moved to Sharon, Connecticut, where the summers were cooler, and they had many friends. That was the beginning of what became Lynden's beautiful gardens in Sharon.

Lynden took away something from her summers in the Hamptons that proved indispensable to her future story: her friendship with Betsy Barlow Rogers. Betsy had a country home in Wainscott right next door to the house the Millers rented. Familiar with Betsy from her book *The Forests and Wetlands of New York City*, and never shy, Lynden knocked on Betsy's door one day to introduce herself. Betsy's son, David, was close in age to Lynden's son Marshall. This was in the early 1970s when Betsy was beginning to develop her role in Central Park. The two women became fast friends.

In the mid 1970s, Leigh took Lynden on a tour of English gardens, and in 1977, his work for American Express took him and his family to London for two years. Even before the move, Lynden had taken some courses at the New York Botanical Garden and Wave Hill. T. H. Everett, whose name runs through many of the stories in this book, was at the New York Botanical Garden at the time; he and his colleague, Miss Elizabeth Hall, suggested that Lynden consult the renowned garden designer Lanning Roper when she moved to London.

Any advice from T. H. Everett commanded respect, so Lynden followed it. The Millers bought a small house in Bedford Gardens that had been restored by the Georgian Group and came with a small garden. When she consulted Lanning Roper, he asked Lynden what kind of garden she wanted. She told him she wanted to grow things that she couldn't have in the cold climate of Sharon, Connecticut. Then Roper asked to see her paintings. After seeing them, he said, "I know what you want. You want careless rapture." This was a fine description for what Lynden would create in the gardens she went on to design.

England is famous for being a nation of passionate gardeners, and Lynden was eager to join them. She bought the famous *Yellow Book*, published annually to provide dates and directions to almost four thousand private gardens open to the public as part of the National Garden Scheme to benefit charity, and she visited gardens every weekend, often to the chagrin of her small boys. Betsy Barlow Rogers came to visit, and they went off to see gardens together; they also visited the people who managed the Royal Parks. Lynden tried to enroll to study horticulture at Wisley, the Royal Horticultural Society garden in Surrey just outside London, but Wisley didn't yet admit women. Instead, she signed up for a nine-month course on plant identification that met in London every week.

As she observed these gardens and worked on her own, she admired the long English tradition of painting with plants. This strengthened her own view that gardening is, and should be considered, an art – a highly demanding art since the "paints" never dry, the palette is always changing, and the composition needs constant maintenance and attention. She went to London, she recounts, "as a painter who gardened and returned as a gardener who painted."

When the family moved back to New York in 1979, Lynden wept. She had only seen the results in her London garden for one growing season. Her sons had gone to the finest schools, Colet Court and St Paul's, and had quickly developed British accents. Her younger son Marshall tried to comfort her, saying, "Don't cry, Mummy. I will go to Oxford or Cambridge someday and you can come back to visit."

After her return to New York, Lynden also returned to her garden in Sharon, Connecticut. One of her first acts was to add windows to the north side of the house to look over a future garden. When the house was originally built by early Connecticut Yankees, they had nothing but fireplaces to provide heat.

They sensibly placed the major windows facing south, closing the north side as much as possible as protection against the elements.

Eager to continue her studies, Lynden went again to talk to T. H. Everett. He counseled her not to go to NYBG's School of Professional Horticulture, whose standards he no longer considered sufficient. Instead, he suggested she go to work in a great garden under a masterful head gardener. He sent her to his friend Don Richardson, who was the head gardener at Greentree, the 438-acre estate owned by Betsy Cushing Roosevelt Whitney in Manhasset on the north shore of Long Island. Betsy Whitney was one of the three famous Boston Cushing sisters: Betsy had married James Roosevelt, oldest son of FDR, before marrying Jock Whitney; her sister Mary ("Minnie") married Vincent Astor; and her sister Barbara ("Babe") married William Paley.

T. H. and Don Richardson, both great horticulturists, were cut from the same cloth. Both men were from the same era, always wearing tweed jackets even when working in the garden. Lynden traveled from Manhattan to Manhasset once a week for a year and a half to apprentice at Greentree. She had to wake up at dawn to get there in time for the day's work and did not leave until 4:30 P.M. or later. Having lost her own father when she was so young, she grew to admire and deeply love Don Richardson.

Lynden continued to make art in her studio as well, and in the early 1980s she had her first one-person show in New York. She produced abstract landscape collages inspired by Central Park. When Betsy Barlow Rogers came to the show and bought a few of her works, Lynden confessed that she didn't really like the art world; she didn't enjoy trying to promote herself and putting up with all of the nonsense. With huge numbers of struggling artists pushing to get into the limited number of good art galleries, the competition was ferocious. She began to wonder what she should do with her life.

In the spring of 1982, Lynden met Rosemary Verey, who was visiting Wave Hill. Lynden was on the board of Wave Hill at the time: Peter Sauer was then head. As she so often did to people she met, Rosemary Verey suggested that Lynden come and stay with her at her famous garden at Barnsley House in the English Cotswolds. Lynden jumped at the chance. She went and stayed for three days, heading out by 5:30 every morning to record and research the memorable gardens of Hidcote, a National Trust property nearby. And in the long light of the evenings, she spent time studying Rosemary Verey's garden.

In that same year of 1982, Betsy Barlow Rogers, Lynden's longtime friend and now founder of the Central Park Conservancy, approached her and said, "I have a project for you. I want you to restore the Conservatory Garden up in the northern end of the park." Lynden replied, "Are you out of your mind? I wouldn't know how to do that!" Betsy presciently insisted that she thought

Lynden could and that she wanted an "artist's eye up there." Then she added blithely that Lynden would not only have to restore the plantings but raise the money to do it. Most important, Lynden would "have to find a way to bring the people back." Just as others had sensed that Betsy had what it took to restore Central Park, Betsy knew Lynden was the right person for the job and that she would succeed. And Lynden realized, "My life would never be the same again."

Before Lynden took on the challenge of the Conservatory Garden, the six-acre formal garden at 105th Street and Fifth Avenue, like the rest of Central Park, was in sorry shape. The Conservatory Garden abutted East Harlem, then a place of crowded tenements, vacant lots, and run-down housing projects. The impressive glass conservatory from which the garden took its name had been built in 1898 but was taken down in 1934 because of the high costs of running and maintaining it.

In 1937, a newly designed garden had opened, an early WPA project. The garden was designed by Betty Sprout, a landscape architect who worked for Robert Moses at the Parks Department. Gilmore Clarke was the consulting landscape architect. Sprout and Clarke later married, so Lynden liked to say, "We got great design *and* romance" in the Conservatory Garden.

Many of the park's gardeners were let go in the fiscal crisis of the 1970s, and by 1980 it had been suffering years of neglect. A few Parks Department gardeners did the best they could, and a cadre of women volunteers from the New York Committee of the Garden Club of America came two times a year to plant annuals and bulbs, but they provided no maintenance. Despite all this, the basic bones of the original Betty Sprout 1937 design remained.

The Garden Club volunteers had done what they could, and some had come to think of the Conservatory Garden as their turf. They hardly welcomed the idea of an outsider coming in to run things.

Betsy was having none of it. She knew the project needed a strong, dedicated leader. She asked Lynden to tackle the situation and take charge of the Garden Club ladies. Lynden agreed. She was ready, both personally and professionally, for a serious project that would employ all her strengths in horticulture and the strong leadership and political skills, which she had not yet had a chance to demonstrate.

Work on the Conservatory Garden took off in the fall of 1982, and the formal opening was scheduled for the following spring. Many well-meaning people advised Lynden against taking on the task, warning that anything she tried to do in the Conservatory Garden would be instantly destroyed by the worst elements in the East Harlem neighborhood. Most told her that "these people will trash it." But Lynden felt the poorer parts of the city also deserved lovely places. She was sure that if she could make the garden beautiful, the community would come together to protect it, and she understood that part of her mission included engaging the community.

Although Lynden first undertook her new role as an unpaid volunteer, she soon began to earn a salary from the Central Park Conservancy, largely so that she would be taken seriously by the Parks Department and the Conservancy staff who would have to work for her. Lynden admired and respected the Parks Department, which had been frustrated for years by the lack of resources. And the department employees, in turn, respected her.

Betsy Barlow Rogers recognized from her own experience when she first received the title of Park Administrator that it was important for Lynden to have an official position and that a title was very important in public and professional life. Lynden became director of the Conservatory Garden, a title she retained for many years.

Lynden faced many ups and downs, but she had fallen in love with the overgrown, romantic place, and Leigh gave her constant encouragement and support. Betsy had wanted an artist's eye and that is what she got. Paula Deitz, the distinguished writer and publisher of the quarterly *The Hudson Review,* recognized this. Deitz, aware of Lynden's early work as an artist, wrote to praise her work in the Conservatory Garden, asking, "What is a garden but a collage?!"

The original Betty Sprout plans for the garden provided an important source for the restoration. The formality of the Sprout design was in strong contrast to the flavor of the Olmsted-Vaux plan for the rest of Central Park. Entered from Fifth Avenue through ornate French black iron gates, the Sprout design divided the six-acre garden into three main sections: the northern section, influenced by French garden style, bloomed in spring and fall with spectacular displays; the central area, more Italian in feel, was primarily green, with a center lawn, yew hedges, and spring color from the crabapple allées; the southern section, often called "the Secret Garden," had a more English flavor and featured perennial beds surrounding a small formal pool with a charming bronze statue in the center. The original design had called for these beds to be replanted three times or more a year with annuals and bulbs, a maintenance demand long since abandoned.

Lynden had her own ideas for what was needed, both for plantings and engaging the community. One of her first acts was cutting down the overgrown tall hedges that blocked the sight lines from outside the garden and made the public feel shut out. She refused to accept the status quo approach to public parks, saying, "There's a belief that we don't need to make them very good, that you can sort of dumb them down, throw in a few marigolds and red salvia and call it a day."

Instead, Lynden created mixed borders using plantings that would look good in all four seasons – not an easy task and one that required ongoing maintenance, although not quite at the Sprout level. Lynden called for a mix of flowering and evergreen shrubs to be planted as a spine in the middle of the perennial beds. Durable perennials were massed for texture, with annuals and bulbs added in spots. Drawing on her skills as an artist, she emphasized color, shape, and texture in her design. She understood that garden design and creation is an art, although, as has been said, "the slowest of the performing arts." Like painting, gardening is all about color, texture, line, scale, and repetition.

First the existing plantings had to be pruned back hard or dug out; many were given to community gardens in the area. Happily, the Central Park Conservancy had for some time before begun composting leaves rather than trucking them out of the park each year at great expense. The rich "black gold" of composted leaves happened to be located right next to the Conservatory Garden, easily accessible to restore the soil.

The garden was a triumph, both in terms of its aesthetics and its appeal to and support by the neighboring community. As Lynden had hoped, the local visitors loved it, and they protected it. She was deeply moved by their reaction, validating her original vision. She never returned to her studio. In recognition of the importance of the garden and its link to the community, Lynden accepted an appointment to serve on the community board of East Harlem in 1983. She served for a dozen years, and Leigh followed her in that role for close to nearly another fifteen years. She enjoyed her time on the community board, found it useful, and when developers threatened to build twenty-six-story buildings along Fifth Avenue from 96th to 106th Streets, shading the Conservatory Garden and tearing down all the existing historic buildings, she joined the battle to stop it. Her skills as a "political animal" proved useful; she testified, enlisted support, got herself named to the Parks Council, and finally persuaded the future mayor David Dinkins to shoot the plan down.

By 1987, the garden was in sufficiently good shape to allow Lynden to undertake an effort to raise an endowment for its ongoing maintenance and improvement. Betsy Barlow Rogers had already established the Olmsted Luncheon as a fund-raising event for the Central Park Conservancy – what Lynden refers to as the "Hat Lunch" – and she often gave tours to people to show them what needed attention and funding in Central Park. Likewise, Lynden was often enlisted to give tours of the Conservatory Garden and that is how she met Alan Weiler and his sister, Joan Arnow. A few weeks later, Joan Arnow donated $25,000 to fix the pergola steps.

Sometime later, the fiftieth anniversary of the Conservatory Garden happened to coincide with the sixtieth wedding anniversary of Alan and Joan's parents, and Joan asked Lynden to suggest some ideas for how they might be honored. Long worried about the future of the garden, Lynden had realized from the beginning that the greatest challenge would be maintaining it. She knew a lavishly planted formal garden on this scale needed an endowment. When Joan asked for a figure, Lynden consulted Kate French, then working for the Central Park Conservancy, and they came up with $1.5 million. (Kate later went on to work at Bryant Park and eventually become the highly successful, long-term president and executive director of Wave Hill at Lynden's recommendation.) After considering it, Joan called to say the family would fund the entire amount! At the time, it was the largest single gift to any public park in the history of the country. It meant Lynden could hire five full-time gardeners to work along with the twenty-five volunteers, and this continues today.

In 1986, as a result of the reputation Lynden had deservedly earned for her work in Central Park, three new challenges came her way: first a garden restoration at the New York Botanical Garden, then a new garden at the Central Park Zoo, and finally the signal challenge presented by Bryant Park.

First came a call from Beth Straus, a gracious, dynamic woman then on the New York Botanical Garden board, who knew Lynden's work at the Conservatory Garden. She said simply, "We need you at NYBG," and came to pick up Lynden at 4:30 that same day. This was before Gregory Long arrived in 1989 to take charge as president of NYBG and revive the entire institution.

The Irwin Perennial Garden needed restoration, and the board had recognized that Lynden was the perfect choice. The garden had so disastrously deteriorated that the family of Jane Watson Irwin, for whom the garden was named, had asked to have the plaque with their name on it removed. Given Lynden's accomplishments, Beth Straus was sure she could restore the area, encourage donors, and attract public visitors again. It was a great joy for Lynden, almost a vindication, for she had been a student at NYBG herself.

Much like Central Park, the New York Botanical Garden had suffered substantial cutbacks in city funding over the years, and priority went to NYBG's scientific programs rather than to the maintenance of its 250-acre public garden located in the Bronx. The half-acre Irwin Perennial Garden was prominently sited, running parallel to the imposing glass conservatory, but its meandering paths were obscured by weeds, and its beds outlined with unattractive railroad ties.

Lynden quickly got to work, employing the many lessons she had learned from the Conservatory Garden. She added four-foot-tall yew hedges to define the space, block the view of the internal road, and create a backdrop for ornamental shrubs and perennials. She removed many ungainly existing plants, there for scientific rather than aesthetic interest, and had them planted elsewhere. Even though the area was designated a perennial garden, she knew that shrubs would be needed to provide year-round interest. She chose plant compositions for different areas according to a color theme.

During the first summer after the replanting, the Irwin family visited and decided to restore the plaque. Lynden and Beth Straus became close friends and the Perennial Garden continues to look beautiful. Thirty years later, Lynden still carries on garden design at NYBG, where she is currently a member of the board.

Situated in Central Park at 64th Street and Fifth Avenue, the zoo, like

Lynden's garden in Sharon, Connecticut

the rest of Central Park, was in terrible shape. By 1983 the Parks Department had decided to close it, ceding management and control to the New York Zoological Society, which runs the much larger and famous Bronx Zoo. The animals were all sent off to much better quarters in the Bronx, and the architect Kevin Roche, of Kevin Roche John Dinkeloo and Associates, was hired to redesign the facility with the generous support of Lila Acheson Wallace, the philanthropist and co-founder of *Reader's Digest*.

The seal pool was being reconstructed, and Kevin Roche reached out to hire Lynden to design a central garden area around it. But first he required Lynden to come to New Haven for an interview. She remembers sitting across from him and a group of his colleagues, answering the many questions asked by his team while he just sat silent, watching her. Then he invited her to lunch. Having heard that the existing crabapple trees at the seal pool were going to be removed, Lynden bravely spoke up, saying that she wouldn't agree to undertake the work unless he agreed to keep the crabapples. After that lunch, Kevin Roche visited the Conservatory Garden, where Lynden showed him the mature crabapples and how, when well pruned and maintained, they added important structure to the space. As an architect, Kevin Roche understood the importance of structure.

Lynden was hired in 1986. She also had to pass muster with the director of the zoo who was skeptical at first, worrying about installing an "itsy-bitsy garden." Lynden remembers that she drew herself up to her "full five feet three inches and replied, 'I don't do itsy-bitsy gardens!'" That ended that conversation.

It was the first time Lynden had to work with a large construction team. She learned much in the process. Her remit was to design a garden in four quadrants around the seal pool. Lynden knew that the pool was a popular destination and that as many people came to see the seals in winter as in spring and summer. Again, this public space had to look good in all the seasons. She added benches; the crabapples remained to provide structure; and she turned to specimen dwarf conifers to sit in the center of each quadrant. She also used Japanese maples, not previously part of her plant palette, for foliage and to make interesting winter forms. The zoo reopened in 1988 and the animals returned. But there was no funding for ongoing maintenance of her garden, and it soon deteriorated from her original design. This was a hard lesson she took to heart in her later work.

Bryant Park was next. A six-acre park behind the main building of the New York Public Library on Fifth Avenue, the space was commonly known by the mid-eighties as Needle Park. It was the home of drug dealers, muggers, and worse. By 1987, it was even closed on the heels of a drug-related murder. The civic leaders dedicated to the restoration of the library understood that they needed to focus on both the building and the park behind it. Andrew Heiskell, chairman of Time, Inc. and the chairman of the library's board, and Dan Biederman cofounded the Bryant Park Restoration Corporation (BPRC) with initial support from the Rockefeller Brothers Fund, which was quickly followed by assessments on adjacent property owners and businesses. Dan Biederman was named to head BPRC. This was the first business improvement district (BID) in the country devoted to a park. It provided the model for private management and funding of urban development projects that expanded to other areas of New York City and has since been widely emulated elsewhere. Biederman hired the architect Hugh Hardy and the landscape architect Laurie Olin to design the space running behind the library building west to Sixth Avenue between 40th and 42nd streets.

Lynden gives great credit for the success of Bryant Park to her friend and mentor, the urban planner William Hollingsworth Whyte ("Holly" to everyone). Whyte lived on 94th Street, not far from the Conservatory Garden, and was among its first donors. His principles had an important influence on Bryant Park, for long before the restoration began, he had written a report for the Rockefeller Brothers Fund about how to bring the park back to life. He and his sociology students at Hunter College had studied New York City's parks and plazas to document how visitors used the spaces and what elements made them successful. He proclaimed simple truths, such as "People sit where there are places to sit;" "What attracts people is other people;" and "Blank walls proclaim the power of the institution and the inconsequence of the individual." His maxims influenced the removal of the walls around Bryant Park, the installation of movable chairs and tables, and the addition of food kiosks and vendors to draw people in. He saw how much people enjoyed the Conservatory Garden and

Lynden Miller

realized he had left out horticulture, and that horticulture had to be a part of the mix. "You make it happen" in Bryant Park, he told Lynden.

Dan Biederman agreed. He liked what Lynden had done in the challenging neighborhood of East Harlem and thought she could do wonders for Bryant Park. Dan Biederman was only in his thirties, and Lynden in her forties, when he hired her in 1987. He asked her to design two three-hundred-foot-long flowerbeds along the balustrade walls flanking the two-acre lawn. This wasn't part of the original restoration plan or budget, so he also asked her to raise the money. The Weiler-Arnow family, the major supporters of Lynden's Conservatory Garden, happened to own a building facing Bryant Park, and once again they generously contributed significant funding.

Laurie Olin cut openings in the balustrade wall on each side so that people could cross the park from north to south as well as east to west. Lynden designed long beds with her now signature mixed plantings, especially emphasizing winter interest here with evergreens and adapting her plantings to predominantly sunny conditions on one side and shade on the other. A series of tall vertical evergreens marched down each side, with benches periodically recessed into the borders.

When Bryant Park reopened in 1992, all of Lynden's tulips bloomed, as if on cue. And everyone had said it couldn't be done. Lynden remembers watching a man in a suit with a briefcase walk into Bryant Park, stop, put his briefcase down, and do two cartwheels. "I was one of those who said it would never work," he said. "I was wrong. I am so glad I was wrong."

Lynden had become the city's go-to person to design important public spaces. Next came Wagner Park, named for Robert F. Wagner Jr., a former New York City mayor, and part of Battery Park City, a ninety-two-acre complex of buildings on landfill along the Hudson River. When first established, a third of the acreage was set aside for parks and open space, and the Battery Park City Authority was created to design and maintain the landscape. In 1988, Jennifer Bartlett had produced a controversial plan for Wagner Park, situated in the southern end of Battery Park City, and had given a talk at Harvard about it. She said she didn't care if it worked or not; she wanted things done her way. Her plan consisted of a series of small spaces enclosed by high hedges, shutting people in or out and obstructing the beautiful views of the Hudson River. When asked by the *Wall Street Journal* about Bartlett's plan, Lynden was quoted as saying it would be a "horticultural jail for plants and people and cost $1 million to maintain." This was in contrast to the $250,000 per year it cost at that time to maintain the Conservatory Garden.

Ultimately, Bartlett was fired by the governor, and David Emil, then president of the Battery Park City Authority, arranged for a design competition. Emil chose Laurie Olin as the landscape architect, Rodolfo Machado as the architect, and Lynden as the garden designer. Lynden worked on the project for four and a half years, and Wagner Park evolved into a lovely small park with two gardens and open vistas to the spectacular views of the Statue of Liberty and Ellis Island.

With all these challenges coming her way, Lynden finally realized she had a design business and needed to hire an assistant. She went on to projects at Madison Square Park, Tribute Park in the Rockaways, and the Heather Garden in Fort Tryon Park, as well beautifying the campuses of Columbia, Stony Brook, and Princeton Universities and much of the stretch of the malls that extends both the length of Broadway and Park Avenue. Over the years, she has worked on about forty public spaces, large and small, all over the city.

After the horror of September 11, Lynden received a call from a Dutch bulb grower who had supplied bulbs to many of her projects. Like so many around the world, he expressed a wish to do something for New York. Lynden recalled that in the past he had sometimes sent free bulbs for people to use in parks and gardens. She asked if he had any extra daffodils to spare and he immediately sent five hundred thousand; the city of Rotterdam gave another five

Central Park: Lynden's borders in the Conservatory Garden

hundred thousand more. Working with the Parks Department, Lynden insisted that the bulbs not be used in already restored parks but in places that hadn't seen a flower in years. More than ten thousand people came out that fall around the city to plant those bulbs with the Parks Department, and the following spring, the sunny blooms appeared as a memorial to those lost that terrible day.

At New Yorkers for Parks, a parks advocacy organization, the Daffodil Project continues each year. Six million bulbs have been planted and the plantings have expanded into housing projects and schoolyards. The idea has now spread to more than fifteen other cities.

In 2004, Lynden began teaching a course at New York University called "The Elements of Successful Public Open Space." Given her background, the course is appropriately in the arts department but is also part of the urban studies program. She attracts about a dozen students each year and keeps track of them. They are her protégés. Her goal is to make sure they will continue as her emissaries, and that they will never approach a public space as they did before her course.

She has also written a book outlining her work and her principles, *Parks, Plants, and People: Beautifying the Urban Landscape* (W. W. Norton & Co., 2009); it is dedicated to the memory of Holly Whyte "for his love of cities and people, and for all he taught us about good public space."

Lynden certainly had many mentors, as well as Betsy Barlow Rogers, not exactly a mentor but important to her career. Lynden's horticultural influences include, first and foremost, T. H. Everett; Lynden is also quick to name the two great Englishwomen gardener–designers – writers Rosemary Verey and Penelope Hobhouse, both known for their painterly herbaceous borders – along with Lanning Roper, who worked with Lynden in London.

Although she describes herself as retired, Lynden is working at the Bayard Cutting Arboretum on Long Island and continues to consult on the Hudson River Park, Wagner Park, New York Botanical Garden, and at Columbia. But the Conservatory Garden is akin to her third child. She is proud that there will be many people she does not know and will never meet who will come to visit her gardens and love them. She believes that there is an unspoken message in these places – "We did this for you and you are worth it." She is sure that beautiful public spaces do something for the soul of all people who use them.

In paying tribute to Lynden's impact on public urban spaces and how she makes them both beautiful and successful, Joanne Kaufman wrote in the *Wall Street Journal*, "She has a kind of full-blooming forcefulness that could get a century plant to reconsider its position and flower annually." Lynden's message has been from the start: "Make it gorgeous and they will come; keep it that way and they will help."

PUBLIC GARDEN INSTITUTIONS

Gregory Long

A great job. Very worthy.

Consistent with his Midwestern, Calvinist upbringing, an ethic that emphasizes commitment to the community and its institutions, Gregory Long chooses the word *worthy* to describe the critical role he has played as president of the New York Botanical Garden. It is an old-fashioned word, suggesting working for something good, meritorious, and of value to others. It reflects his view of the importance of what he calls "anchor institutions," those that are essential to the life of any vibrant community, and in some cases, of a country.

Like many other great New York City cultural institutions, the New York Botanical Garden was founded in the late 1800s, a time when New York aspired to become known as a world-class city on a par with the great cities of Europe, one where major cultural institutions could be visited and appreciated. It is the era when, in addition to the botanical garden, the Metropolitan Museum of Art, the American Museum of Natural History, the New York Zoological Society, the New York Philharmonic, Carnegie Hall, and the New York Public Library all began. Gregory's early interest in art brought him east to study in New York, and there he remained to play an important role in reviving four of the city's anchor institutions before becoming president of NYBG.

His Midwestern background probably also accounts for his calm, gracious style that does not immediately reveal the strength of character, powerful drive, and determination that led him to transform the venerable New York Botanical Garden during the twenty-nine years of his leadership. From his prior experience at other great New York cultural institutions, he developed skills he would draw upon and bring to NYBG, including the arts of nonprofit corporate governance and successful fund-raising, and most important, an ability to articulate an inspiring vision for the future.

Gregory Long was born in Kansas City, Missouri, on October 3, 1946, the older child of Robert Long and Elizabeth Breed Long. Unfortunately, his father died early, leaving his mother a young widow. As a result, all four grandparents, who lived nearby, were important to his upbringing, especially his father's parents, as Robert had been their only child. The Longs were well established in Kansas City and lived in the nearby countryside where they maintained chickens, grew vegetables, and were surrounded by woods and wildflowers. Both the Longs and the Breeds were proud of their family history; their ancestors had arrived in America in the 1630s. Gregory's grandfathers served on the school board and were deeply involved in the Presbyterian Church. With this family heritage, it is not remarkable that Gregory came to think of himself as "American, Presbyterian, Protestant, and committed to the well-being of the community and its institutions."

Kansas City was a sophisticated Midwestern city comparable in many ways to St. Louis. As Kansas City expanded westward between the two World Wars, it was influenced by the City Beautiful Movement, adopting city planning to carefully design parkways, parks, and attractive water features. The city also boasts a very good art museum, an excellent orchestra, and an impressive stockyard. Gregory believes Kansas City's sophistication gave him one foot in the east with another deeply tied to the Midwest, where his relatives still live on farms in western Missouri. His great-grandfather's farm was part of the original tall grass prairie, with sod that had never been cut, out near what is now the Flint Hills National Wildlife Refuge in Kansas.

This happy extended family existence came to an end when Gregory's mother, Elizabeth, moved with her two children to Minneapolis. Gregory was eleven, and it was hard to leave his grandparents and his roots in Kansas City behind, but there were excellent schools in Minneapolis, where he attended high school.

Gregory's description of his mother could well apply to himself; she was and continues to be an important role model. She is involved in her church and her book group, and inclined to "tell everyone what to do." He describes her as a highly cultivated woman, "smart, funny, charming, strong, level-headed, and intelligent," as well as "very formidable and independent." She was also skillful at managing budgets, never accepting financial help from any of the grandparents. When Gregory became president of the New York Botanical Garden, Elizabeth particularly bonded with the chief financial officer there.

From his early days, Gregory was interested in art. In Kansas City, he used to ride his bike to hang out in what is now the Nelson-Atkins Museum of Art (then two museums, the William Rockhill Nelson Gallery of Art and the Mary Atkins Museum of Fine Arts, but already known locally as the Nelson-

Atkins Gallery). After he moved to Minneapolis, he discovered its Institute of Art. He became particularly fascinated by Italian art and architecture. When it was time to go to college, he chose to go to New York City to enroll at New York University; H. W. Janson, the noted scholar of Renaissance art, was the lure, having published the definitive classic textbook of art history.

Not surprisingly, Gregory's family thought he should remain in the Midwest and go to Carleton College, an excellent small residential liberal arts college in Minnesota. If not Carleton, then definitely Harvard. But this was 1965, and Gregory saw himself as a student radical. He did not want to be part of the kind of homogeneous community he had experienced in high school, which he considered boring. He wanted the diversity of New York University and New York City; both proved to be good for him.

Gregory immediately fell in love with New York. He lived in the dorms on Washington Square with a congenial roommate from Long Island. He quickly made many friends, especially with several of the international students and his professors. For the first time, he began to travel. He spent a few summers in London thanks to one of his roommates, whose mother had a house in Chester Square, Belgravia. From his time in England, his interest in art expanded to architecture. He explored the London antique shops, getting to know several of the dealers who drew him out to the countryside. It was on one of these forays that he first saw Chatsworth, the historic grand sixteenth-century house owned by the Duke of Devonshire, with its magnificent art collections, imposing architecture, and extensive gardens, including majestic water fountains and a cascade; he also visited nearby Hardwick Hall, built by Bess of Hardwick, which had its own important landscape, once also owned by the Duke of Devonshire. Gregory was bowled over.

After graduating in 1969, he made another trip to England and for the first time visited Sissinghurst and many of the other great English gardens. He was particularly drawn to Sissinghurst because of its ties to the literary Bloomsbury set, which included Vita Sackville-West, who, with her husband, Harold Nicolson, created its famous gardens around the remains of a derelict Elizabethan tower in the 1930s. Both wrote eloquently about them. Now a National Trust Garden, Sissinghurst is among the most popular gardens in England. Its combination of striking architecture and the artistry of color-themed plantings so captivated Gregory that many years later he insisted that George Schoellkopf go there, thus having a major impact on the creation of the gardens at Hollister House.

Gregory thought it logical to continue his studies in art history and applied to NYU's Institute of Fine Arts for graduate school. To be admitted, he had to demonstrate proficiency in two foreign languages, and although his Italian was passable, he flunked the German exam three times. He wasn't really sure he wanted to become a professional scholar anyway. Art scholars, primarily Germans, ruled the roost at the institute; committed to training other academics, they thought it essential for any scholar to be able to read Latin and other sources in the original language. Their world was the academy; they viewed museums as too worldly and were condescending to the curators who worked there.

With graduate studies ruled out, Gregory thought he might do library work since he had done a bit of that after college and enjoyed it. He had made friends with some of the NYU faculty who had gone to work as curators and historians for the Metropolitan Museum of Art, right across the street from the Institute of Fine Arts. And the museum had jobs.

Although it wasn't surprising his interest in art would lead him to the Met, it changed his life in ways that *were* surprising. The first job he was offered in 1969 was cataloging in the European painting department; it seemed an excellent fit. The salary was princely at four thousand dollars per year. But there was a different job available in administration that offered a salary of eleven thousand dollars. The decision was clear.

Ashton Hawkins, then General Counsel and Secretary of the Corporation, hired Gregory to work for him with the title of Executive Assistant to the Secretary of the Corporation and President of the Board. Wealthy, patrician Douglas Dillon – head of Dillon, Read & Co., the investment firm his father had created, and former ambassador to France and Secretary of the Treasury – was then president.

Gregory did continue some graduate school studies at Columbia as well as at the Institute of Fine Arts while working at the museum, but he never finished his Ph.D. He was having too much fun at the museum. He stayed for two and a half years and loved working in the Met's management: "It was fabulous! I adored it."

He worked hard, and he learned about corporate governance firsthand, especially the importance of having prominent, generous members of a board. In 1970, the museum was about to celebrate its centennial, and Brooke Astor was chairing that committee, with George Trescher as the committee's secretary. This was a major effort involving highly prominent and influential New Yorkers. Over the course of the campaign, Douglas Dillon himself would donate $20 million. It was a time of great change. Gregory recalls, "The Met wanted to open its galleries to more people and new constituencies. It was the centennial of the museum, and the era of the blockbuster exhibitions and open houses had begun."

Gregory also learned to negotiate contracts, to be an effective liaison and convincing communicator. He was noticed as "an exceptional writer who could synthesize historical facts, institutional narrative, and a sense of the museum's vision into an elegant pitch to donors." Naturally, he was drawn to and became friends with the art historians; they had lunch together. But the curatorial staff and the administration didn't interact very much. Gregory became a go-between, understanding both curators and the administration and bringing them together.

The work was exhilarating but endless. Friday nights were almost always work nights; Ashton was a demanding taskmaster. Gregory was responsible for the overall preparation for all the board meetings. He also became the captain of the typing pool. When Thomas Hoving came in as the director of the museum, he and Gregory did not get along. Gregory also grew restless with a job that didn't have a clear upward trajectory. He eventually left, but he has always loved the Met.

After taking the summer to travel to Europe, he went to work at the Brooklyn Museum to help put together two major exhibitions. He reported directly to the director, Duncan Cameron, as he had before with Ashton Hawkins and Douglas Dillon. He had learned the importance of reporting directly to the powers who ran institutions.

The Brooklyn Museum had never mounted a special exhibition before and had a very small curatorial staff. That made it a very exciting time for Gregory. One exhibit was on Norman Rockwell; the other was on prints and drawings from the museum's permanent collection. Gregory always arrived early, nicely dressed in his blazer to work with his three volunteers, one guard, and one person from finance (who also sold postcards – there wasn't even a museum shop). The organizers hoped the exhibits would draw more people to the museum, and that lesson – that special appealing exhibits serve to attract new and larger audiences – would serve Gregory well when he had to find ways to bring more visitors to NYBG in the Bronx.

Gregory "loved being in the front of the house." Even though he does not have a flashy style, he understood he was putting on a show. He saw himself as the "floorwalker" and was there early every morning to be sure that "everything is beautiful and all and everyone is in place." But the job was specific to those two exhibits, so he left at the end of six months.

Although it is not arts related, the Museum of Natural History then hired Gregory, thinking that he had fund-raising experience from his time at the Met. Even though he told them they were wrong, that he hadn't worked in the development office, he failed to dissuade them and so accepted the job. After all, a lot of the major fund-raising was orchestrated out of Ashton Hawkins's office. Major donors were either recruited for election to the board or invited to become members of the corporation, thereby becoming part of the institution's governance, cementing their relationship and encouraging their ongoing financial support. Gregory had learned from Ashton that fund-raising was intrinsic to corporate governance.

The American Museum of Natural History had never had a development

NYBG: Peggy Rockefeller Rose Garden

office but wanted to organize one. Gardner D. Stout, a partner in the investment bank of Dominick & Dominick and the descendant of a prominent New York family, was the unsalaried president. The museum's focus was very much on scholarship and research, but its leadership was beginning to sense that it needed to emulate the example of its neighbor across the park and have a more active public presence, as well as an ambitious fund-raising program. It too embarked on a centennial campaign. David Ryus, the executive vice president, had worked with the existing Men's and Women's Committees that organized small parties and cultivated friends, but these were very informal operations. Much more needed to be done. Gregory came in to establish a professional development program. My husband, Charlie, was then on the Men's Committee, which is how we first met Gregory. It was clear to both of us that the still young Gregory had far too much energy and drive for what was then a very sleepy institution.

Gregory stayed for a little over two years, and he did build a small development office. In the process he learned more about corporate fund-raising and how to write grant proposals to foundations. The museum was very generous, supporting him as he hired and trained staff and dealt with corporate CEOs and other potential big donors. The board was enthusiastic about his progress, but he was soon wooed away.

The New York Zoological Society (now the Wildlife Conservation Society and better known as the Bronx Zoo) courted him, offering him more money than he had thought he would ever earn. He really liked the people and especially the board. It included gracious civic leaders and philanthropists such as Howard "Howdy" Phipps, Laurance Rockefeller, and, once again, Brooke Astor. Gregory signed on as the deputy director and stayed for seven years. This time, he built a big development office. He also ran the public education programs and worked on increasing membership, audience development, public and government relations, and marketing. The director, Dr. William G. Conway, was a fine role model; he was a hard worker who was determined to create a new and better zoo. He was also very charismatic and smart. Together, Gregory and Bill established a new donor constituency, and, significantly, they created a strategic plan to set goals, establish priorities, and state the case for a shared vision of the future. The strategic plan was necessary to both energize the organization and excite potential donors. Gregory says they just made it up as they went along. There were no models to turn to, but Gregory could sense that big changes were afoot. Under Hoving, the Met was "cooking with gas," and everyone was trying to follow that example.

In the end, as successful as Gregory was at the zoo, he found it was not the right niche for someone who still thought of himself as an art historian. It was 1981, and Vartan Gregorian had just taken over as president of the New York Public Library. His first hire was Gregory Long. Under Vartan, great things were clearly going to happen at the library, and Gregory had only worked for institutions undergoing big change. Once again, Gregory thought the library was emulating the Met's example and believes he was hired because of his experience there. The library was trying to build an equally glamorous new constituency and to raise funds.

Gregory was the vice president for public affairs; he stayed for eight years, his longest tenure thus far. As always, he worked closely with the board – then chaired by Andrew Heiskell, chairman and CEO of Time, Inc. – and also handled public education, exhibitions, and fund-raising, conducting the largest fund-raising campaign of any American library. Vartan, recalling a holiday party Gregory organized for all library cardholders at the main building on Fifth Avenue, said, "People loved it. People felt a real ownership of the institution." The party wasn't designed as a fund-raiser but it moved people to care and to donate. Perhaps most important, Gregory created a strategic plan for the entire library system, eighty-six libraries spread across all five boroughs. "I used everything I had learned," he recalls. And with great success.

In 1989, Vartan Gregorian decided to leave the library to become president of Brown University (he later went on to head the Carnegie Corporation of New York). Gregory also began thinking of leaving when Linda Gillies, then president of the Vincent Astor Foundation, and Brooke Astor, who was on the library board, approached him about taking the top job at the New York Botanical Garden and told him his name was on the short list. Ultimately, it was Beth Straus who, in her role on the search committee, engineered his hiring. Straus loved NYBG and having visited most of the great European botanical gardens could see all its possibilities. She cared about both horticulture and science and wanted to restore NYBG, to build it up to be an internationally recognized botanical site.

NYBG was chartered in 1891 with a grant of 250 acres of land owned by the City of New York. Located in the Bronx, it is a naturalistic landscape, marked by forest and rolling terrain with the Bronx River running through it. A Columbia University professor of botany, Nathaniel Lord Britton, and his wife, Elizabeth, had visited England and seen the Royal Botanic Gardens at Kew, and they started the effort to make a botanical garden for New York. Calvert Vaux, Frederick Law Olmsted's partner on the design of Central Park, came to design NYBG's landscape and early gardens. Over time, many significant garden designers have lent a hand to its evolution.

When Gregory interviewed for the job, NYBG had always been headed by a distinguished scientist/botanist, and Gregory appeared to be an unlikely candidate. However, he convinced the board it was important *not* to hire a specialist. The board had always supported the important research of NYBG's botanists and scientists, as well as the operation of its major research library and herbarium, but the gardens had suffered from lack of attention. The infrastructure, including the imposing glass conservatory, was in poor condition. In the Bronx, which Gregory describes as the poorest urban county in America, NYBG had functioned more as a public park for dog walkers and immediate neighbors than a botanical garden. Roads cut through the historic landscape, allowing cars to drive across.

After accepting the position, Gregory perceptively observed, "In my previous jobs, I had learned how to manage complex institutions. I discovered that I had the gift of being persuasive, of being able to tap into the history of an institution in a way that was relevant to its current needs. The garden was financially insecure. Yet it had this wonderful history. But the garden was being used as a park. I sought to strengthen its identity as a botanical garden and a museum of plants. I became a spokesman, and an agent, for change in a city that I can claim as my very own." Always quick to credit others, he added, "And it certainly helps to have a brilliant board of trustees to partner with in a characteristically New York spirit of cooperation." Among his earliest initiatives were to fence in the grounds, ban cars and dogs, and begin charging admission to generate much-needed revenue

Gregory thought the institution had become very balkanized, with the science side not interested in the horticulture side and vice versa. Staff morale was understandably low. Neither a specialist nor a scientist, Gregory understood he could not be identified with any one side, insisting that they had to stop quarreling and "make this one institution."

Drawing upon his earlier experience, he promptly began a strategic planning process. He sought to "build endowment, and to fund program initiatives; widen our audiences and develop capital projects." All segments of the NYBG community were engaged in the effort, including the board and the staff. The programs had been divided into three separate camps – science, horticulture, and education – with a lot of competition among them for the minimal funding available. Gregory knew that they had to come together to develop a coherent plan for the overall institution, a plan to provide a shared vision and establish long-term goals. Engaging the staff from the three camps as well as the board members, he set priorities for fund-raising and restoration improvements, with measures for success. The process was prolonged, involving more than 150 people, but the garden eventually adopted a seven-year plan.

Importantly, the process was inclusive and revelatory. Longtime board members learned more about the institution; the scientists learned about gardening and the gardeners about science. Everyone had to listen to everyone else. The board members loved it and were willing to invest more. The then vice chairman of the board recalled, "When Gregory came, the whole nature of the place changed. It was his mind-set that caused us to look at things differently." The science staff started out expecting almost all the available funding, but Gregory managed to engage them in thinking about the overall institution. He knew it was essential to restore the gardens to attract the public, and only that would make it possible to attract more funding. More funding was essential – for everyone! He was very careful about spreading the budget among all three camps. He viewed them "like your children – you have to treat them fairly and give them equal shares."

Gregory gave credit to all involved. As one board member observed, "With Gregory, it is never 'I.' He is always crediting the staff, the board." Gregory made it clear: "It's not about me. It's all about the institution. I feel as strongly as I do about the New York Botanical Garden because precious though it is, it's an undervalued resource. I'm part of a team with a purpose." And he kept everyone focused, faithful to the plan. Whenever anyone tried to stray and reshuffle priorities in their own favor, he would simply say "NIP," which meant "not in plan." It kept them in line.

Gregory understood public relations and kept the focus on the future of the garden and its strategic plan; he was always optimistic, avoiding discussion of problems. He described what was indeed the greatest library on plants in the world, and the second largest herbarium. He emphasized that NYBG was also a museum and a cultural institution, points that had long been overlooked. He would turn that articulation into reality.

The Getty Museum Management Institute so admired Gregory's long-term plan that it invited him to teach, which he returned to California to do for many years. His strategic planning method is still the core curriculum at the Getty. He also finally received his Ph.D., an honorary one, from the City University of New York's joint Ph.D. program in recognition of his "inspired stewardship in helping to make culture flourish in New York City."

As things were jelling at NYBG, Gregory's personal life also took a happy turn. In 1993, he met his partner, Scott Newman, on a snowy Saturday in a Manhattan restaurant. It was practically a blizzard, so Gregory couldn't make his usual weekend drive to his country home on a hundred acres in the rural farm country around Cooperstown, New York. Instead he met Scott Newman, a distinguished architect, partner in the Cooper Robertson firm and fellow of the America Institute of Architecture. They have been together ever since. Eventually, they sold the farm in Cooperstown and bought a home in Ancramdale. The house inspired Gregory to write his book *Historic Houses of the Hudson River*

Valley: 1663–1915 (Rizzoli, 2004) and is included in that book. Called the Silvernail Homestead, it coincidentally once belonged to Lynden Miller before she moved to Sharon, Connecticut. Gregory found it helpful to have a writing project to focus on, instead of "obsessing about NYBG all the time!"

His book grew out of his early interest in architectural history and the convenience of having all the houses nearby, which allowed him to visit and talk with the curators on weekends. Eventually, Gregory would like to find time to write another book, one about his strong interest in Italian architecture.

That time might be coming soon. Not long after a major yearlong celebration of NYBG's 125th anniversary in 2016, Gregory informed the Board that he would step down in June 2018. In the public announcement, Maureen Chilton, chair of the board, noted that his twenty-nine-year tenure will be the longest since the original founder (almost one-quarter of NYBG's entire history) and "one of the most transformational." She went on to say that under Gregory's leadership, NYBG carried out forty-three major capital projects (including the addition of fifteen new gardens), completed major landscape restorations, and thoroughly revitalized the 250-acre living museum of plants. Attendance and membership quadrupled, with more than 1 million visitors each year, and the endowment grew more than twentyfold. Scientific and scholarly programs flourished, and a series of widely admired exhibitions married botany and horticulture to the arts and humanities. Gregory raised more than $1 billion for these many initiatives, most of it coming from the private sector.

Throughout, NYBG has stayed true to its role as a world-class center for botanical research and education. Succinctly summarizing the impressive range of NYBG's role, its broad categories of goals for the future are 1. Creating a Green Urban Oasis; 2. Connecting Gardening to the Arts and Humanities; 3. Teaching Science to City Kids; 4. Saving the Plants of the World; and 5. Anchoring the Community (supporting growth in the economy and stature of the Bronx).

One of Gregory's first projects was the major restoration of the imposing glass conservatory, built by the renowned greenhouse company Lord & Burnham and originally completed in 1902. In the 1970s, it was in such dire condition it had to be torn down or largely rebuilt. Enid Haupt endowed the conservatory, saving it from demolition, and after restoration it was renamed in her honor. In 1993 Gregory supervised the modernization of the conservatory, which upgraded all the mechanical systems and redesigned the space to better house special exhibits. With its many tiers of glass domes, the highest standing ninety feet tall, and more than seventeen thousand windowpanes, the iconic conservatory is at the garden's core, showcasing tropical and desert plants. Additional greenhouses were built to expand NYBG's living plant collections.

The ornamental gardens are more beautiful under Gregory's tenure and

NYBG: Enid A. Haupt Conservatory and greenhouses

new ones have been added. The famous modern garden designer Piet Oudolf created a new border in 2014. The rose garden has been modernized, and the new Native Plant Garden has been integrated into the landscape. While the Native Plant Garden is hard-edged in steel and concrete, Gregory believes it has slipped into the "historic landscape in an elegant way; it feels as if it were always there but it is very contemporary."

In addition to being a site for showcasing plant collections and orna-mental gardens, NYBG is also a historic landscape. Much of that landscape has been restored, and the work continues. The lay of the land at NYBG is very exciting and romantic. It is a topography of rivers, rocks, and large trees, a big naturalistic landscape. The people of the city love that and Gregory loves that they do.

Although NYBG is one of the great New York cultural institutions, it had not been associated with art – except to those who believe that gardens are works of art. Gregory has made a priority of linking the garden to art and the humanities through outstanding exhibitions and special events that have attracted huge crowds. A recent show featured the Mexican artist Frida Kahlo, exhibiting some of her paintings along with a stunning display in the great conservatory of a recreation of a portion of the garden she created with Diego Rivera in Mexico City. Before that there were exhibits related to Monet and his famous Giverny gardens, the Impressionists, and Emily Dickinson. No doubt there will be more. But even Gregory was surprised by the turnout for the Frida Kahlo exhibit: "We thought Frida Kahlo would be a wonderful thing but we never thought she would outdo Monet!"

Even the more traditional floral exhibitions have been linked to art and cultural history, becoming annual extravaganzas. The Chrysanthemum Show is now called the Kiku event, with each highly structured floral display – the result of months of training the plants into amazing shapes – tied to Japanese culture and art. The dazzling Orchid Show often has a larger theme, a recent one being the history of intrepid orchid collectors. During the show, the conservatory and the greenhouses are packed with a profusion of orchids of every size, shape and color, skillfully hung from tall palm trees or tucked in and among the existing plant collections.

For the winter holidays, the Train Show draws huge, enthusiastic crowds, with model trains chugging through ever more of the greenhouses. Tiny locomotives snake in and out of miniature replicas of iconic New York City buildings, such as Grand Central Terminal and the 42nd Street Public Library. All these cityscapes are fashioned out of natural dried-plant material, such as bits of pinecones, seedpods, and bark.

NYBG had always taken justifiable pride in its scientific strength. Its superb Mertz Library holds more than a million cataloged items available to the public. The library also maintains extensive archives, collections of historic photographs, rare books, folios, botanical engravings, and illustrations. The Steere Herbarium holds 7.8 million dried-plant specimens that are essential to plant research. It is the largest herbarium in the Western Hemisphere and the second largest in the world. The library and herbarium are being digitalized to better serve researchers worldwide. In addition to its highly regarded Ph.D. program, NYBG supports scientists globally in areas as far away as the tropical forests of Myanmar and the western Amazon in collaborative efforts to document and conserve plants, especially endangered species, and to promote biodiversity.

Gregory particularly cherishes the education programs that teach city kids. He notes "that for some kids, it is their only opportunity to be outside in nature." The new Edible Academy will allow for better year-round programs teaching plant biology, ecology, conservation, and sustainability. Hands-on classes in organic vegetable gardening and cooking promote healthier eating. NYBG also helps teachers create gardens at their schools and community groups plant neighborhood gardens. NYBG periodically monitors and helps active local gardens in what Gregory calls the "Hortmobile."

NYBG added amenities to expand its visitor base by making their experience easier and more welcoming. An impressive visitors' center is now at the main entrance, and there is an attractive café to serve the public as well as having the catering capacity to accommodate special private events, producing revenue and goodwill. An adjacent parking garage for 825 cars was built – the first NYBG structure ever built off the grounds – to facilitate visitation and earn money.

Gregory speaks eloquently about NYBG's role as an important economic force in the Bronx, thanks to employing full-time and seasonal staff and the visitors it attracts throughout the year. The many capital projects have provided construction jobs, and the new parking garage, in addition to providing revenue for the garden, makes it easier for visitors to come to the Bronx.

When asked about his mentors, Gregory generously gives credit to those who have been important in his life, but he is too modest to claim his own credit for mentoring so many others, many of whom have gone on to head other great institutions.

Gregory's early mentors certainly include Ashton Hawkins at the Met and Bill Conway at the Bronx Zoo.

Then, bigger than life, there is Vartan Gregorian. He believed in the importance of his mission and loved his central role in restoring the great New York Public Library. He is also a master manager of people, something Gregory does brilliantly, too. Vartan remains his great friend.

Then of course there was Mrs. Astor, as Gregory always refers to Brooke Astor. He says simply, "She got it!" She understood what great institutions mean to New York City. Gregory had initially been worried that if he wanted to leave an institution she supported, as for example when he left the zoo, she would be angry. But instead she helped him. She was very constructive and creative, and she understood the importance of power and how to use it. She was a marvelous generalist and smart about life. She saw the big picture and understood that people of wealth and other civic-minded citizens had to work together with government and business leaders, so she kept her foot in all camps. Whenever there was an opening party, Mrs. Astor always wanted to have the mayor come, along with the head of a major bank, and an intellectual figure. Above all, she always wanted David Rockefeller. She relished her role as a middleman and loved introducing people.

Gregory's personal taste in horticulture was shaped by his interest in literature and architecture, especially the English Arts and Crafts movement and the Bloomsbury Group. He was moved by his visits to the gardens created by Vita Sackville-West at Sissinghurst and Lawrence Johnston at Hidcote, with their strong structural elements and carefully designed plantings. He learned from them and other like-minded gardeners. Rosemary Verey was a special friend and teacher. She often stayed with Gregory and Scott when she came to

America, many times also en route to stay with me. We all went to see her at Barnsley House whenever we traveled to England. "She was so fastidious! I loved that," he recalls. *Fastidious* is a word he also uses to describe himself, when he admits, "I've been known to pull out weeds, even though I realize there is staff for that."

In an article for the English magazine *Gardens Illustrated,* Paula Deitz described Gregory as a man with the knack of making organizations work for specialists and the public. As Mrs. Astor taught him to do, Deitz wrote, "he sees NYBG as an apolitical platform where all kinds of people meet each other a community of inclusion located in NYC's least-affluent borough."

Gregory's grace, modesty, and insistence on always giving credit to others make it look as if it has been easy, but for his twenty-fifth anniversary at the garden, he did confess, "I wish I could say it's just flown by, but a lot of it went slowly and there was hard work to do." Hard work indeed: the magnificent revival of a great institution. Once again, the New York Botanical Garden has become both an oasis and a proper botanical garden, the equal of all the greatest of the world.

Gregory Long

Elizabeth Scholtz

Plants were always important in my life.

I T'S HARD TO imagine a bigger transition than leaving South Africa in 1960 during the height of apartheid and moving to the heart of Brooklyn. It is even harder to think that a brief visit to the Brooklyn Botanic Garden while on a yearlong fellowship in Boston would lead someone to return to Brooklyn and spend the rest of her life there, eventually becoming the much-celebrated director of the Brooklyn Botanic Garden. Betty Scholtz might say this was all pure serendipity, but others who know better would credit her intelligence, enthusiasm, and ability to rise to a challenge to the transformation of the BBG into a vibrant institution.

Elizabeth Scholtz was born in Pretoria, South Africa, on April 29, 1921, to Dr. Tielman Johannes Roos Scholtz and Vera Vogel Roux Scholtz. She was their first child, followed by two brothers. Her father was a successful surgeon who had studied botany as well as zoology before becoming a doctor, and her mother was a nurse. Although her father had a botany background, it was her mother who was the devoted gardener. From an early age, Betty loved her time in the garden helping her mother. Given the interest of both parents, Betty says, "Plants were always important in my life."

Tragically, Betty's father died when she was only eleven as a result of operating on a patient with septicemia. Despite his usual careful precautions, somehow Dr. Scholtz was stricken. Within two weeks, he was gone. Betty's mother was only thirty-two, with three young children to raise.

A bright student, Betty went to university when she was only sixteen years old, graduating from the University of Witwatersrand in Johannesburg in 1940 at nineteen. Betty had hoped to become a doctor like her father, but even though she was the oldest, her mother told her she couldn't afford the tuition for medical school. She had two younger sons to educate. Instead of going to medical school, Betty graduated with a B.S. degree in zoology and botany; she had studied science like her admired father. Upon graduation, she did the closest thing she could to practicing medicine: she went to work as a medical technician in Johannesburg. At one point she worked for Dr. Christian Barnard, who later gained fame for performing the first human heart transplant. For the next eighteen years, Betty worked in various venues in South Africa as a medical technician doing research.

Although Betty's life in South Africa was relatively peaceful and pleasant, it was a turbulent time for that country. Nelson Mandela began the Defiance Campaign in 1952 and endured the Treason Trial in 1956, before being sentenced to his long incarceration in the infamous prison on Robben Island for the next eighteen years. But very little of that turbulence impinged on Betty's young life.

As a medical researcher, Betty worked for Dr. Merseky, who brought her to the United States for a year fellowship in 1957 to join him at Boston's Beth Israel Hospital on research being conducted by Benjamin Alexander, a famous hematologist. During her time in Boston, a friend of Betty's family in South Africa put her in touch with Dr. George Sherman Avery, a distinguished plant physiologist and then the director of the Brooklyn Botanic Garden. The family friend knew Dr. Avery from research they had done together and, considering Betty's degree in botany, thought the two of them should meet. So Betty traveled to New York to visit Dr. Avery and the Brooklyn Botanic Garden one very hot day in August.

BBG was initiated in 1897 when New York State set aside thirty-nine acres for the purpose, but it finally became a reality only in 1910, when Alfred T. White donated $25,000, and the City of New York contributed a like amount to build a garden on what had been wasteland and a smoldering garbage dump. The garden would later become part of Prospect Park, which was designed by Frederick Law Olmsted and Calvert Vaux, with its early landscape designed by the Olmsted Brothers. By the time Betty went to see it in 1957, BBG had grown to fifty-two acres in a very much more developed and urban Brooklyn.

She returned to South Africa at the end of her fellowship. Apart from this brief stint in America, her entire life had been in South Africa. There she might well have remained had she not, during her visit to the garden, toured the entire operation, including the education department, where she met its head, Miss Frances Miner. She recalls, "I must have made the right kind of noises because I went back to South Africa and got a letter from Miss Miner whom I met on that occasion, offering me a job." Betty was surprised, thinking "these people are out of their minds" since she had not worked in botany for eighteen

BBG: Betty at groundbreaking of Elizabeth Scholtz Woodland Garden

years. She later learned Miss Miner was always short of staff, since most were very young women who stayed for only a year or two and then left to get married. Betty was then a mature thirty-seven and, by the time she agreed to come, thirty-nine.

Something must have touched Betty's sense of adventure, because she accepted and moved to Brooklyn. Although she probably never imagined the garden would occupy the rest of her life, she agreed to be an instructor under the direction of Miss Miner, whose official title was the charming "Curator of Instruction." Brooklyn Botanic Garden had long included a commitment to public education in its mission of horticulture and research.

Before she arrived, Betty wondered how she was going to be able to do the job, so she wrote to Miss Miner and asked, "Is there anything that I should read? Is there anything that I need to know before I come?" Miss Miner's odd reply was that "cultivated plants are the same the world over." Perhaps this was purely salesmanship, but Betty quickly discovered it was not true. When she arrived in America she found "a completely different flora – things I'd never seen before." Strange trees, shrubs, flowers; she knew oaks and pines. "What did I know about *Parrotia*? What did I know about *Oxydendron*? What did I know about *Pieris*? I could name a thousand plants that I had never seen before. You can imagine the culture shock when I came."

Worse was to come. After Betty arrived in 1960, Miss Miner called her into her office to explain that in the education department "everybody teaches a course. What are you going to teach?" Some taught pruning, others propagation and the like. Betty had been a hematology technician: "Nobody was interested in learning how to count blood cells." But Miss Miner could be stern. She asked what Betty's special interest was and Betty spontaneously replied, "Wildflowers." That ended the conversation. Betty was to teach a course in American wildflowers, plants about which she knew almost nothing. She was terrified. "I spent that winter reading books, going home and crying at night, thinking I'm going to fail, I'm not going to do it."

But it was not in Betty's nature to fail. She reached out to Dr. Avery and asked him how she was going to be able to do this. He had an idea. He called Elizabeth Van Brunt, a descendant of one of the original Dutch families who settled New York. She had long been a member of the BBG auxiliary of volunteers, active in the herb garden, her particular interest and area of expertise, but she also loved American wildflowers. She lived on a large property of roughly two hundred acres in Westchester County, far north of Brooklyn, near the town of Mount Kisco. Well over an hour's drive away, it was called the Kitchawan Research Station; Elizabeth's family had donated the entire property to BBG to own and manage in the 1950s. BBG in turn had given her the title of Honorary Curator of Herbs. Years later, Betty would have the garden name the *Magnolia* x *'Elizabeth,'* developed by BBG, in her honor.

Betty began traveling to Westchester every weekend, and she and Elizabeth drove around the countryside to acquaint Betty with American wildflowers. When her course began, she managed to stay just one step ahead of her students, some of whom, like Elizabeth Van Brunt, were experts, one having written a book about wildflowers. She says, "It was my baptism of fire."

Betty's maturity and strong, clear voice, as well as her obvious intelligence, must have impressed Miss Miner, who was running both adult and children's education with a very limited staff that had to manage the Children's Garden, all the children's classes, and all the adult education programs. The Children's Garden, begun in 1914 on one acre, was among the first of its kind, a place where city children learned how to grow their own food. Betty began by helping with all of it: staffing the Children's Garden and teaching children's as well as adult classes. Little by little, the adult education program grew, and she found herself handling all the adult classes, while continuing to work in the children's program. Her low, deep voice and South African accent appealed to her audiences, although a staff member pulled her aside one day to say, "In this country they're called tom-*AY*-toes, you don't call them tom-*AH*-toes." Betty predictably replied she had "been calling them tom-*AH*-toes for a hundred and fifty years, and I'm not going to change."

The Brooklyn Botanic Garden had long depended upon its auxiliary, a cadre of volunteers, primarily women, who worked in the garden and also provided financial support. Many of Betty's educational programs were important to the auxiliary, and, in addition to the fifty-two acres of gardens in Brooklyn, BBG was also the owner/administrator of the Kitchawan Research Station and two other properties, all located quite a distance away, each of which had its own auxiliary group and educational programs.

By 1964, Betty was traveling regularly to Kitchawan and found that working with the Kitchawan auxiliary volunteers proved "quite a challenge." Betty recalls that "fitting in with the membership was quite different from BBG." Always resilient, she soon adapted to the different culture of the suburban ladies of Westchester and the homogeneous makeup of the group, and, always quick to credit the best in others, made many good friends.

Gerard Swope, a neighbor of Elizabeth Van Brunt's, so admired the gift of Kitchawan to BBG that he wanted to do the same with his own nearby property, which became known as the Teatown Lake Reservation. He gave his property of about two hundred acres to BBG; it became a second regular destination for Betty where she dealt with another set of auxiliary volunteers.

In 1966 Grenville Clark decided that he, too, wished to donate his property to BBG. It was not only much smaller, about eighteen acres, but was also located in an entirely different direction from Kitchawan and Teatown Lake, far to the east in the town of Albertson in Nassau County, Long Island. Managing what became known as the Clark Botanic Garden meant she had to drive east to get there, run its programs, and oversee the work. "I was constantly on the road," driving north to Westchester County and then east to Long Island to check up on the Clark Garden. Eventually, Betty played a diplomatic role in having all of these become separate, stand-alone institutions or close, and was quite happy when she could finally "shed all that responsibility."

Early on, Dr. Avery had counseled Betty that the key to success with Miss Miner was good communication. Betty followed his advice. She was sure to let Miss Miner know in advance her work schedule and any ideas she came up with for new programs. That was a good procedure for any working relationship, and it came to stand Betty in good stead for her future role at BBG. Miss Miner quickly came to appreciate Betty's capabilities, and before long her habitual response to anything Betty proposed was a succinct "More power to you, kid!" Which meant full steam ahead.

Eventually, Miss Miner promoted Betty to be head of all adult education – or more precisely she created the position for Betty, since there had never been any division in the department between programs for adults and children. The emphasis had always been on children's education; the adult education programs were more limited. Miss Miner confessed that she personally preferred working with children and had hoped Betty would be more comfortable with adults. That was in fact the case. Being older than most of the other instructors helped. Betty was given the new title of Assistant Curator of Instruction, and she would increase the number of people in the adult education program from a bit over a thousand to more than four thousand.

In the 1950s, long before other botanical gardens were offering programs on bonsai, BBG began featuring lectures. Kanichiro Yashiroda, a bonsai master from Japan, had come on a short-term fellowship to lecture, and people flew from as far away as Chicago to attend his full-day course. BBG was also the first public garden in America to have a Japanese garden, opening its Japanese Hill-and-Pond Garden in 1915. A combination of the original hill-and-pond garden design and the later stroll-garden concept, with its striking red torii, or gateway, the garden was considered a masterpiece of its creator, Takeo Shiota.

BBG: Torii in Japanese Garden in winter

Many years later, in 1961, Takuma P. Tono, a Japanese landscape architect, was invited to come to BBG from Tokyo to design a replica of the Ryoanji garden in Kyoto, famous for its simple walled area of raked sand and carefully placed rocks. In the course of his work in Brooklyn, Mr. Tono felt he needed some detailed information about the appropriate characteristics of the raked sand, the correct placement of the rocks, and other details, so in 1964 Dr. Avery asked Betty and another colleague, Anne Birdsey, to travel to Japan to study the original Ryoanji design, take photographs and obtain all the necessary information, and agreed to pay their airfare.

When the Ryoanji replica was installed at BBG, Betty demonstrated her flair for marketing. Dr. Avery had suggested it might be nice to have Japanese hostesses there to welcome the visitors. Betty managed to produce a kimono-clad bevy of Japanese beauties. Sadly, while the rest of the Japanese garden remains, the Ryoanji look-alike did not survive. It proved very hard to maintain, and its understated subtlety failed to attract much interest. While the public appreciated the other parts of the Japanese garden that looked more like a landscape, they understandably preferred to look at green plants rather than precisely raked sand and rocks.

Betty loved to travel, and while she was still an instructor had toured as many other gardens in America as she could. Before leaving for Japan in 1964, through her role in the garden's education department, she had been in communication with people in Thailand about plants used to make dye, a subject she had been studying because she thought it would make an interesting topic for a BBG handbook. She planned to have the handbook feature reports from various countries around the world where native plants were still being used to produce natural dyes. She suggested to Anne that after their three weeks in Japan, the two of them should travel on to visit her contacts in Thailand, as well as stop on the way to see friends in Hong Kong and Taiwan. So they did.

On their return, Betty gave a report to Dr. Avery on her travels, and he thought that would make an appealing trip for BBG members. In his typical manner, he queried Betty, "How about offering this as a tour for members?" He would then leave it for the other person to decide whether the idea was worth pursuing. He never nagged or checked in to see if they had done anything more. But if they did, and the implementation of the idea proved successful, as was true in this case for Betty, he inevitably said later, "Thank you for your great idea!"

Thus began BBG tours abroad. In 1966, five leaders – Betty, Anne, Dr. George Avery and his wife, Virginia, and Lynn Perry, from the staff of the U.S. Agricultural Department office in Tokyo – took sixty-two people on the tour. Some chose only to go to Japan, but many opted for all the offered destinations

At the time, the idea of international garden tours was new. It proved enormously popular, and they are now commonly offered by many organizations. Betty went on scouting trips to plan these tours. She loved her exploratory trip to France with a woman who became a dear friend, Faity (Esther) Tuttle, who was president of the auxiliary volunteers. Betty recalls that "Faity drove and spoke French. I navigated and spoke botany." In the years since, Betty has been on at least thirteen tours to Japan, many to South Africa, and well over a hundred tours total to forty-six countries. A large map hangs in her office with flags indicating each tour she has led.

George Avery stepped down as director of BBG in 1969, having served since 1944, a twenty-five-year period Betty describes as the "golden years." After a few years, it was clear that things were not going well with his successor, who suddenly quit. In 1972, Betty was asked to take on the job. She refused at least three times. She had never acted in an administrative capacity before – but then, she had never worked in botany before coming to BBG, either. She didn't want to do it. Why not ask Miss Miner, who had been there forever? But Miss Miner felt she was too old for the job, and Betty finally agreed. She stipulated that she would only serve for three months until a worthy candidate could be found to replace her. She says, "I was there on the spot, but I was scared out of my wits!" She stepped in because she felt she was needed.

She was the first woman named to head a major botanical garden in America. And she was faced with quite a challenge. Not only did she have to lead the institution after her immediate predecessor had suddenly resigned, but she had to learn how to raise money and how to work with the chair of the board of directors. When asked what was her biggest surprise in taking on the job, Betty replied, "Immediately after I took the job, New York City went broke! Here I was with no experience, and I had to step in and raise enough money to survive."

It was the fiscal crisis of the early 1970s, in part the result of a sudden, dramatic rise in oil prices but also the consequence of too many long years of financial mismanagement of New York City. The funding for BBG dried up, along with that of the many cultural institutions, public parks, and others accustomed to city support. Running the garden was hardly business as usual! The outlook was bleak.

Under Betty's leadership, her board – then chaired by her friend Faity Tuttle – launched an ambitious $25 million campaign for a new conservatory and endowment. In today's dollars, that would be almost $143 million! This was long before there was a deep professional development staff to support a major campaign. Betty recalls that Dr. Avery had been against fund-raising. "In his view, you didn't ask for money. You made it possible for people to give." But it was definitely time to ask people for money, and Betty made sure the campaign was a success.

BBG: Native Flora Garden

The funds raised were used to improve and add to many areas of the garden, including moving the original Shakespeare Garden to a better location. Donated in 1925 by Henry C. Folger, once chairman of Standard Oil of New York, a collector of Shakespeareana and founder of the Folger Shakespeare Library, BBG's Shakespeare Garden had languished in what had become a shady spot. It was successfully moved to a sunnier place, where it continues to be a much-admired part of BBG.

The Cranford Rose Garden was also revitalized and improved, and it was decided to develop a rose specifically in Betty's honor. Elvin McDonald, then the director of special projects at the garden, had initiated this effort and said, "I wanted a rose with qualities most like Betty, who stands tall, looks elegant in all weather, and is strong and vigorous. Yellow is her favorite color rose." When the yellow floribunda rose 'Elizabeth Scholtz' was presented to her, she was completely surprised, saying, "When I was a sixteen-year-old botany student, I was intrigued with the naming of plants and dreamed of finding one that would be named after me. But until last week that was something I'd long forgotten."

Having run education programs for adults, Betty also understood the importance of bringing more people into the garden. She expanded the auxiliary program that enlisted volunteer docents to conduct guided garden tours. She added events to entice people to make a special visit to the garden. The one that continues to be the most popular is called Sakura Matsuri, the annual cherry blossom festival. BBG has a long history of ties to Japanese horticulture and culture, and boasts an important collection of flowering cherry trees, making it the perfect place to celebrate the brief, transporting moment when the trees are in full bloom.

Thanks to Betty's leadership, and the work of many others she is quick to credit, BBG now proudly includes many distinctive garden areas, as well as a handsome glass conservatory, and holds more than ten thousand taxa of plants. Close to one million visitors come through every year. Its education programs continue to maintain the highest standards and reach broad audiences.

By 1980, after eight years, BBG was on a solid footing and Betty stepped down as director, becoming director emeritus and vice president. She continues to be a voice and deeply admired presence at BBG and has garnered just about every prestigious honor in the field. She received the Scott Medal from the Scott Arboretum in 1981, the Liberty Hyde Bailey Award from the American Horticultural Society in 1984; the Garden Club of America Medal of Honor in 1990, the Hutchinson Medal from the Chicago Horticultural Society in 1991, the Award of Merit from the American Association of Botanical Gardens and Arboreta in 1992, and the Gold Medal from the Massachusetts Horticultural Society in 1994.

She didn't stop leading garden tours abroad. The book she worked on with Rae Spencer-Jones published in 2007, is entitled *1001 Gardens You Must See Before You Die*. It was on one such garden tour that Betty and I connected in England. I was on my once-in-a-lifetime sabbatical in 1991, working first for Rosemary Verey in her famous garden at Barnsley House in the English Cotswolds, followed by a shorter stint working for Penelope Hobhouse at Tintinhull House, a National Trust Garden in Somerset. I recall working busily away at Tintinhull, kneeling over one intensely planted herbaceous border, only to hear a busload of American visitors arrive. When I looked up, I recognized Betty. She was leading the group, calling out directions in her strong, booming deep voice. I stood up to introduce myself, and I think she was surprised and amused to find me there in my gardener's guise. She quickly explained to the group that I was a well-known and highly regarded New York lawyer who had escaped into a new life as a working gardener. We have been fast friends ever since, and she still laughs about the encounter.

Betty is generous in her praise of her mentors – certainly, Dr. Avery and Miss Miner, along with Elizabeth Van Brunt and Faity Tuttle.

She is modest about people she claims as her protégés, although others describe her as the mentor for "generations of North American public garden professionals." In one way or another, they are all part of what became Betty's extended BBG family. Any list will fall far short but should include Judy Zuk, who became head of the Scott Arboretum before returning in 1990 to serve as director of BBG. Betty names people who worked with her for Miss Miner, such as Daphne Drury, who was Miss Miner's longtime assistant, and Mollie Harker and many other young women who were interested in horticultural education. She also played an important role in the life of Fred McGourty, a young man with no background in horticulture, who Betty enlisted to edit the invaluable BBG handbooks; he went on to write many other garden books and operate his own specialty nursery in Connecticut. Others she names include Alice Ireys, a landscape architect who worked and taught at BBG, and who designed the Fragrance Garden; Frank Okamura, who ran the Japanese Hill-and-Pond Garden and the Bonsai Collection; and Bob Tomson, head of the gardeners, who ran a

BBG: Osborne Garden with azaleas and wisteria

wonderful team. Peter Nelson, a botanist who became a particularly close friend, shared similar interests, especially in music; they had dinner together almost every week.

Betty continues to work out of her office at BBG, where she serves as a vital resource for staff, volunteers, and visitors, who treasure her vast knowledge and the good humor for which she is famed. On occasion, she can be seen giving out to visitors one of her buttons that reads *ibotpul* – which stands for "I Bend Over To Pick Up Litter." Every member of the staff, from the current director to the security guard, knows Betty by sight and name, raising their hand to say hello whenever they spot her. As always, she knows them all as well, making each and every one feel valued and important.

Betty Scholtz with author

Marco Polo Stufano

Less is more? Not true. More is more, if the original idea is not lost.
Rules for using color in the garden? I never learned them.
I want the entire paint box, the giant Crayola.

MARCO POLO IS A NAME that rings out rich with history, recalling the intrepid Italian who traveled to Asia and came back with riches and the amazing tales that inspired others to follow in his footsteps. Our modern-day-Marco Polo is an Italian American who came back from his travels with plant riches that he used to create the extraordinary public garden at Wave Hill and to inspire others to follow his example.

Marco Polo Stufano was born in Queens, New York, on September 15, 1938, to Michele and Isabella, the youngest of their four children. Michele, the oldest of seventeen children, left his family farm near Bari, Italy, where his father grew olives and almonds, to travel to America with only seven dollars in his pocket. There he met Isabella, who came from a village in Puglia, not far from his original home.

Like many Italian immigrants from the region around the city of Bari at the time, Michele first found work as an iceman but moved on to supplying heating and fuel oil to his customers, developing a successful business and establishing a small but comfortable home in Richmond Hill, Queens, for his wife and children.

By the time Marco arrived, his parents were both involved in gardening around their modest house. His mother had an ornamental garden in the front and along the side, while his father grew vegetables – tomatoes, of course, as well as basil, squash, and the rest. The Long Island Rail Road ran on an embankment behind the house, and Michele first expanded his garden to the flat area at its base behind the garage. With the permission of two neighbors, he then cultivated the areas behind their houses, all on LIRR-owned land. Eventually, he carried on farther and terraced his vegetable garden right up the embankment.

Marco seems to have been the only sibling even slightly interested in the family gardens, but he recalls they were always a big topic of conversation around the family dinner table. However, Marco was annoyed that his father always gave the best vegetables to the neighbors, saving the ugly, blemished ones for the family. His mother's garden was quite artistic; she also sewed and painted murals. He remembers playing in her garden and creating imaginary landscapes.

His mother must have passed along her artistic tendencies to Marco; he has always been a visual person. He attended Public School 54 where, he says, "My first recollection of my own plant was a cutting I stole from the windowsill of my class at P.S. 54. That hasn't stopped. I take cuttings everywhere. Plastic bags are an essential part of a gardener's backpack."

After attending P.S. 54 he went on to Richmond Hill High School, where he was fortunate to have a teacher who steered him to Brown University. He remembers her looking like a "schoolmarm" right out of a Dickens novel, with a round bun formed tightly behind each ear. She had studied at Brown herself, earning her Ph.D., and Marco must have been a bright light to impress both her and the admissions committee at Brown.

While at Brown, Marco studied art history, but he was less interested in the scholarly approach to art than in creating it. Brown only offered one studio art class, which he took, but Marco had been raised to be practical and frugal, and he froze up when he tried to paint. He was paralyzed, terrified about messing up and wasting canvas as well as expensive art supplies. A public-school boy from Queens, he also felt a bit intimidated by many of his classmates, most of whom had come from fancy private schools.

He was only a freshman when he signed up for art history as an elective among the then required courses. It proved to be a nineteenth-century survey course of American architecture taught by a marvelous professor, Dr. William H. Jordy. Jordy, the author of a series of five volumes titled *American Buildings and Their Architects,* had once been on the Yale faculty with Vincent Scully, another legendary architecture professor.

Professor Jordy was so enthusiastic about his subject and would become so excited in his lectures as he pointed out some wonderful details on a slide that he would lose track of what he was saying. He would stop, turn around to the class, and ask them where he had left off. Marco was captivated. He took to strolling through the streets of Providence to observe the architecture – while avoiding his schoolwork. One Victorian mansion is still fresh in his mind's eye, with its entire three-story façade covered in a magnificent wisteria vine.

Professor Jordy was a major influence on Marco; he still regrets never having had the chance to tell him so.

Gardening was never far from his life. While at college, he earned money during his summers by working for local gardeners in Queens. It was nothing fancy, he notes, just basic lawn maintenance and servicing suburban properties. But he was never completely removed from the hands-on pleasure of working with plants.

After graduation in 1960, Marco enrolled at Columbia to earn a graduate degree in art history. He returned home to live with his parents, commuting into Manhattan for his courses. He dropped out of Columbia early in the semester and started working at the Museum of Modern Art. He had simple jobs there, but at least he continued to be surrounded by art. Directly across the street was the Donnell Library, where he took his breaks. During one of those breaks, he stumbled across the seminal book *Landscape Architecture: A Manual of Environmental Planning and Design,* by John Ormsbee Simonds, an early and visionary landscape architect. Marco was fascinated. He had never heard the term "landscape architecture" before. And he was hooked!

Marco enrolled at the University of Pennsylvania, where Professor Ian McHarg had recently founded the department of landscape architecture, then among the very few such programs in the country. Marco was thrilled; this was a program that married his interest in visual, structural concepts with his early love of gardening. Without an undergraduate degree in architecture, landscape architecture, or city planning, Marco was first required to take a one-year introductory program before he would be permitted to continue on to the two-year graduate program.

The additional year was discouraging, and so was Professor McHarg's emphasis on ecological design, as eventually articulated in his influential book *Design with Nature.* McHarg criticized classical garden design that he said "subjugated nature"; he was less interested in the visual and aesthetic than in plans sensitive to the environment, with attention to the conditions of soil, drainage, climate, and sustainability. Marco could not bring himself to enjoy the focus on such things as draining land for parking lots and planning corporate headquarters. He sarcastically renamed the course "How to Hide the Parking Lot." Plants were incidental. As is often true of landscape architecture, the program was as much about the hardscape as the plantings. Only a dozen or so plants seemed to be used in every design. Marco didn't want to quit midstream, so he finished one semester and left.

It was the early sixties, and the war in Vietnam was escalating. Marco went back to the Museum of Modern Art while waiting for the draft to find him. In 1963 he was inducted into the army, where he spent the next two years.

Wave Hill: Flower Garden and Marco Polo Stufano Conservatory

Guardian angels kept Marco from being sent to Vietnam. Instead, he had a wonderful stint in Europe. For some reason, those in charge of his putative talents thought Marco had an aptitude for electronics. He says, "They were wrong!" Nevertheless, they sent him to microwave repair school, and because he was good at languages, they shipped him off to Germany. Truth be told, Marco was pretty good at Spanish and French thanks to his Italian, but he didn't know much German. However, he was clever. There was a test to pass for each language. Since he could tell from the first tests that each of them contained exactly the same questions, albeit in the language being tested, he simply memorized the questions from his tests in Italian, Spanish, and French, and thus passed the German test, which came last.

Those two years in the army as a private first class were happy ones for Marco. He spent half of one year in Heidelberg, that charming university town, before being sent off to Kaiserslautern, in the middle of nowhere. Happily, his unit had no supervising officers other than a single staff sergeant, and his duties weren't onerous. He didn't do much more than wax floors and stand watch on the machine that maintained the hotline from Moscow to Washington, D.C. Watching for what, he wasn't sure. He says, "I didn't have a clue if it was working, unless by touching one of them I found that a tube was cold and needed replacement." Fortunately, there were no international crises or mishaps, and he managed to travel all around Europe, wangling a pass for every weekend he could.

When he was discharged, Marco returned to New York without a clear idea of what to do next. He knew he loved the art of gardening. While working at the Museum of Modern Art, he used to make little bouquets from flowers he cut from his mother's garden to bring to his friends there. He always placed a vase of fresh flowers on the front desk. He began to think he might be a good floral designer.

He wasn't sure where to turn for advice, but, not being shy, he went straight to the top at the New York Botanical Garden. He had no appointment and wasn't sure exactly where to go, but he walked right into the office of T. H. Everett, the director of horticulture and education. Three secretaries guarded the inner sanctum: Lillian, Nancy, and Hette. Marco must have charmed Lillian, the private secretary to T. H., because she sent Marco off to talk to Miss Elizabeth Hall, then in charge of education at NYBG. This was the same Miss Hall who earlier had introduced Frank Cabot to the nascent American Rock Garden Society.

T. H. Everett was born in England, studied at the Royal Botanic Gardens at Kew, and arrived by boat to America in 1927 for his first job as a gardener on the estate of Samuel Untermyer in Yonkers, New York. He went on to work on another estate, returning to England in 1930 to take his final exams and earn his National Diploma of Horticulture, awarded by the British Government and the Royal Horticultural Society. He returned to be the head gardener and horticulturist at the New York Botanical Garden in 1932, where he remained for the rest of his career. He became Director of Horticulture and Senior Curator of Education while compiling his important ten-volume *New York Botanical Garden Illustrated Encyclopedia of Horticulture*. He was also one of the founders of the American Rock Garden Society, designing and installing NYBG's rock garden, as well as its rose garden, and numerous displays and exhibits. For many decades, T. H., his secretary Lillian Weber, and Miss Hall were a forceful triumvirate, and T. H. proved a major influence on many others besides Marco.

As a young woman, Elizabeth Hall had wanted to become a doctor, but few medical schools accepted women in her day, so she went to the Ambler School of Horticulture, now part of the University of Pennsylvania, where she studied horticultural therapy instead. She never practiced but went on to become the librarian at the Horticultural Society of New York.

When Marco encountered Miss Hall, she was busy filing cards in the card catalog. Marco now asks, "Can anyone remember card catalogs?!" He kept up a steady stream of conversation as Miss Hall worked until finally she agreed to talk to T. H. about him. She did. Marco often recounts that she walked into T. H.'s office and announced, "T. H., I think we have a live one!"

Miss Hall and Marco would develop a lifelong friendship. She lived with her father in Douglaston, Queens. Marco recounts that years later she told him that she commuted to work every day by ferry before the construction of the Bronx-Whitestone Bridge. Miss Hall and T. H. hung out together until midnight before Miss Hall went back home, often with the people who managed the grounds at Princeton and Vassar, along with Harold Epstein, the impressive plantsman who had helped found the Rock Garden Society. Apart from her work and her horticultural friends, Marco thinks "Miss Hall lived like a monk." Marco became one of her closest friends, and when she died, he was the executor of her estate.

If so much in life is luck and timing, Marco's meeting with T. H. was providential. T. H. was just reviving a program to train professional gardeners. He had initiated it in 1932, but it had been interrupted by World War II. His plan was to have the students work in the garden all day and study at night. T. H. hired Marco to work in the native plant garden that summer and then enroll in the newborn program when it opened that September; he was one of just three students.

The job that summer was completely hands-on, backbreaking labor. Marco found that almost as hard as the toil itself was learning how to relate to his coworkers, most of whom were juvenile delinquents there as part of their parole requirements. Marco became an expert in the art of "double digging," an approach to soil preparation that requires first digging a two-foot trench as long as the intended planting area, piling the topsoil being removed along one side and the rest of the soil along the other. Finally, what had been the topsoil is shoveled into the bottom of the trench, while the rest of the removed soil is enriched with compost and then shoveled back on top. This daunting and exhausting approach deters most gardeners from indulging in such procedures.

In September Marco's daywork didn't stop, and his studies began. The other two students both already had horticultural degrees. The program lasted for two years. Marco's salary for his daytime job supported him so he could study at night.

Marco loved it all. He instantly connected gardening with his love of the visual, and he felt none of the intimidation of possibly wasting precious art materials that had so paralyzed his early efforts to paint on canvas. Painting with plants was something else entirely. As he observes, "You can always dig it up and start again." He sees the process of gardening as being as important as the product – the process of playing with plants, of weeding, pruning, deadheading, and even double digging. Marco is just as happy working with vegetables as with perennials or with rare greenhouse plants. It is growing the plants, watching and nurturing them, that provides him so much satisfaction. It is a sheer joy to just be in the garden.

T. H. instructed some of the classes, and Marco found him an excellent teacher as well as a great writer. He believed that the world was filled with marvelous plants of all kinds. His most important advice to Marco was to avoid becoming a specialist, to instead remain a generalist, open to learning about every kind of plant. Most profoundly, he urged, "Don't be a snob!"

T. H. has sometimes been called the patron saint of Wave Hill because he helped persuade then Parks Commissioner Newbold Morris to preserve the former private garden for the public. Others know the real reason: he sent Marco to Wave Hill. This was 1967, and Marco had just earned his certificate from the program at NYBG.

Wave Hill is now a public garden and cultural center on twenty-eight acres in Riverdale on a magnificent site high up and overlooking the Hudson River and the Palisades. It had been a private estate, acquired by George W. Perkins, a J. P. Morgan partner, in 1903 and owned by his family until 1960, when his daughter, who had been on the NYBG Board, and the other heirs donated the property to the City of New York. She also provided a modest endowment in a private trust, but that barely made a dent in Wave Hill's overall financial needs.

During the first few years, Wave Hill barely hung on. Two determined women in Riverdale, Hannah Williams and Martha Munzer, who ran a program called Riverdale Outdoor Labs, were civic-minded and concerned about its future. They went to their neighbor Gil Kerlin, a prominent New York City attorney, for help. In 1965, he established a separate nonprofit corporation to manage the property and raise additional private funds. The structure is like that of the other thirty-two city-owned cultural institutions, including NYBG, the Metropolitan Museum of Art, and the American Museum of Natural History. Ned Ames became the first director and still serves on the board.

When Marco arrived to become the first head of horticulture, Wave Hill's future was uncertain. It could easily have become just another neglected city property or, worse, been split up into small parcels and sold off to developers. While there were some handsome trees, there *was* no horticulture, mostly mowed lawns with some derelict greenhouses. It was just beginning to define itself as an institution.

Land rich and cash poor, Wave Hill had almost no money to transform into a public garden. Marco's only help was a small crew employed by the New York City Parks Department, and, in addition to working on the grounds of Wave Hill, he was also expected to take on the maintenance of the adjacent parkland that ran along the Hudson River. He recalls he would sometimes "feel sheer desperation, panic really, about how am I going to get anything done." Over time, as funds were raised, Marco finally replaced the Parks Department crew with two young men he hired, both graduates of a NYBG work-study program for potential high school dropouts. The two came and stayed for the next twenty-five years.

After he finished up at NYBG but before he was scheduled to begin work at Wave Hill in September 1967, Marco made his first trip to England. He really had no deep interest in going because he accepted the stereotype that the English were distant and cold, but he felt it was his duty to observe the gardens there and perhaps to visit Italy as well. T. H. laid out an ambitious itinerary of many important gardens, including Calderstones Park in Liverpool, where he had started his own career. He also equipped his young protégé with introductions to many of the important people in charge. Marco was deeply struck by this first exposure to the great gardens of England and the wide array of plants found there. He admits he has become "an Anglophile. A real gardener has to be. The English took a love of plants and ability to grow them and turned it into an art form."

He was even more surprised to discover how nice the English were. He still recalls waiting for a bus while visiting Liverpool and watching one go by with a sign saying its destination was Penny Lane. He broke out in a smile and began to hum the popular Beatles song. Feeling quite lost, he asked a woman standing near him if this might be the right bus for where he wanted to go, and

Wave Hill: Flower Garden view to the Palisades and Hudson River

she took him by the hand and walked him three blocks to get him to the right bus stop. No doubt he looked very needy, but he was hugely grateful. He changed his thinking about the cold Brits; he loved them. He did also find time to visit the gardens in Italy but was very discouraged by all the bureaucratic red tape that made access so difficult.

Marco would return to England virtually every year thereafter, each time bringing back plants not then available in America. No one else was bringing herbaceous plants into the United States, particularly half-hardy and silver-leafed plants. Marco brought them back just because he thought they were so beautiful. Then he raised them, learned how to grow them, and displayed the best of them in the gardens he was developing at Wave Hill. Not surprisingly, it became a gardening destination for anyone interested in seeing the latest horticultural novelties.

In the 1960s and into the 1970s, there wasn't much adventurous horticulture in the United States. New and exciting plants were primarily being introduced in England and on the Continent. America didn't yet have many serious specialty nurseries. Although Marco scoured catalogs and started plants from seed, he routinely found his plant sources were coming in from England. Of course, there was NYBG and other botanical gardens, but they focused on science rather than on ornamental gardening or on disseminating plants to the public. Longwood Gardens in Wilmington was an exception, and a few private gardens, like the one Frank Cabot was establishing at Stonecrop, were beginning to do great things. But England was still the mecca for finding plants.

Plants that now seem commonplace were completely unfamiliar, plants such as *Helichrysum petiolare* (one of Marco's gray-leafed loves) and the now omnipresent *Verbena bonariensis*. Many of the best English gardeners were enormously generous to Marco and eventually became his friends. The great plantsman Christopher Lloyd in particular gave Marco seeds and many plants from his garden at Great Dixter. Although Marco was generous as well, when he first acquired some new treasure, he liked to keep it to himself, to be the only kid on the block to have it – at least for a while. But after a few years of enjoying his monopoly, he would always share his bounty with admiring and covetous fans, spreading the wonderful plants he introduced more widely through nurserymen and other gardeners.

When Marco began working on the gardens at Wave Hill, the early pictures confirm that he planted row after row of tough, but very pedestrian, marigolds. They were certainly bright and cheerful but nothing unusual. Over time, as he acquired more staff (often people pursuing second careers) and raised more funds, he began to create the masterful borders that were so innovative and visually appealing.

He developed his own exuberant style, mixing rare treasures he had brought back from England with everyday tough doers; he planted annuals between perennials and used woody shrubs to add height and strength to the compositions. Marco emphasized shape and structure, and he liked to "let the plants mingle, to climb on each other, to consort with each other. That's the way it is in nature."

For the tasteful types who say that less is more, Marco retorts, "Not true! More is more, if the original idea is not lost." Texture, foliage colors, and shapes were all brilliantly combined. As for the "rules," Marco asks, "Rules? Rules for using color in the garden? I never learned them. I want the entire paint box, the giant Crayola!"

The Wave Hill gardens were exciting and different, looking more like someone's private garden than a public display. People began to come from near and far as the news of what was happening at Wave Hill started to spread in horticultural circles.

Marco's style of gardening is certainly not low maintenance. He believes "a low-maintenance garden is a low-interest garden," or what his friend Christopher Lloyd called a "low-brain-tenance garden." Marco was composing pictures: "I love placing things in relation to others. Some kind of architectural framework is important so the plants can escape from it. But you never know what they're going to do, where the self-sowers will pop up or look best. It might be in between the cracks in stones. The art is in getting rid of what doesn't belong. A good garden is about editing."

Now visitors coming to enjoy Wave Hill will find the same stunning site overlooking the Hudson and the Palisades but with multiple gardens reflecting years of Marco's creative and innovative work. They will be welcomed by a new visitor's center and shop, and admire the two original estate buildings, now restored to host art exhibitions, concerts, and educational programs as well as a café. The gardens include formal herbaceous borders; terraced herb, dry, and alpine gardens; an aquatic garden; a wild garden; and woodland walks. The flower garden just outside the restored conservatory that now bears Marco's name reflects his philosophy of mixing ordinary plants with the rare and allowing things to just rip.

Just two years after Marco arrived at Wave Hill, Miss Hall would play another important role in his life. Although she no longer worked at the Horticultural Society of New York, Miss Hall continued to volunteer there. She didn't like to leave any job unfinished. Before she left the society to go to NYBG, she had been the librarian and had received a collection of books from a Mr. MacKenzie. The books had never been properly unpacked and cataloged, so Miss Hall volunteered and returned from time to time to finish the job. One day

Wave Hill: The Pergola with Wave Hill Chairs

while she was working there, John Nally wandered in. He was a young man from Missouri with a master's in printmaking, not long out of school in Lawrence, Kansas. He had arrived in New York to work for a print dealer, but he hated his job. His daily commute took him past the society and that day he decided to stop in. His mother had been a great gardener, and he was curious what the society did. And there was Miss Hall to tell him and to elicit his story. She thought he would be perfect at Wave Hill and sent him to meet Marco.

John had no gardening experience other than his familiarity with his mother's garden in Excelsior Springs, Missouri. But like Marco, he was a visual person, and Marco hired him to work at Wave Hill two days a week. At the time, Wave Hill was open only on weekends, charging a twenty-five-cent admission. One of John's jobs was to sit at the front gate and take tickets. Marco then hired him to work in the garden that summer.

Over time, John became an important colleague in developing the gardens at Wave Hill as well as Marco's life partner. Marco and John would fight over ideas and plans, but Marco credits John with having an equal influence on everything that developed at Wave Hill before his untimely death in 1988. They also collected nineteenth-century furniture, porcelain, and pottery and shared what Marco calls "a reverence for beauty." Wave Hill honored John by creating a program to train gardeners; the students are known as the John Nally interns.

Though Wave Hill is on the opposite side of the Bronx, when he began working in Riverdale, Marco lived in a rented apartment near NYBG. Finally, after twenty years of traveling back and forth, he moved into a small cottage behind a large house right across the street from Wave Hill, practically living in the garden. He was on constant call, available to be woken up in the middle of the night if the heat shut off in the greenhouse during winter.

He hung out with the gardeners he hired, and they all became good friends. John Emmanuel, an aspiring playwright and poet, came as a volunteer; when he was finally hired for the summer, he remained on the team for twenty years. José Concepcion was another. He came from a New York City program for troubled youth. Going with his positive gut reaction, Marco hired José. José stayed for some twenty years and became a valued gardener, gifted pruner, and a heaven-sent mechanic, keeping the mowers and tractors running. There are many others who passed through and grew under Marco's tutelage.

Marco has had many protégés over the years and a far-reaching influence on American gardening. One of his stars is Timothy Tilghman who, long after his training at Wave Hill, has been enticed by Marco to head up the work at the embryonic Untermyer Gardens in Yonkers, where Marco serves as a horticultural advisor without pay and Stephen Byrns, once on the Wave Hill board, is president. Timothy is replicating Marco's early days at Wave Hill, restoring and creating a wondrous garden there.

Best of all, Louis Bauer came back to Wave Hill after a brilliant stint creating a public garden at Greenwood Gardens in New Jersey. Marco served on the Greenwood board while Louis was director there. Louis now serves in Marco's role as director of horticulture at Wave Hill. He is carrying on the great tradition and the high standards Marco established so many years before.

Marco credits many mentors in addition to T. H., especially J. C. Raulston, an important influence on him and so many others. J.C. started teaching horticulture at North Carolina State University in Raleigh in 1975 and began an arboretum there. The arboretum eventually grew to ten and a half acres and became known for artistic plant displays. It was February 1988 when Marco first went to lecture there and then invited J.C. to do the same at Wave Hill many times. J.C. always stayed with Marco and introduced many plants to Wave Hill. Some years later, Marco went back to Raleigh. He was scheduled to fly back to New York that night, but J.C. insisted Marco stay over instead, and Marco relented. A week later J.C. died. Marco is forever grateful he stayed.

Frank Cabot, who shared Marco's love of plants, was another important figure in Marco's life. He was involved with Wave Hill from the beginning,

Marco Polo Stufano

since the property had been a gift from his wife Anne's family. He also established the Friends of Horticulture Committee, an ongoing part of Wave Hill. Despite his patrician background and style, Frank loved to hang out in the potting shed with the gardeners. There, Frank, like Marco, was just another passionate gardener.

Marco decided to retire in 2001 and moved out of the cottage across the road into a house around the corner just a block away, a house he'd bought a few years before in anticipation of his retirement. He continues to drop in to have coffee in the potting shed with his gardener pals. He serves on the boards of George Schoellkopf's Hollister House, a Garden Conservancy project in Washington, Connecticut, and of Greenwood Gardens in New Jersey, as well as being horticultural advisor to Untermyer Gardens just a short drive north of Wave Hill in Yonkers, where T. H. Everett first worked.

Marco has received many honors over the years for his influence and important contribution to the world of horticulture. The most recent is particularly precious because it is the highest honor awarded by the Royal Horticultural Society in England. On February 2, 2016, Marco received the Veitch

Memorial Medal for outstanding advancement of science and the practice of horticulture. In its 150-year history, it has rarely been given to an American. The Brits are justifiably proud of their own gardening tradition and have almost always awarded this medal to their own, very rarely to anyone from the "colonies." Marco was an exception, following his mentor Frank Cabot, who received the award in 2002, and his friend Dan Hinkley, who received it in 2007.

Among his many other awards, Marco also received the Scott Arboretum Arthur H. Scott Medal, the Garden Club of America Distinguished Service Medal, the Massachusetts Horticultural Society Thomas Roland Medal, and the Pennsylvania Horticultural Society Distinguished Achievement Award.

Marco continues to be a bright spirit in horticultural circles. He is just as enthusiastic as ever. During Wave Hill's celebration of its fiftieth anniversary, Marco was honored as the founding director of horticulture and for the dedication and artistry he brought to the spectacular gardens. He now holds the title created for him, director of horticulture emeritus. Speaking from the heart, he modestly said, "It's about providing someplace beautiful for the people of the city … it's not about a collection of plants. It's about making pictures, putting things together in a way that's pleasing."

Wave Hill: The Pergola in winter

Stephen F. Byrns

It was an amazing sight ... It captured my heart.

IN A DEEP SLEEP for half a century, Untermyer Gardens, like the princess in *Sleeping Beauty*, was just waiting for a prince to come to bestow a kiss to awaken it from its slumbers. Stephen Byrns was that prince, and although he fell in love at first sight, the garden, unlike the princess, couldn't spring to life in an instant. Although in ruin, enough remained to reveal the basic structure of a walled Indo-Persian garden with classical elements that spoke to Stephen's architect's heart. Little did he realize when he fell in love that the garden's resurrection would take over his life.

What he first saw in 1988 gave him only the smallest hint of what had once been the magnificent gardens created in Yonkers for Samuel Untermyer in the early 1900s. By the time Stephen arrived, the property was owned by the city of Yonkers, and the gardens were long gone, although some work had been done to preserve part of the original design. Impressive crenellated walls still stood, incised with a diamond-lattice design and punctuated by octagonal towers in the corners enclosing a large space now called the Walled Garden. Passing through an imposing entrance gate, modeled after the famous Lion Gate at Mycenae in Greece, Stephen saw a three-acre space divided into quadrants by intersecting canals, a common water feature in Persian gardens, though by then no water coursed through them. Stephen instantly appreciated the surviving classical architectural elements. It was, he recalls, "an amazing sight" that drew him in. Ultimately, he would become the full-time president of the Untermyer Gardens Conservancy, the organization he created to restore this extraordinary place.

Samuel Untermyer purchased the property called Greystone in 1899, with its ninety-nine-room mansion and 150 acres of land overlooking the

Hudson River, from the estate of Samuel J. Tilden, once governor of New York. In 1916, he hired the Beaux Arts architect, William Welles Bosworth, who had already designed the Rockefeller gardens at Kykuit in Tarrytown, New York, to design his gardens. Competitive by nature, Untermyer didn't live far from John D. Rockefeller Jr. in Manhattan, and he commissioned the very same architect with instructions to make Untermyer's gardens "not less than the greatest gardens in the world." After the Untermyer project, Bosworth was sent off by Rockefeller to France to work on the restoration of Versailles, where he spent the rest of his life.

Among the most successful lawyers of his time, Untermyer was a founder of the firm Guggenheimer, Untermyer, & Marshall, then the leading New York Jewish law firm, and is credited with reforms leading to the establishment of the Federal Reserve system and other important financial regulations. A Zionist, he supported a Jewish homeland in Palestine. In 1933 he'd become an early crusader against the Nazis and remained one until his death in 1940, establishing the Non-Sectarian Anti-Nazi League, which called for a boycott of German goods. At a time when mixed marriages were unusual, he married Minnie, a Protestant, and a strong supporter of the arts and of the women's suffrage movement.

The original garden design incorporated themes from Persian to Greek to Renaissance, with clear references to the Alhambra, Taj Mahal, Boboli Gardens, and Villa d'Este. The gardens were opened weekly to the public, as well as for cultural events and social gatherings. The *New York Times* reported that one event, a free flower show on October 29, 1939, drew more than thirty thousand people on a single day. To maintain the gardens at their full glory, Untermyer employed sixty full-time gardeners and sustained sixty greenhouses. His chauffeur drove to his Manhattan office every afternoon to deliver a fresh orchid for him to wear in his buttonhole after his morning orchid faded.

Public-spirited and justifiably proud of his gardens, Untermyer tried to donate them to the public during his lifetime, offering them first to the State of New York, then to Westchester County, and finally to the city of Yonkers. They all turned him down. When he died in 1940, the provisions of his will attempted to carry out the same plans but failed, and the garden fell into limbo. Six years after his death, Yonkers finally agreed to accept sixteen of the total 150 acres. The rest were sold. The original ninety-nine-room mansion and all the greenhouses were demolished.

Happily, a small bit of the Untermyer garden lives on in Central Park. Walter Schott, a leading German sculptor of the early twentieth century, created a beautiful bronze called the *Three Dancing Maidens* that Samuel Untermyer bought on a trip to Berlin to stand in the fountain at his main entrance. After he died, his children gave the fountain to New York City, and it has become one of the delights of the Central Park Conservatory Garden so wonderfully restored by Lynden Miller.

Perhaps if the Garden Conservancy had been in existence to help, Samuel Untermyer's plan might have succeeded. Instead, rehabilitation of the gardens for the public had to wait many decades until Stephen founded the Untermyer Gardens Conservancy.

Horticulture became part of Stephen's life in early childhood. He was born on December 4, 1954, in St. Joseph, Michigan, a few hours away from Evart, where Dan Hinkley grew up. St. Joseph is on the eastern shore of Lake Michigan, facing Chicago across the lake to the west. As a result, Stephen describes it as "closer to Chicago in culture than to Detroit," further away to the east. He was the firstborn and only son, followed by three sisters.

His first gardening experience began when he was in sixth grade, living in a house near Lake Michigan. One day, a young friend came to visit and said, "Your yard looks really dead." As Stephen looked around, he realized the grass really *did* look dead. When he dug into the soil, he saw that it was almost pure white sand. Any water drained away immediately. Relishing a challenge even then, Stephen tried to revive the grass by watering it every day until it finally began to look green. Then one day, a package of free seeds came enclosed as a giveaway in a loaf of white bread his mother bought. The seeds were called Near White Miracles. Stephen planted them, and watched with delight as they emerged as marigolds. He thought it was a miracle to see those seeds germinate.

A few years later, his family moved across the street into what had been his great-aunt's house. A serious gardener, she had created a sophisticated garden. Stephen's aunt had been among the first to recognize the "lake effect," causing the climate along the lake to be more even and less extreme than further inland. She even thought she could grow rhododendrons, and did, quite successfully. Others followed her example. Even though she employed a full-time gardener, as she aged the garden fell into disrepair.

Although he was only a teenager when his family moved into his great-aunt's house, Stephen took it upon himself to restore the garden. His parents began to pay him for his work, and then some of the neighbors followed, hiring him to mow their lawns and help with their gardens. He learned hands-on as he went. Over the next four or five years, Stephen managed to restore his great-aunt's garden and nearly doubled its size.

Stephen's father hailed from the east, and the family was well off, so Stephen was sent to boarding school at Hotchkiss in Connecticut, graduating in 1973. He went on to Princeton, where he studied history and architecture, graduating in 1977. From his studies, Stephen learned to view history as cultural, a discipline in which literature, music, and art are integral parts of historical currents and context. His history curriculum at Princeton was called Western Historical and Cultural Studies, and he was required to write a thesis to graduate. He chose as his subject William Butterfield, an English architect (1814–1900) and designer of High Victorian Gothic churches, who was influenced by the Oxford Movement that promoted High Church practices as well as by the Cambridge Camden Society (later the Ecclesiological Society), an architectural society that promoted a revival of Gothic style.

At Princeton Stephen took a single course in landscape architecture, in which he was required to design a park. Returning to his roots in St. Joseph, once a thriving factory town, he found the city had created a public park where the factories once stood. But there was nothing in the park except grass. Not even trees. He decided to design a proper park for that site.

Stephen approached his grandfather, a successful businessman with his own charitable foundation, to ask if he would fund his intended design. His grandfather, still grieving for his late wife who had died in a terrible car crash only a year before, agreed to fund the park in her memory. The total cost would be $100,000 (or just over $400,000 in 2015 dollars). When Stephen graduated from Princeton, he came home to implement his park design. Without any experience, he hired laborers, supervised the work, and retained an architect to design a gazebo that still stands. The park is called the Margaret Upton Arboretum.

After the park was finished, he returned to New York to study architecture in graduate school at Columbia. After graduating in 1981, he worked for the architectural firm of Kohn Pedersen Fox, known for major projects around the world. As a beginner, Stephen did a lot of the basic grunt work before computers, spending many hours hunched over architectural drawings. He observes that this is why architects have a tradition of wearing only bow ties. So much of their work was spent leaning over drawing boards that anyone wearing a traditional tie would have to tuck it in to ensure the tie did not fall into the mess of the lead dust. Bow ties worked better. Even now, Stephen is only seen sporting a bow tie.

Stephen met Tom Lollar in 1983; they have been together as partners ever since. A sculptor, teacher, and art dealer, Tom likes to look at gardens, but Stephen says he "has zero interest" in hands-on gardening.

In 1985 Stephen left Kohn Pedersen Fox and founded BKSK Architects. Given the focus of his academic interests, it is not surprising that the firm is renowned for designing buildings that take into account the social, ecological, and historic context of the setting.

Stephen and Tom bought a house and in 1988 moved to Yonkers, where

Untermyer Gardens: The Walled Garden

Stephen was bound to discover Untermyer Gardens. Even on first encounter, he immediately appreciated the stunning architecture that still remained, though much of it was overgrown and covered in graffiti. Earlier in the 1970s, the City of Yonkers had engaged an architect to restore some of the original elements, particularly the Walled Garden and its imposing entrance gate. The effort took place during New York's financial crisis and Yonkers could not afford to maintain it, but at least this work kept some of the essential structures in place. Otherwise, Stephen thinks, "Yonkers might have leveled it all to build a football field."

The enclosing wall had been vandalized so many times that the garden was locked up tight at night for security. Outside the Walled Garden, young woods had sprung up and mature trees lay where they fell. Weeds and worse triumphed. Because the Yonkers workers who maintained the property were members of the Teamsters Union, the garden followed Teamster hours; it was only open from 7:00 A.M. to 3:00 P.M. weekdays and rarely at all on weekends.

In addition to supporting some structural restoration, Yonkers had also made a modest attempt to grow a few annuals along the edges of what had once been the central water feature, the intersecting water canals inside the walled enclosure. Bosworth had called this section an Indo-Persian garden, referring to the traditional *charbagh*, which literally means "four gardens." This ancient design, a walled garden divided into quadrants by intersecting water canals, is most famously embodied in the Taj Mahal.

A semicircular columned amphitheater with traditional classical Greek elements stood behind a reflecting pool at the opposite end of the entrance gate and the central canal. It had been the venue for concerts, galas, and dance performances during Untermyer's day but was almost impossible to see underneath a veil of overgrown junipers. In front of the amphitheater, a pair of sphinxes faced each other, carved by the prominent sculptor Paul Manship; each sphinx sat atop handsome marble twin columns soaring tall above the reflecting pool.

On the western side of the walled enclosure, was the Temple of the Sky with its roofless circle of Corinthian columns and beautiful mosaic floor, looking down to the pool and terrace garden below; the pool also featured beautiful mosaic tile. Beyond was a view of the Hudson River and the Palisades. The temple, too, had once been the venue for entertainments, and although many of the tiles were missing or broken the basic design survived.

Outside the Walled Garden some distance away, the remains of the Temple of Love, covered in graffiti and weeds, stood on land that had been acquired by a developer who planned to build apartments there. Luckily for the future of Untermyer Gardens, that developer went bankrupt, but he was followed by another with an even more threatening plan to build a high-rise tower. That developer went bankrupt as well. By the 1990s, there was a major effort to retrieve that land and convert it for public use. Local environmentalists worked with the Open Space Institute and Yonkers agreed to buy back that parcel of roughly twenty-seven acres for $30,000. The gardens went from sixteen acres to a total of forty-three, and the Temple of Love was saved for future restoration.

There was also a battle in the 1990s to save the northern part of the gardens, an area that had once been the Italian Gardens, a series of ornamental terraced gardens with water rills, that was now owned by a hospital that announced plans to build a nursing home there. Although no longer visible, Stephen was sure that the original rills must still exist. All that could be seen were some walls, marble basins, and a bit of the stairs. Stephen decided to excavate to see if he could find the rills, and digging into the ground, he was excited to find some cobalt blue tiles, confirming they had survived.

Trying to be reasonable, Stephen led the charge to try to stop the hospital from building the nursing home. He didn't push to stop construction but urged the hospital to adopt a design that would shift the building, so at that least some of the garden could be saved, including its existing vista to the Tappan Zee Bridge. Fearlessly, he even debated the hospital's president on cable TV. But the president was adamant and insisted on sticking to the original design. The nursing home was built, but in the end, it proved to be so unprofitable that the hospital sold it off. Only the top terrace of the Italian garden remains.

By 1998, Stephen and Tom had moved from Yonkers to Riverdale. They bought a house that had once belonged to Ruth Rea Howell, who during her lifetime was a skillful and committed gardener. There is still a garden named for her at the New York Botanical Garden, the Ruth Rea Howell Family Garden. She had died five years before, and her garden, like that of Stephen's great-aunt, had decayed over time. Once again, he set to work; he restored and doubled the size of her garden.

He also soon joined the board of Wave Hill, not very far south of the Untermyer site in Yonkers, where he met Marco Polo Stufano and they became good friends. When Marco retired as head of horticulture at Wave Hill in 2001, he continued to live in Riverdale, not far from Stephen, who became a member of the New York City Landmarks Preservation Commission and was also occupied with his architectural practice.

Then one night at a Yonkers party, Stephen learned that some of the water had at long last been turned back on at Untermyer. He had not seen water there for twenty years and was thrilled by this major step Yonkers had taken to restore the water feature at the core of the Walled Garden. He quickly went to visit and recalls, "It was an amazing sight. It transformed my summer." However, he also realized that the Untermyer Gardens would never really be fully restored unless he undertook to do more himself.

Recognizing his work as a volunteer was "taking more and more of my time," and that the gardens "had captured my heart," he resigned from the Wave Hill board and the Landmarks Preservation Commission to start the Untermyer Gardens Conservancy. It was an ambitious idea, creating a nonprofit organization to work in partnership with the City of Yonkers, following the Central Park Conservancy model and undertaking responsibility for what he calls the gardens' "rehabilitation" rather than restoration, since a full restoration is no longer possible.

By coincidence, Stephen learned that he and Tom and Marco Polo Stufano happened to be planning a trip to Rome around the same time in 2010. They agreed to meet up, and once in Rome, they hired a car to visit important Italian gardens, including the Villa d'Este and Villa Aldobrandini. During that garden tour, Stephen braced himself and finally bravely asked Marco if he would be willing to become involved in the work at Untermyer pro bono.

"Absolutely. It would be like coming full circle," said Marco. He then disclosed his own early ties to Untermyer Gardens. Marco's mentor T. H. Everett's first job in America was at Untermyer Gardens. Untermyer used to send an agent down to the docks to find gardeners to hire, and T. H. was one such hire. In the 1960s, T. H. took Marco to visit the gardens to show him where T. H. had first worked. While there, Marco remembers seeing a rare sight, a handkerchief tree (*Davidia involucrata*) in full bloom. As a tribute to that memory, Marco later planted a handkerchief tree at Wave Hill that still stands. Marco was on board.

One of Marco's first important moves at Untermyer was to attract Timothy Tilghman to come on full-time as head gardener. Timothy has been in charge ever since. Having worked at Wave Hill for four years, Timothy views Marco as a mentor and works easily with him as an advisor. Rather like Marco's early efforts at Wave Hill, when he used easy, bright marigolds to make a splashy display when little else was yet planted, so too early on Timothy had an exuberant planting of masses of marigolds along the central water canal in the Walled Garden. Since the marigold is a flower used in Hindu offerings, Stephen viewed this as wonderfully appropriate to the Indo-Persian spirit of the place.

Now each year the plantings are particularly lush along the canals and around the large reflecting pool in front of the semicircular amphitheater. Many pots of exotic tropical plants provide vibrant color, some growing right in the waters of the pool. Deep borders line the perimeter of the Walled Garden with a wonderful mix of shrubs and perennials.

Just outside the northern end of the walls is the Vista, a stairway 650 feet long descending to the Hudson River and ending at the Vista Overlook, graced by a handsome pair of ancient Roman monolithic cipollino columns that frame the view. This part of the garden's design was modeled after the stairs at

Untermyer Gardens
Left: The Vista with the Hudson River below
Right: The Temple of Love

the Villa d'Este that descend to Lake Como, but the Vista had been buried under trees that blocked the view. The space has now been cleared and new plantings begun. To the north of the Vista are the two remaining Color Gardens, yet to be restored. Originally there were six terraced Color Gardens, each planted in a single color, and Stephen hopes to effect a land swap with the hospital to restore three of them. The sixth has been irretrievably lost, buried under a road. Below the Color Gardens, the former rose and dahlia garden can be only imagined from the twelve standing columns in the distance, once part of an elegant pergola cloaked in climbing roses. Further below are the ruins of the gatehouse, linking the carriage trail to the old Croton Aqueduct.

Much of the restoration is like an archaeological dig or history research project. In addition to Untermyer's files, there are photographs of the gardens in the Smithsonian archives. Stephen would like to recreate the sundial, which was made up entirely of plants so perfectly placed that Samuel Untermyer often set his watch there. Stephen has also begun to uncover the original carriage trails that loop through the property and link the Overlook at the bottom of the Vista back up the hill to the Temple of Love. Timothy Tilghman and a crew from the Yonkers Parks Department have begun to uncover the remains of an extensive rock garden long buried under soil and vegetation. Once a naturalistic grouping of stones tumbling downhill along the sides of a small stream, the rock garden also had stone paths crisscrossing the stream on rock bridges. A small seating area on a curved stone bench remains partway up the hill.

The most recent success story is the restoration of the Temple of Love, a circular temple topped by a dome of lacy wrought iron that sits high atop a manmade creation of boulders simulating a giant rocky outcropping, with a marvelous view of the Hudson River and the Palisades. The outcropping was once an elaborate water feature, with water coursing all around it in various waterfalls and ponds. The Temple of Love was created by Carlo Davite, a Genoese stonemason who did work in the Paris Exposition, the St. Louis Exposition, and at the Frick Museum. Many of the rocks were hollowed out to form planters that were lushly planted. There are three bridges in the rough stone and a small seating area with a stone bench that can be reached through a rocky tunnel. An additional bridge crosses the pool at the base of the temple.

Stephen Byrns

This is the conservancy's most important restoration project to date. The temple was replaced and the dome restored. New electrical, plumbing, and mechanical systems were installed. Massive masonry elements were hoisted into place, and new railings and a rustic arbor finished things off. Best of all, water runs through it again, with five waterfalls and six cascades.

While much remains to be done, Stephen has led the Untermyer Gardens Conservancy from strength to strength. On February 1, 2016, almost thirty years after his first encounter with the gardens, Stephen resigned as a partner of BKSK Architects to become the first full-time salaried president of the conservancy.

After starting as the only gardener in 2011, Timothy Tilghman now oversees a staff of six. More than sixty thousand visitors a year come to see Untermyer Gardens. The first year's budget was $100,000; it is now more than $1 million a year. Restoration work continues apace as the budget grows; the challenge is to coordinate and obtain approval for any work with the New York State Department of Parks, Recreation, and Historic Preservation as well as the city of Yonkers. The gardens are listed on the National Register of Historic Places. Success breeds success.

With Stephen Byrns bringing his vision and energy to the effort as its full-time president, Untermyer Gardens is already well under way to once again becoming among the most spectacular gardens in America. Looking back, Stephen says, "All of my lifetime interests in architecture, history, historic preservation, and horticulture have come together."

Dr. Richard W. Lighty

I knew by the age of ten that I wanted to grow up to be another Luther Burbank.

ALWAYS FASCINATED by variations in nature, Dr. Richard W. Lighty "knew by the age of ten that I wanted to grow up to be another Luther Burbank." He still has the book his scientist father gave him entitled *Luther Burbank: Plant Magician*. Plant genetics, or to be more precise, cytogenetics, was inevitably his academic focus, first as an undergraduate in horticulture at Pennsylvania State University and then in his doctoral program at Cornell. But Dick, as he is known, a unique combination of scientist and plant lover, has broad interests. His lively blue eyes sparkle as he recounts in his warm, rich-timbered voice that his professional life took place in "three fifteen-year segments – the first spent learning, the next teaching, and the third, the last, in developing and running a public garden." Although Dick may think of these segments as distinct careers, there is continuity and overlap among them. His teaching career connects his time in research at Longwood Gardens, one of American's greatest public gardens, with the University of Delaware's Longwood Graduate Program in Public Garden Administration, a program he began and ran, to the third segment, his work creating a new public garden, Mt. Cuba Center. Throughout the three segments he went on many plant-finding trips where he discovered, brought back, and introduced wonderful plants new to American horticulture.

Dick was born November 8, 1933, in Freeport, Illinois, the second of three children and the only son. His father, Paul, was an important role model, since he was what Dick calls "an above average gardener," working with both vegetables and ornamental gardens around the house. Most important, his father loved the process of gardening, while his mother, Florence, liked the products. The nature of Dick's father's work caused the family to move many times in the eastern United States. Dick's grandfather was a professor at the University of Wisconsin with a Ph.B. (bachelor of philosophy) from Cornell who envisioned and developed Wisconsin's exemplary extension program, seeking to raise the quality of life for residents in far-flung areas of the state. He was the first to use radio to reach them. He must have been a little disappointed when his son dropped out of the university to marry Florence. A few years later, the Great Depression set in and Paul, after losing his job at the Burgess Battery Company, bought a Sears Roebuck prefab cottage and erected it on his farm in Madison. Paul and Florence moved in with three-month-old Richard and his sister, Delma, and continued to raise their family, attended college classes, and earned a living by operating a photo-finishing business at night in the basement.

Upon completion of his Ph.B. with a major in chemistry, Paul moved the family to New Jersey, where he went to work for Thomas A. Edison, Inc., in battery development. The family moved a few more times, first to West Virginia, where he worked as a spectroscopist for International Nickel, then to Long Island to join Sperry Corporation (originally Sperry Gyroscope) during the war, and finally to northwestern New Jersey, where Paul bought a hundred-acre farm and commuted daily fifty miles each way to his work for ITT in Nutley.

It was while Dick was living in West Virginia that he first met his sweetheart, Sally; he was five, and she was three, and they were playmates. Years later, when he enrolled in undergraduate school at Penn State, Sally followed him, studying there for two years until they married upon his graduation in 1955 and then joining him at Cornell to complete her B.A. degree while he did his graduate studies. They have been married for more than sixty years. He says, "I believe in long courtships – and I definitely recommend them."

Dick and Sally first began to visit the Adirondacks while he was in graduate school at Cornell, not that far away. At first they stayed in houses owned by the parents of good friends at Cornell, but eventually, after they moved to Pennsylvania, they bought a "summer camp" on five acres above a river near Elizabethtown, New York. Many years later, in 1995, they built a house of Dick's design there, perched on a rock ledge thirty-five feet above the Boquet River. They have gone to the Adirondacks every summer since 1958, and now spend at least four months of each year there. Both their children have gone into horticulture.

Like Burbank, who developed what Dick believes is still the best baking potato, Dick worked with potatoes and other agricultural crops, but his deeper interest has always been in ornamental horticulture. He studied plant breeding and genetics but

Dick Lighty on Mt. Sorak, South Korea 1966

minored in ornamental horticulture and horticultural taxonomy. Professor George H. M. Lawrence was an important mentor who supervised his work in his minor subjects and was himself a horticultural taxonomist of international reputation, who helped develop the International Code of Nomenclature for Cultivated Plants.

Working under Lawrence on his Ph.D. dissertation, Dick analyzed the chromosomes of Madonna lilies, proving that all of them grown in this country originated from a single clone. He still loves lilies and grew quite a few when he had his own marvelous garden just outside Kennett Square, Pennsylvania, in the Red Clay Creek Valley, where he and Sally moved in 1961. His house and garden happened to be at the far edge of the property known as Hartefeld, which belonged to my husband's parents and was where he grew up. Dick would play an important role in the life of the young Darrell Probst, who lived nearby.

Dick had assumed that after leaving Cornell he would find a job with a seed company, but Walter Hodge, then head of education and research at Longwood Gardens and another important mentor, came to Cornell to interview students. He urged Dick to consider a position at Longwood. Situated in the Brandywine Valley of Pennsylvania, on the outskirts of Wilmington, Delaware, Longwood Gardens is one of the great public gardens in America and indeed the world. I think of it as the Versailles of American gardens. Thanks to Dick's work, others see it as the American equivalent of the Royal Botanic Gardens at Kew, not only for its plant research, but particularly for its educational training programs in professional horticulture, in which Dick came to play such an important role.

Created in the early 1900s by Pierre S. du Pont, Longwood became his ongoing legacy and was the principal beneficiary of his substantial wealth when he died in 1954 without children.

Longwood Gardens spreads over a thousand acres and contains many extraordinary features, including its major conservatory complex and formal outdoor ornamental gardens, as well as vast acres of natural meadows and woodlands. There is an outdoor amphitheater created inside formal hedges and the Italian Water Garden with playful fountains and geometric pools that provide respite from the summer sun. The Main Fountain Garden displays a more energetic use of water, with its towering jets that are especially vivid at night when the fountains, choreographed to dance to music, are illuminated by colored lights. The Main Fountain Garden has recently been reconstructed in a manner true to Pierre du Pont's original intent. With an annual budget of more than $50 million and a staff of more than 1,300, Longwood is not only a much-visited public garden, but also among this country's leading centers of horticultural research and education.

Right out of Cornell in 1960 with his newly minted Ph.D., Dick went to

Longwood and became the geneticist in charge of the research greenhouses, conducting horticultural research and breeding. But he also began to pay attention to the cultivation methods used by the old gardeners who had worked at Longwood for many years while it was still a du Pont private domain. Many of these gardeners were reluctant to share their secret techniques, nor would they easily abandon their tried and true methods, even when better ways were suggested to grow display plants. Since Longwood had become a public institution, Dick worked hard to convince these skeptics that modern, scientific methods could produce the quality plants needed for the public seasonal greenhouse displays in less time and for less money by using new growing mediums, fertilizers, environmental techniques, and disease control measures.

As part of a cooperative program at Longwood with the U.S. Department of Agriculture, Dick went to Korea in 1966 on a plant-finding expedition. It was his first trip outside the United States other than to Canada. The flora of Korea, like that of China and Japan, evolved under conditions similar to the eastern United States but had been long overlooked by Western botanists. Communist China was then inaccessible, so Korea became Dick's base of operations for four months during the growing season while he studied and collected desirable plant material.

Heat prostration, sore muscles, food poisoning, severe dysentery – Dick lost more than twenty pounds – primitive living, and challenging road conditions did not deter him. The plants were sent back to the United States to be evaluated and distributed after inspection for any problems, so that they did not inadvertently introduce invasive plant material, fungus, insects, and the like. In total, Dick mailed back cuttings, live plants, and seeds of 450 different woody plants, ferns, and other herbaceous treasures. Dick smiles, saying proudly, "We lost only a few of the plants we sent back."

Dick has been an outspoken critic of nonprofits that sponsor plant-finding expeditions but fail to adequately absorb and evaluate the results and get the worthy new species out into public use. He thinks they are "planning the next trip before they've had time to digest the previous trip – that's the crux of the problem." By selecting plants that performed well in his own garden, and through his own personal efforts and connections with private gardeners, nurserymen, and plant societies, he has disseminated his favorite discoveries across the country. One of my own favorites is a tough and beautiful little woodland plant he brought back from Korea, *Aruncus aesthusifolius,* while Dick's friend and fellow plantsman William H. Frederick Jr. treasures Dick's *Iris ensata* var. *spontanea* with its color that Frederick describes as "electric mauve."

Dick's other great Korean finds from other trips that are particularly popular are the grass *Calamagrostis arundinacea* var. *brachytricha, Hydrangea serrata*

Longwood Gardens
Left: Dick pollinating Delphinium 1964
Right: Working with F. Joseph Carstens in the Experimental Greenhouses 1965

'Blue Billow,' and the lovely *Caryopteris incana* 'Blue Billow.' The original plant specimen of this *Caryopteris* was found by Dick and Edward G. Corbett, then at the U.S. Plant Introduction Station, when they were on a plant-finding trip and spotted it along the beach on Cheju Island in Korea. Its form caught their keen eyes when they noticed its prostrate stems arched upward at the tips, displaying tight clusters of soft blue flowers that also proved to be an excellent nectar source for late-season butterflies.

Recognizing that controlling weeds is a constant challenge, Dick also encourages the use of ground covers as the most effective "green" solution. Some of the best of these came from his and others' plant-finding trips. "When I say 'ground cover' I mean a planting that will control weeds when it reaches maturity," he explains. So rather than the omnipresent *Pachysandra terminalis,* he recommends vigorous forms of both clump-forming and stoloniferous sorts of *Tiarella* and selected cultivars of *Vinca minor,* such as 'Miss Jekyll's White,' that will not burn out and can fill in thickly enough to allay the germination and spread of weeds. As others came along to promote new ground cover ideas,

Longwood Gardens: Exhibition Hall Fern Floor

Dick provided strong support, especially enthusiastic support for *Epimedium,* with the several new forms introduced by Darrell Probst and certain examples of *Asarum* brought in from Japan by Barry Yinger.

There are many other plants Dick brought back that are not as well known but reflect what he is seeking with his high standards. He looks for plants that are "quite free of disease and cultural problems," and that also "make a good, basic palette for gardens in the Middle Atlantic region." But his interests have always been broad so "finer, more finicky plants are welcome to enhance composition and orchestrate the garden."

In 1967, Dick began the teaching segment of his career. He became the founding director of the new Longwood Graduate Program at the University of Delaware, which would train graduate students who, at some point in their careers, wished to concentrate on public garden management. Sending him to his interview for this position, the director of Longwood told him, "We've interviewed a number of people and the ones the university likes, we don't like. The ones we like, the university doesn't like." The university wanted academic credentials while Longwood wanted someone with experience in public gardens. Dick, of course, had both.

As the founder of the graduate program, Dick built it, administered it, and taught classes in public garden management. Despite his position as the program's head, Dick also taught undergraduate courses in horticulture and botany. He began to take students on a series of tropical study trips, usually in the winter months during the school break, often to Central America and Brazil, and occasionally to Florida or California. Even when he traveled abroad for other reasons, he generally managed to fit in some time for collecting plants.

Over time, Dick's broader interests led him to introduce business and economics courses into the program. What had been Longwood's Graduate Program in Ornamental Horticulture became the Longwood Graduate Program in Public Garden Administration. He is justifiably proud that so many of his protégés have become leading figures at major horticultural institutions in their own right. It is an impressive list that includes more than twenty people, including Richard Brown, director of the Bloedel Reserve; David Scheid, executive director of the U.S. Botanic Garden; the late Judy Zuk, past president of the Brooklyn Botanic Garden; Jane Pepper, longtime and now former president of the Pennsylvania Horticultural Society; Paul Meyer, executive director of the Morris Arboretum; Claire Sawyers, director of the Scott Arboretum of Swarthmore College; and others in major horticultural institutions in locations throughout the country: Washington State, Ohio, Texas, Tennessee, Missouri, Michigan, North Carolina, and more.

Dick has also applied for patents for a few plants he either found or spotted growing as an unusual cultivar. One is *Hydrangea serrata* 'Annie's Blue,' no doubt related to the popular *Hydrangea serrata* 'Blue Billow' that he had discovered earlier in Korea. There are also a few *Epimedium* cultivars, *Epimedium* 'Conalba' Alabaster and *Epimedium grandiflorum* 'Purple Pixie,' speaking to his long friendship with Darrell Probst. He has served on thesis committees, including the one that supervised Barry Yinger's thesis on Japanese *Asarum*, and has been an enthusiastic supporter of plant societies, noting that they "can encourage nurseries and greenhouses to provide good plants they long for and become the repositories of last resort for cultivars as they go out of vogue."

As he became increasingly well known, Dick joined the board of the American Association of Botanical Gardens and Arboreta; he became its president in 1978. He was sought after by countless organizations for advice, lectures, and expertise. Then, in 1982, Dick received a call from Mr. and Mrs. Lammot du Pont Copeland asking for a consultation in connection with the future of their property. They had been thinking of establishing an arboretum or some kind of public garden on their estate, which was located in the village of Mount Cuba, outside of Wilmington.

He agreed to consult and asked them about their particular interests, urging them to select a particular focus for their property. He wisely concluded that the Copelands needed to create a unique identity that was distinct from the already well-established important public gardens nearby, Longwood Gardens and the extensive gardens at Winterthur, which had previously been funded by members of the du Pont family. Learning of Mrs. Copeland's lifelong love of wildflowers and devotion to conservation and land preservation, Dick thought the family should continue to develop their property, already a significant and beautiful garden, but then added, "Your love of the Piedmont topography, evidenced by the choice of Mt. Cuba as the site for your home, and the wonderful array of Piedmont wildflowers you've already incorporated into your garden, suggest these as a suitable focus for future development." They loved the idea of featuring the native Piedmont flora, and who better to execute the plan than Dick?

The Piedmont is a plateau along the East Coast, between the Atlantic Coastal Plain and the Appalachian Mountains. The word means "foothill," coming from the Latin word *pedemontium,* literally "the foot of the mountains." Dick's suggestion was very timely as the interest in native plants was just beginning to emerge, a movement that has continued to grow in strength and popularity.

The Copelands first bought 126.7 acres near the village of Mount Cuba, Delaware, in 1935 and built a handsome manor house there. Over the next few decades, they hired outstanding landscape architects and designers, including Thomas W. Sears and Marian C. Coffin, to develop appropriate formal gardens around their imposing home.

Longwood Gardens: Flower Garden Walk in spring

As ideas about the importance of conservation and sustainable ecology began to take hold, the Copelands started to think about the larger landscape. Mrs. Copeland, in particular, was increasingly concerned about wildflowers and the impact development was having on them. They added an additional 17.72 acres and began to create a more naturalistic garden there. The landscape architect Seth Kelsey came in to design a woodland wildflower garden with native plants, ponds, and paths.

In 1983, the Copelands asked Dick to become the first director of Mt. Cuba Center with a focus on the study of the native plants of the Appalachian Piedmont. Unfortunately, Mr. Copeland died shortly before Dick reported for work. Mt. Cuba Center, beginning as a botanic garden on a private estate, evolved under Dick's leadership into a public attraction, hosting visitors in the late 1980s and offering docent-led tours during the spring. The horticulturists began documenting their increasingly diverse native plant collections. In 1989, Mt. Cuba Center for the Study of Piedmont Flora was incorporated as a charitable foundation and began its transition from a private estate to a public garden over the remaining span of Mrs. Copeland's life.

After fifteen years as the founding director, Dick stepped down in 1998, after what he calls a wonderful "partnership" with Mrs. Copeland, "each learning important lessons from the other." In 2001, Mrs. Copeland died, and Mt. Cuba Center was no longer a botanic garden on a private estate but entirely a public garden. For her legacy, Mrs. Copeland said, "I want this to be a place where people will learn to appreciate our native plants and to see how these plants can enrich their lives so that they, in turn, will become conservators of our natural habitats."

Mt. Cuba carries on as an important public garden, fulfilling its mission "to inspire an appreciation for the beauty and value of native plants and a commitment to support the habitats that sustain them." In addition to welcoming visitors to enjoy the beauty of the fifty acres of display gardens, there are five hundred acres of natural land used for public programs and conservation. Considering Dick's earlier role as an educator, it is not surprising it also includes an important educational component, offering many classes as well as a certificate in Ecological Gardening.

While he was still at Mt. Cuba, Dick had his serendipitous encounter with Frank Cabot at a meeting of the Association of American Botanical Gardens and Arboreta (now the American Public Gardens Association). That was in the late 1980s, just as Frank was beginning to dream about what would become the Garden Conservancy. The chance meeting occurred at the Missouri Botanical Garden. As Dick recalls, they happened to be walking toward each other, each fully aware of the other's credentials. They hit it off immediately,

Dick Lighty at Mt. Cuba Center

both sharing the same passion for plants. When Frank later sent Dick a letter outlining his idea for a national organization to preserve exceptional American gardens, he asked Dick for a critique. Dick replied honestly that he didn't think it had much chance for success. He particularly thought it would be very hard to be a national organization and handle all of America, pointing to the difficulties the American Horticultural Society faced trying to manage programs on the West Coast from a home base in the east. Frank's response was to invite Dick to join the incipient board.

He was the perfect choice. With his ongoing experience in creating a public garden from what had been a private estate, and his having founded and run the Graduate Program in Public Garden Administration, he brought insights vital to the organization to preserve exceptional American gardens. His experience would prove central in helping private gardens transform themselves into public institutions or, at the very least, into gardens that inspire public involvement and support. Through his network in the horticultural world, Dick would also become an invaluable advisor in identifying those gardens worthy of attention and preservation. He accepted Frank's invitation and was a founding member of the board of directors and became the first chair of the Garden Conservancy's Garden Oversight Committee.

It wasn't long before Frank asked Dick to serve on the board of Stonecrop, Frank's private garden in Cold Spring, New York, which he planned to organize as a pubic charitable organization, open to visitors and, on a small scale, a training ground for professional horticulturists. Dick still serves on that board and is now also director emeritus of the Garden Conservancy. When he was elevated to emeritus status, the Garden Conservancy paid him tribute by observing that he "never hesitated to add creativity, insight, botanical erudition, and a welcome touch of wit to every occasion, even in emails under the sly handle of the botanical name of the dandelion genus, *Taraxicum* – and at Earth-Link, naturally!"

Dick is quick to name Walter Hodge and Professor George Lawrence as important mentors and role models, although he credits his dad as his first mentor. Equally important is Charlie Emmerick. Charlie worked at the Sperry Corporation when Dick's father worked there. Brooklyn born, before going to Sperry, Charlie had owned a machine shop that made such things as a candy-cutting machine and a packaging machine. He was also very interested in gardening and encouraged Dick in many ways. Whenever Dick needed help on a question about materials or machines, he knew he could call on Charlie. If the necessary tool or machine didn't exist, Charlie would create it!

Dick has been recognized with many awards for his work. In 1999 the American Horticultural Society gave him their Liberty Hyde Bailey Award, and in 2016 the American Public Gardens Association gave their Service Award to Dick and Sally jointly, recognizing their important partnership through the years. In 1983 he had received their Honorary Life Member Award. The association said of Dick, "He has contributed greatly to some of our most prestigious member institutions, enriching their research programs, collections, and serving as a mentor to many staff and students."

Despite his credentials and impressive accomplishments, Dick remains passionate about plants but modest about himself. Looking back on his role as part of the younger generation that took over leadership in the early 1970s of the American Public Gardens Association (then still the Association of Botanical Gardens and Arboreta), when the "old guard stepped aside," he wisely counsels, "it is very important in the evolution of any organization that after it puts faith in you and gives you power, and you do what you think is right, then the proper thing to do is to step aside so that the organization can move on to the next higher level." Dick has always done what he thought was right and contributed enormously to the organizations fortunate enough to have him, stepping aside at the right time and leaving his successors with a strong foundation.

PLANTSMEN, PLANT FINDERS, NURSERYMEN

Windcliff: Ceonothus, roses and succulents

Dan Hinkley

When all is said and done, it will forever be the garden
that sustains me and provides my purpose.

PLANTSMAN EXTRAORDINAIRE Dan Hinkley has traveled the globe hunting for plants to bring back to Heronswood, the much-beloved and now much-mourned nursery he founded on the Kitsap Peninsula on Puget Sound across from Seattle, Washington. Even though his nursery no longer exists, Dan continues his plant-exploration adventures, hunting for plants to bring back to America to introduce to the public. A self-described "plant nerd," Dan couples his deep knowledge and passion for plants with the wicked sense of humor that made reading the Heronswood catalog such a delight in its day.

It's hard to imagine, but a catalog that listed over seventy-eight different hydrangea offerings, each with Dan's brief but clearly written description and growing advice, could make the reader laugh out loud. For example, he describes the mounding habit of *Rosa soulieana* as useful "for covering an old tree, VW Bug, or neighbor's fence!" And for a new variety of rosemary, he insists it "simply demands you cook a chicken." Anticipating the reader's reaction to a more ordinary evergreen, the catalog listing opens with "(Soooo boring, you say to yourself.) And you are in such a hurry to get on to *Arisaema, Campanula,* or *Tradescantia* that you bypass this handsome creature. Well suffer this for a moment." Dan's impact on American horticulture is beyond measure and endures through his ongoing plant introductions, writings, and lectures. He says his life is still "a perfect madness of plants."

Dan's passion for plants started when he was a young child, growing up in northern Michigan. He was born on September 6, 1953, to Ralph and Vivian Hinkley in the small town of Evart, along Lake Michigan. His father, grandfather, and great-grandfather all came from Evart; Ralph was the town pharmacist.

Everyone called him Doc because he gave good advice and was always available and willing to deliver needed medicine at all hours. Dan's mother, Vivian, was a nurse in the local school but also in the local rest home. They had four children, a daughter and three sons – Dan was number three.

He was the only gardener in his family. Both parents were busy working and raising a family, so he planted the family vegetable garden himself each year. He grew seeds of oranges and avocados, and, like so many children, recalls, "I impatiently waited – in fact, I would repeatedly exhume the seeds, wondering why they had not germinated. When they finally did emerge, I would watch, in awe of the miracle as it unfolded." He marveled at the lifting of the soil as the tiny seedlings emerged and displayed their first leaves. "Nothing could quite compare with this mystery, and I am happy to say that the emotions summoned in these early interactions with plants have remained unscathed through the trying realities of adulthood."

It wasn't long before this very young gardener decided to build a greenhouse himself. Enterprising even then, he did it without a kit. This was to be his own creation; he built the greenhouse as a lean-to against the house so that he could hook it up to heat and plumbing.

As a portent of things to come, Dan didn't choose to grow ordinary plants in his greenhouse. He grew orchids! Orchids were then a rarity, very hard to find, and certainly, a challenge in frigid northern Michigan. At that time, there were no big box stores selling them by the hundreds. Dan discovered orchids when he went to work after school in a local nursery that grew them for corsages, then a required item for proms and other special events. Thanks to this nursery, Dan could grow many species.

He graduated from high school in 1971 and went on to Michigan State University to study ornamental horticulture and horticultural education, graduating in 1976. His passion for plant exploration took root while he was still in college. In his sophomore year, he and a friend, along with the friend's dog, set off to see if they could find the last stand of eastern white cedar that was reputed to grow on a pristine island in Lake Michigan. The search required three days to find the cedars, and it set his life's path: "I had searched for plants and had discovered my quarry. My perceptions of what my life could and would be were dramatically altered. The excitement of finding, observing, describing, and ultimately cultivating such plants is what has guided me in my life's pursuit."

After college, Dan taught secondary school in southwestern Michigan as part of a vocational training program for three years, earning the princely salary of $12,000 a year. While he was teaching, all his siblings moved to Washington State. He began to visit them there each summer and eventually found it hard to leave and return to Michigan.

He was the last of his siblings to leave Michigan when he moved to Wenatchee, Washington, a small town in the eastern part of the state, where he went to work at a fruit tree research center. There he conducted research trying to prove that a virus was the cause of a particular pear tree disease. Once this could be proved, the center would then work to find a way to treat the virus or breed virus-resistant pear trees.

Dan thought he wanted to teach at a community college and he knew that would require a graduate degree, at the very least a master's. He also aspired to owning a nursery someday and began to collect a lot of plants while he was working in Wenatchee. Many of the plants that he collected and grew in these early days became like his family. They would follow him on his many subsequent moves. Just recently, he was pruning a small Japanese maple that he realized he had transplanted several times over the years until it finally settled at Heronswood. It is still there.

By 1983 he had enrolled in the University of Washington in Seattle to earn a graduate degree in urban horticulture. He found the perfect living quarters in the university's arboretum, a part of the university's botanic garden and also a city institution. Thousands of plants moved there with him, all in pots.

Dan Hinkley at Brush Hill, Connecticut

He lived in a charming, picturesque stone cottage, but it was right on the main artery so there was traffic rushing by all the time. Never mind. Dan had 350 acres to play in and learn about all the plants there, along with plenty of space to grow his own. In the early days of his studies, he was given an assistantship title, but he wasn't required to teach so he had a relatively easy time.

During his first year in graduate school, Dan met Robert L. Jones at a square dance. Square dancing was hugely popular at the time, and there was a gay square dance virtually every weekend. Robert and Dan were good enough dancers to reach the dance challenge level, although they never won. Both men were no doubt too busy with their demanding careers, Robert as an architect and Dan as a teacher. Dan and Robert have been together ever since and were married on August 3, 2013.

After graduating with his master's in 1985, Dan went to work at the Bloedel Reserve, an internationally renowned public garden and forest preserve on 150 acres on Bainbridge Island, a short ferry ride from Seattle. He lived at Bloedel, along with his thousands of peripatetic plants, until 1987. That year he moved away from Bloedel, Robert went off to work on a project in Saudi Arabia, and Dan began teaching part time at Edmonds Community College and at a local high school.

While carrying his heavy double teaching load, Dan began to look for land and saw a plot that would eventually become the site of his Heronswood Nursery. It was not love at first sight. He turned it down. However, in that summer of 1987, after Robert came back from Saudi Arabia, the broker took them both to that same property. Somehow the stars were aligned on this visit. Maybe the sun came out. Whatever the reason was, Dan thought the place just fine. He recalls, "This smoldering passion burst into full flame only after I came to own land." They bought the property that fall just as Dan began teaching full time at Edmonds Community College. Naturally, thousands of plants moved with him again.

There was a house on the property that was livable, but the location in Kingston on the northern end of the Kitsap Peninsula was a challenge. Robert had to get up at 5:00 A.M. every day to catch the ferry to Seattle while Dan had to take a ferry north to Edmonds. The two men barely saw each other. When Dan started full time at Edmonds, he gave up his high school job and often didn't have class until 1:00 P.M., leaving him free to garden all morning. That first November, only a few months after they had moved in, Robert's whole family arrived for Thanksgiving, and they were immediately enlisted to help build a fifty-foot greenhouse in a single day. This time Dan used a kit to create a plastic hoop house. One member of the family, an electrician, was able to hook up power, and somehow they figured out how to dig trenches and lay pipes for the plumbing. Finished before everyone sat down to Thanksgiving

Dan in Vietnam 2013

dinner, the greenhouse confirms Dan's status as an overachiever. It was the beginning of what would become the world-famous Heronswood.

Six years later, Dan began his countless plant-hunting explorations abroad.

According to academic rules, Dan had earned a six-month sabbatical from Edmonds Community College, and for his first organized plant-finding trip he decided to go to South Korea. Four years earlier, he had gone to Japan to buy plants and collect seeds, but he knew that was nothing like true plant hunting in the wild.

That first trip to South Korea in 1993 had a profound impact and would incite his appetite for many more. He made at least two plant-finding trips each year thereafter, and in some years more than two; he traveled to places like China, Taiwan, Korea, South and Central America, Mexico, New Zealand, South Africa, Nepal, Vietnam, Sikkim, Bhutan, Tasmania, Canada, and more recently Myanmar. He has been to Vietnam and China at least ten times each. He chooses destinations where the climate and growing conditions are likely to support plants that can do well in America, seeking what he calls the "Goldilocks Zone" where it is "not too hot, and not too cold" but just right. At the same time, he has also ridiculed a strict adherence to planting zones, scoffing, "Zones, schmones!" He believes gardeners should be brave enough to break the rules and test things. In a way, he feels "it is our duty as gardeners to kill as many plants as possible!"

He realizes that many may consider plant-finding expeditions glamorous: "People have an idea of plant hunting as romantic, wandering through the woods with a wicker basket, but when the rains come, the leeches are everywhere!" And worse. His descriptions of climbing along narrow precipices at high altitudes in pelting rain and fog (despite his deep fear of heights) are riveting. Seed cleaning is done in "a tent at night and it's raining cats and dogs outside and the only light is a headlamp." Andrew Bunting, Darrell Probst, and Pierre Bennerup have been fellow travelers on some of Dan's trips. Tales abound of getting lost, even with a guide, and surviving on almost no food in very cold temperatures. But the thrill of the hunt keeps him returning for more. "A sort of emotional overload confronts me as I set out to explore the botanical riches offered by a particular slice of the globe – marveling in its landscapes, hearing the songs of its birds, witnessing the night sky, and embracing the human interaction with the whole."

Windcliff Garden Path

On that first trip, Dan was fortunate to have an important patron in Ferris Miller, an American who had a private arboretum in Korea and was the go-to man for anyone plant hunting in that country. Miller helped Dan with funding and put him up when Dan was in the vicinity of the arboretum. By the time of this first trip, Dan had already begun publishing a catalog of plant offerings from Heronswood Nursery. Ferris had seen one and was impressed. He helped him come to Korea and introduced him to James Compton and three of Compton's colleagues. Trained at the Royal Botanic Gardens at Kew, James Compton had been the supervisor at the Chelsea Physic Garden in London, and had already made several plant-exploration trips, so he had the protocols down to a science.

Thanks to this introduction, Dan spent the first part of his trip to South Korea working with James, who is still a good friend, and who, along with the others on the trip, helped teach Dan the protocols of recording each plant collected, with specific details as to the site, the elevation, and other relevant information. Dan also learned how to carefully clean and process the plants he collected, although he was always slightly envious of the British as their rules for importing seeds are far more lenient than America's. The Brits can take in uncleaned seeds and even fruit!

To be exact, Dan collects seeds, not plants (with a few exceptions). The process for extracting seed varies, depending on whether it is contained in a pod or inside fruit. Once extracted, it is critical that the seeds be as fully dried as possible, for if they mold, they will not germinate. In what are often rainy conditions, drying seeds can be challenging. Even in dry weather, it is rare that the seeds can be spread out in the sun as collecting usually carries on from dawn until dark, requiring the seeds to dry out inside the tents. Once dry, the seeds are packed in paper so they can breathe. If the collectors use plastic bags, the seeds are first wrapped in paper towels.

Ferris Miller had seen a Heronswood catalog thanks to another of Dan's important role models and mentors, the renowned J. C. Raulston, who had begun teaching at North Carolina State University around 1975 and created a highly influential arboretum there. J. C., as he was always known, had gone to Seattle to give a talk, and someone urged him to go see the nascent nursery at Heronswood. He did, and as Dan recalls, "He recognized another plant nut!"

J. C. invited Dan to come to visit him in Raleigh, both to see the arboretum and to visit some mail-order nurseries nearby. Thus, Dan was able to acquire many of J. C.'s plants for Heronswood, and, of course, many from Heronswood ended up at what is now called the J. C. Raulston Arboretum, in memory of J. C., who died in 1996 and who served as a role model for many others. In admiration, Dan says, "J. C. knew, he sensed what a good plant was."

When Dan first met J. C., Heronswood was not yet a mail-order operation. It was J. C. who urged Dan to issue his first catalog to offer plants by mail. Dan followed that advice, sending out his first limited mail-order catalog in 1988. A year later, it had grown into a very large mail-order list, and by the time Ferris Miller helped Dan's trip to Korea in 1993, the Heronswood catalog had a wide and enthusiastic audience.

Another important mentor to Dan was Roy Lancaster, the English plantsman. Early on, Dan read his books and came to know him as a deeply knowledgeable fellow lover of plants. Christopher Lloyd, another great English plantsman and creator of the marvelous gardens at Great Dixter, was yet another special friend and role model. Christo, as he was called, also happened to be a superb writer with a very sharp wit, very much like Dan's. Anyone reading the Heronswood catalog with its hilarious asides can infer Christo's influence.

Dan views this part of his story as being in "the right place at the right time." There was a real scarcity of nurseries offering truly interesting and unusual plants. Heronswood's success coincided nicely with a burgeoning interest in gardening in America.

Another piece of serendipity occurred on that same 1993 trip to South Korea. After the first part of the trip with James Compton, Dan took off on his own, setting out into the bush. When two people stopped to ask him for directions, he learned that they were heading to the same destination and with the same purpose. It proved to be Bleddyn and Sue Wynn-Jones, who themselves had started the Crûg Farm Plants nursery just two years before in North Wales, offering unusual, desirable plants. The three of them were immediate soul mates and stuck together for the rest of the trip, and they have been fast friends and fellow travelers ever since.

After South Korea, Dan went the following winter to Mexico. In 1995, two years after his sabbatical, Dan left Edmonds Community College and began to work full time at Heronswood. Robert also left architecture to join the enterprise, taking on the mailing lists, account books, and commercial operations, allowing Dan to focus on plants. Dan had enjoyed his teaching career; some of his closest friends were once his students. That's not surprising, since he recalls seeing more of his students in a class that met four hours twice a week than he saw of anyone else. He remains proud of his progeny, as he thinks of his students – as he should, since many of them, as well as countless interns at Heronswood, have gone on to important careers in horticulture, including Richard Olsen at the National Arboretum and Jonathan Wright at Chanticleer in Pennsylvania.

Dan's travel schedule continues apace, and he keeps extensive journals of each trip containing all his collection notes along with his observations. These form, in effect, a diary of all those extraordinary experiences. But he was to work full time at Heronswood for only five years.

In this short and intense time, Heronswood was riding the crest of its publicity and the American gardening fervor. In 2000, Heronswood was sold to Burpee's to be run by George Ball. Part of the deal required Dan and Robert to continue operating Heronswood for five years after the sale. Dan's hope was that with its much-larger commercial marketing capacity, Burpee's would be able to disseminate his best plants more widely. Along with many others, he recognized that many of the botanical gardens and arboreta supporting plant-collection efforts kept them for study but were reluctant to release them to the public. A rivalry exists, and has always existed, between public gardens and private nurseries, a gap between those who consider themselves scientists and think of others as being merely in "trade"; as Dan puts it, there is a very real difference between "exclusivity and openness."

Five days after closing on the sale of Heronswood, Dan and Robert bought their Windcliff property in Indianola, also on the Kitsap Peninsula. The property had been owned by two women who ran a kennel for German shepherds. Although Dan and Robert continued to live at Heronswood during the week until 2004, they immediately began spending weekends at Windcliff. Dan started to map out a garden and Robert began to think about designing a new house. Although only a few miles away from Heronswood, and its shady woods, the five-and-a-half-acre Windcliff is on the coast looking south-south-east over Puget Sound with astonishing views of Mount Rainier (when it's clear) and the Seattle skyline in the far distance, in full sun and subject to high winds.

There, Dan created a very different garden from the wooded property at Heronswood. The excitement of planting a garden with a palette of different plants thrills him. Every spring as the perennial plantings re-emerge, he "equates the excitement of the herbaceous border to that of unpacking each year the trunk in which we store our collection of antique Christmas ornaments,

The house Robert Jones designed at Windcliff

accumulated from friends and family over many years. The unwrapping of each is in essence its rebirth, of its heritage and intrinsic beauty."

The original house was finally taken down to its foundations and a new one of Robert's design begun in 2003; they moved in by 2004. While they continued to work at Heronswood they were paid a salary that Dan remembers being much better than the profits he generated when they owned it. He was also paid travel expenses for his ongoing plant expeditions.

Sadly, it ended badly. George Ball was furiously spending money but not generating adequate returns. In 2006, Ball fired Robert, probably expecting Dan to quit. Dan refused. So two weeks later, Ball announced that he was shutting down the nursery and fired everyone, including Dan. That momentous day was June 6, or for those inclined to believing in portents, 6/6/6. Dan recalls this as an "unnecessarily sad time"; the way it was handled provoked deep anger in the community at large. Heronswood limped through the summer, and the gates were closed in the fall. Ball sent some of the plants back east to sell but then tore down all the greenhouses.

Dan decided to find solace by taking off on another trip to Vietnam. Before he left, Monrovia contacted him to see if he would consider working for them; they were interested in expanding access to plants that Dan introduced. Founded in 1926 and headquartered in California but with operations in Oregon, Georgia, and Connecticut, Monrovia is a vast commercial enterprise, offering four thousand plant varieties, with sales of 22 million plants to garden centers across the country. Dan was initially dubious after his Burpee's experience. After all, Burpee's had purchased Heronswood with the identical concept. Instead, "far from expanding the presence of our plants in American gardens, that short-lived relationship resulted only in the complete abandonment of our highly stylized brand within a very few, yet exasperatingly long years." But on his return from Vietnam, Monrovia persuaded him that they were different and Dan accepted their offer. And they have kept their promise, proving to be very good about propagating and growing the plants he finds on his ongoing trips and making the best of them available to the public. So good, in fact, that he says he can hear a "palpable and collective sigh of exasperation when I appear from my travels with seeds of yet another species." Since they began the relationship, Monrovia has produced over a million of Dan's plants. Meanwhile, Robert has gone back to designing single residential homes for clients.

Dan continues his annual plant explorations and his writings. He has published three books and written countless articles for magazines such as *Horticulture, The American Gardener,* and *Garden Design* and was on the payroll for *Martha Stewart Living* for two years. His book *Winter Ornamentals* was published in 1993 by Sasquatch Press; *The Explorer's Garden: Rare and Unusual*

Garden view of Puget Sound punctuated by pennants

Perennials was dedicated to J. C. Raulston and came out in 1999 from Timber Press, which also issued *The Explorer's Garden: Shrubs and Vines from the Four Corners of the World* in 2009.

After Heronswood was closed in 2006, the property was put on the market for $11 million, but the price began to drop every few months thereafter. At one point, there was an attempt to save it by a local group that formed a non-profit for the purpose. They tried to raise funds to buy Heronswood and carry it on; they asked Dan to join them but he found it all too stressful. He didn't really see the place as a viable proposition without a nursery business to support it. It had grown to fifteen acres after Ball added land to the original holdings. When an offer for $4.5 million fell apart, Ball tried reducing the price to $3.5 million, but that too failed. Dan remains grateful to those who tried so hard but he is not sure how it could have worked. He still felt responsible, so it was somewhat of a relief that a struggle didn't ensue.

When 2008 rolled around with its severe financial crash, Ball kept lowering the price, and finally in 2011 the Native American Port Gamble S'Klallam Tribe grew interested. But they still couldn't arrive at a deal even when the price dropped to $1.1 million. Ball finally put the place up for auction and the tribe was the only bidder, a low bidder. Heronswood belongs to them now.

Dan pitched in and volunteered to help the tribe. By 2014, he became the director of the property. The Port Gamble S'Klallam Tribe pays him a salary, and the property is now part of a tribal trust, removing it from the jurisdiction of the county planning department and placing it under tribal rule. That allows the tribe to proceed without public hearings and other red tape. The tribe is very environmentally sensitive, especially to the nearby waters because they harvest shellfish. In due course, they hope to open a small convention facility and to use the place for weddings and other celebrations. It will never be a nursery again, but Dan was pleased to help restore the display gardens with the work of many enthusiastic volunteers. Restoration is not likely to return to the high horticulture of the original, but it should be close in overall aesthetic. A beautiful Welcome Pole has been carved and is now raised in place. It sports a heron and a frog, symbols of Heronswood and its rebirth. And Dan, delighted, thinks, "The garden is looking fantastic!" Many of his original plants have survived and remain.

Dan is currently breeding *Agapanthus* the easy way in what he calls "Redneck Breeding!" which means he lets the bees do the work and then observes what comes out of the crossbreeding that results. His role is merely to observe carefully, select the best, and allow Monrovia to acquire and offer the results. He does admit to getting enmeshed in one genus at a time. He "finds something that sucks me in." For a time it was hydrangeas. I still have a numbered no-name one from Heronswood in my garden that I love. *Abelia* had its day, as did other genera, but now it's *Agapanthus*.

Dan carries on with his writing, lectures, and ongoing plant-finding trips. Part of his motivation is to preserve genetic diversity and plants that are threatened by ongoing environmental devastation through construction, clear cutting, climate change, and worse. His website describes him as "plantsman, writer, lecturer, consultant, nurseryman, naturalist, gardener." As a writer, he "is uncertain how one can possibly know enough about a plant to discuss it in writing if one does not first tend it." It is perhaps that last word *gardener* that names what is the closest to his core. From his travels, he believes that "seeing plants in their rightful place makes me a better gardener and teacher"; it shows him how a plant wants to grow. His passion endures because, he says, "my libido for plants that virtually no one else finds remotely ornamental has not lessened in age." So "when all is said and done, it will forever be the garden that sustains me and provides my purpose."

Windcliff water feature overlooking Puget Sound

Pierre Bennerup

Our Connecticut Yankee ingenuity has never led us to assume that good
can't be made better and we're usually the first ones to figure out how to do so.

AN EXCELLENT WINE connoisseur displays the same qualities as an
excellent plantsman. Both always seek to find the great, not merely
the good; both have a taste for subtle nuances, for what makes a *grand
cru* as opposed to *vin ordinaire*; both have refined senses and set standards followed by others. Pierre Bennerup sharpened his ability to differentiate the great
from the mundane first as a marketer of wine. His skill in mastering the precise
names, origins, sources, and special characteristics of the wines he sold served
him well when he turned his talents to the world of plants. In place of introducing fine wines to appreciative audiences, he has for decades offered a wide array
of outstanding perennials from Sunny Border Nurseries in Kensington, Connecticut, setting a high bar for nurseries and gardeners across the country.

Pierre has earned recognition and honors both for introducing exceptional plants to the public and also for encouraging a greater use and appreciation of perennials. He couples his deep knowledge of plants with an infectious
sense of humor, one often in evidence in the Sunny Border catalogs he writes.
He is almost bigger than life, and his sparkling blue eyes, sense of humor, and
joie de vivre are irresistible. He exudes boundless energy, deep knowledge,
infectious excitement, all communicated in his rapid-fire speech. No wonder he
was so successful as a wine salesman and now as a marketer of plants.

Unlike many plantsmen, Pierre was not particularly interested in gardening as a young man, but, as the son of a nurseryman, he did grow up surrounded by plants. In fact, it was his father, Robert Bennerup, who began Sunny
Border Nurseries in the 1940s. An immigrant from Denmark arriving in the
1920s, Robert came to be a gardener on the grand estates in New England. His

Pierre Bennerup

credentials included the highly respected title of "gartener," which he earned in Europe after six years of serious study and practical training at the Vilvade Trade School near Copenhagen. On one of those estates, he met and married Claudia Audet, a French Canadian governess and cook also employed there. Neither spoke the other's language but somehow they managed to communicate.

Robert Bennerup began to work for Beatrix Farrand on some of the gardens she designed, as well as for other garden designers. An enterprising man, he traveled to Florida in the slow winter months to offer his services as a flower arranger to his clients in their winter homes in Palm Beach. Eventually, when he couldn't source the plants called for by the New England garden designers for whom he worked, he decided to start his own nursery. Undaunted by the Depression, he opened a small nursery in Norwalk, Connecticut, in the mid-1930s specializing in bare-root perennials, along with some woody plants and small conifers; it was called Norwalk Perennial Garden and was principally a wholesale nursery with a small retail clientele. In 1945 he moved his young family and the nursery to Kensington, Connecticut, optimistically naming it Sunny Border Nurseries although he had only one small site. Sunny Border has had the same name ever since. Over time Pierre has made that optimistic plural a reality, expanding to nine different properties, with eight in Connecticut and one in far-off Ohio.

Pierre was born in Yonkers Hospital on January 12, 1934, following his older sister. The family lived in Tuckahoe, New York, for his first few years, until Robert moved his family to an area near the Wilton and Norwalk line in Connecticut to open his nursery and then on to Kensington to open Sunny Border. Although not an enthusiastic gardener as a young boy, Pierre was pressed into weeding chores by his father. He hated it! But he now admits that however grudgingly he tackled weeding, plants unwittingly got into his blood. He "was infected." He went on to Princeton on a full scholarship and contemplated taking botany but was told he needed to have a prerequisite course in biology. Since that meant repeating a course he had already taken in high school, he chose instead to concentrate on English, and that major shows in the high quality of the Sunny Border catalogs.

After graduating in 1956, Pierre tried selling silverware, taught in a private school in California, and returned to New York to work in the advertising business. There, he met Alexis Lichine and worked for him as a sales manager in the wine import business. Just as Pierre was settling into this career, his father died in 1967, leaving his mother widowed and virtually penniless. She became the sole proprietor of the nursery but knew nothing about plants. Pierre was just thirty-three years old. His sister, who had married before their father died, had moved to Denmark and was reluctant to return. It was left to Pierre to step in, take charge, and rescue his mother. He quit the wine business and worked on salvaging the nursery for two years. It really didn't generate enough to support them, so he returned to marketing wine, joining Banti Vintners, the firm that distributed Riunite Lambrusco, then the largest-selling Italian wine in the United States. But he continued to run Sunny Border Nurseries at the same time, usually from a distance, for ten long, intense years, from 1970 through 1980. Fortunately, he hired Marc Laviana, then a high school student, who stayed on, remained an important part of running the place, and became the president of the nursery until his untimely death in 2017.

Never having formally studied plants like his father had, Pierre was forced to learn on the job, and he knew he had a lot to learn. An important early mentor was the great guru of perennials, the Englishman Alan Bloom. Known for growing perennials in island beds, Bloom created or named 170 new perennials during his career. Pierre asked if he could travel to visit him at his famous nursery, Blooms of Bressingham in Norfolk, England. Alan encouraged Pierre to visit and took him under his wing. Pierre spent three full days, recorder in hand, taking notes and learning the names of all five thousand plants growing in Alan Bloom's famous garden! It was a crash course in perennials. By now, of course, Pierre says, he would know them all.

Pierre was interested not only in a plant's proper identification and its Latin name but also how it grew and what it required to flourish. This was in 1969, the nadir of the American public's interest in perennials. Following World War II, the American suburbs had begun to develop, but the emphasis was on maintaining a fine lawn and low-maintenance gardening that featured foundation plantings around the base of the house. Some predictable annuals might be perfunctorily added each year for a little color. A few brave souls with plots large enough grew vegetables, but almost no one cared about perennial plants or creating an herbaceous border. That all came later, thanks in large part to Pierre's leadership and marketing skills, assets that were foundational in shaping the evolving sophistication of American gardening.

While juggling his two careers, and after a brief first marriage and divorce, Pierre married Susan Sawicki in 1974. They had his only child, Brooke.

As a result of Pierre's leadership and the expanding interest in perennials, Sunny Border began to make enough money to justify Pierre's returning to work at the nursery full time. Although he left the wine business for good in 1980, he still appreciates and understands fine wines. Looking back, he thinks he was always more interested in the vineyards and how the grapes were grown than in the distribution end of the business. But his considerable marketing expertise proved invaluable, helping Sunny Border survive, and then thrive and grow. He sees gardeners and wine lovers as cut from the same cloth. The person with a taste and pocketbook for fine wine is often one who appreciates the artistry of garden design and appropriate plantings.

In 1983, Pierre founded the Perennial Plant Association. He first proposed the idea at a symposium held at Ohio State University, in Columbus, Ohio, along with Steven Still, who was head of horticulture there. A year later, the association was officially established, and he was elected president for the first two years. This was the first organization concentrating solely on perennials, and 250 people came to the association's first symposium. The organization was structured with a separate director for each of the seven growing zones of the United States and one for Canada, with an annual symposium that rotated among them all. In 1990, in a brilliant marketing move, the association started announcing the Perennial Plant of the Year, making each plant chosen that year's must-have plant for consumers.

Not surprisingly, one of the great Perennials of the Year is *Veronica* 'Sunny Border Blue,' a plant originally introduced by Pierre's father and still popular to this day. Named in 1993, *Veronica* 'Sunny Border Blue' was not a recent discovery but the result of Robert Bennerup's hybridizing efforts that crossed *Veronica longifolia subsessilis* with a very dark blue *Veronica spicata*. Because 'Sunny Border Blue' is sterile and cannot produce seeds, it requires vegetative propagation, ensuring that each plant remains true to the original. Unaware of its own sterility, the poor *Veronica* vigorously keeps on blooming in a futile effort to produce seed. Other plants have also been named for Pierre or Sunny Border, such as *Pulmonaria* 'Pierre's Pure Pink,' a tongue twister but strong growing, and *Chrysogonum virginianum* 'Pierre.'

By now the Perennial Plant Association has more than 2,500 members and continues to select the Perennial Plant of the Year, a concept also copied by others (for example, the best woody plant of the year). Pierre intended for each choice to be a relatively new, undiscovered, or underused plant, provided it was not too difficult for nurserymen to propagate and grow. He regrets that the association too often selects plants that, though worthy, are hardly new, and already very well known and widely used. Pierre is direct and often blunt, and his outspoken observations have on occasion provoked irritation in others whose views are more conventional.

Thanks to his Yankee ingenuity, Pierre became an inventor and innovator, transforming the nursery business. His father, Robert, like most nurserymen of his time, only sold bare-root plants to customers since appropriate containers were not readily available and there were no good soil substitutes to use in pots. Most plants were grown in the ground and dug up "bare root" for sale. Pierre's first innovation was to turn to growing plants in pots. Pierre observed that in Connecticut, "our soils are less than perfect so we've learned to grow in containers in which we recycle a whole range of waste products which otherwise might be clogging our landfills. Fifty years ago plants and trees had to be fresh dug in the field before they could be sold." Pierre was instrumental in developing successful potting soil mixes, and he worked with the nearby University of Connecticut to figure out how to design proper pots. When he began, the only pots in use were made of either tar paper or terra cotta, the latter heavy and prone to breaking, especially if kept outdoors in the cold winter weather of Connecticut.

Pierre began experimenting with plastic pots. At first he found some possible suppliers but quickly discovered they only produced round pots, not an efficient shape for a large grower. The producers used blow molding to make the pots, a process somewhat similar to glass blowing, and the molds were all round. Searching for suppliers

Pierre on white faced yak in Sichuan, China

Pierre riding a camel into Cappodocia, Turkey

willing to produce square pots, he approached several companies. One finally agreed to try to produce his desired square design, but only if he would guarantee to buy one million pots! Not discouraged, Pierre set to work to figure out how to use the blow mold system to produce square pots much more cheaply. Once he succeeded, the usual rectangular carrying trays were soon transformed into square divisions that could hold each pot firmly upright without wasting space. By 1986, Pierre had switched entirely to growing perennials in pots that were plastic and square.

Always the great marketer, Pierre chose to use brown as his signature color for Sunny Border's pots, rather than the more usual green or black. By now, his signature brown square plastic pots have been copied by others, but those in the know have learned to look for his particular shade of brown to be sure they are buying a Sunny Border offering from their local retail nursery. He also initiated his Gold Pot Plants in each year's catalog to indicate those that bore his special seal of approval, a sure signal of an outstanding new offering deserving special attention.

One of the high-tech innovations of its day was the development of tissue culture to propagate plants. Once again, Sunny Border took the lead. Before tissue culture was introduced, nursery propagation was limited to the traditional techniques of growing plants either from seed, by taking cuttings, or by making divisions. Pierre established the first tissue culture lab in Connecticut for the propagation of perennial plants at Sunny Border in the early 1970s. It operated for thirty years, but now, like most other tissue culture operations, much of the production is outsourced to places like India and Turkey because the work is so labor intensive.

For a high-volume wholesale grower like Sunny Border, tissue culture could produce many more plants in much less time and in much less space than traditional methods. According to Pierre, "It takes half a year to grow the same amount of plants that it would take twenty years to grow using traditional propagation methods." At one point, he produced more than a quarter of a million plants each year either in his own tissue culture center or in outsourced labs. In an extraordinarily small space, a few skillful people carefully dissect tiny bits of green from the mother plant, placing the small bits in test tubes filled with plant hormones and kept under sterile conditions. The goal is to produce branching and then roots. As these develop, the tiny plantlets are then grown in rich nutrients under light and heat in 100 percent humidity. Thousands of tiny plants in small tubes occupy layers of shelves in a closed area kept sterile to avoid possible disease that could wipe out the entire crop. As a result, any new, worthy plant introductions can be quickly produced in large volume and sold to a wide and appreciative international audience.

Today Sunny Border produces less than 20 percent of its crop from seed, the rest coming from tissue culture, basic cuttings, and divisions to ensure that each plant offered is truly the named cultivar. Pierre observes that there are only a few basic ways new plants come to the marketplace. One is by identification. Plant-finding expeditions set out to locate and identify plants not known to Western horticulture and bring them back. A plant might also be spotted growing in a garden by a sharp-eyed gardener who notices a "sport," or an unusual variety of a familiar plant. Then there is deliberate hybridization, such as the efforts of Pierre's father to develop *Veronica* 'Sunny Border Blue.' This requires skillful crossing of one plant with another, then painstaking observation to select the best of the offspring. Finally, there is generational selection, where a known plant happens to produce variation among naturally produced offspring that over time prove to be superior.

In addition to his innovative propagation techniques, Pierre has also been a plant identifier. Some of Sunny Border's plant offerings are the fruits of Pierre's plant-finding expeditions to remote regions of the world, but he has also discovered and brought back worthy plants from frequent visits to specialty nurseries in other countries. He dubbed one group who often travel together hunting for plants the "Ratzeputz Gang" after "an evil-tasting concoction for which we named ourselves!" Pierre has "traveled to many countries on at least four continents in search of new and unique plants with a curiosity for what grows where and why." Satisfying that curiosity helps inform how he then grows those plants at Sunny Border.

Pierre's trips are usually scheduled in the fall when the nursery business is quiet and the wild plants are setting seed. The fall season also means that, since the flowers are over, the only way to identify plants is by their foliage and what remains of their pods or fruits containing their seed. He has been to China on such forays at least seven times, including the southwest, Hunnan, Sichuan, and Kunming, as well as taken numerous trips to Patagonia, South Africa, and New Zealand.

Hunting plants in the wild requires endurance under challenging circumstances. Pierre has traveled in the company of Dan Hinkley. When he was first asked to join Dan and other members of his impressive traveling group, he felt deeply honored, validated as the fine plantsman he had become. While his fellow travelers were principally interested in finding new plant material, Pierre was equally interested in learning how the plants grew in their native environment, allowing him to imitate those conditions in his nursery. But he also enjoyed the sheer adventure of trips that required everything from scaling high peaks to collect a plant that someone's discriminating eye had discerned in an impossible spot to living under primitive circumstances in a cold, wet tent in the remote region of western mountainous China. There, even the roads were terrifying, requiring them to snake through challenging rough terrain in a rickety vehicle or on foot.

Each day begins in a state of excitement, each member determined to be the first to identify some new treasure. The spirit of competition is fierce, even though they all share their finds at the end of the day. Usually the muscle-weary but exhilarated participants show off their prizes and then clean their seeds, an arduous and labor-intensive process. On one China trip alone, Pierre collected hundreds of plants, mostly rock plants or alpines, a particular interest of his. That's a lot of seed to clean! Wet weather often makes it nearly impossible, especially while living in leaky tents. The plumbing is often absent and the food unspeakable. But the thrill of the chase carries them on.

On one plant-finding trip in the Andes of Argentina, Pierre spotted an appealing mountain-type viola and collected a large paper bag full of seed. Traveling on to the beautiful lake country of Bariloche, he spread the seed out on a windowsill to dry. That night he was awakened by a loud popping sound, as the seedpods had heated sufficiently to explode, much like popcorn, scattering seed everywhere. After the challenge of finding and retrieving the small seeds, neither he nor his companion, Kurt Bluemel, another great nurseryman, was ultimately able to germinate a single plant!

Pierre and his fellow travelers are nurserymen, plant lovers, passionate gardeners, and sensitive to the environment they visit. They strive to leave the native environment intact, principally collecting seed and on rare occasion a piece of a plant, only when there is enough left behind to grow on undisturbed. Local botanists and experts guide them.

Pierre gets mad when he gets wind of criticism from the "professionals" who view these trips as made by "semi-professionals." He thinks such criticism unjustified, coming from people who don't, or refuse to, understand what is at stake. Because he sells plants for profit he knows he is viewed with disdain or at best with mistrust by many academics or those in nonprofit institutions, such as arboreta and botanical gardens. He suspects they feel that they should have a monopoly on plant finding. Like other plantsmen, Pierre believes that all too often plant-finding efforts sponsored by nonprofit horticultural institutions fail to share their findings with the gardening public. Great plant material identified and brought back too often languishes for lack of attention to or any interest in disseminating these discoveries for general use. By contrast, it is the nurserymen who are motivated to provide worthy garden material to the public. Pierre believes the groups he has traveled with help preserve and protect the plant diversity of our planet. They grow the plants they have identified and encourage their use; they try to save many that are under threat of extinction due to local development and environmental degradation.

Pierre at Woolong Panda Preserve, China

Critics also raise fears that introducing new plants can bring in noxious, invasive species, but Pierre knows this underestimates the seriousness of purpose and knowledge of these plant explorers. Each accession is carefully identified, and its exact growing location is recorded. They respect advice from local experts, but subject all finds to further testing, since a plant that can behave sedately in a harsh climate can easily grow out of control in one more benign. No one wishes to be blamed for the next kudzu or mile-a-minute vine epidemic, although Pierre is quick to point out that kudzu was introduced by our government, which wrongly assumed the plant would be useful in erosion control.

Pierre does not confine his hunt for exciting new plants to exploration trips to remote destinations. He also travels to specialty nurseries in the United States and abroad. Each year, he scours Europe, focusing his trained eye to discover plants that will work well in American gardens, finding many wonderful plants in nurseries that have been either neglected or are unfamiliar to Americans. In Germany and the Czech Republic, many fine nurseries have been revived thanks to improved economies. The countries' climates are similar to the tougher conditions of the colder zones in the States. Pierre has been particularly pleased at finding many varieties of his beloved alpines that thrive in the mountain ridges of the Czech Republic. One great example is a *Dianthus* he spotted in a German nursery. In 1987, he bought two small plants of what was in Germany known as *Dianthus gratianopolitanus* 'Feuerhexe' and offered it as *Dianthus gratianopolitanus* 'Firewitch.' It was named the Perennial Plant of the Year in 2006.

He has written humorously but with gripes about what he calls the "native plant Nazis." To quote a piece he wrote called "My Turn" under his sometime nom de plume Evers O'Greedy, "There's a bunch of crackpots out there saying we should only plant stuff that's always grown around here, even since long before the Indians got here." He points out that this would also dictate not growing most vegetables, such as beans, peas, squash, celery, potatoes, tomatoes, parsley, kale, Swiss chard, cucumbers, melons, and peppers, and the list goes on. Even sweet corn didn't grow wild here before the Native Americans brought it. "I guess I'll just have to starve." He continues, "Having a good mix of plants and vegetables in the United States is as important as having a good 'salsa' of ethnic, religious, racial and nationality groups. For one thing, it allows us to have the most varied diet in the world as well as some of the most diverse and beautiful gardens known to mankind." He does admit that some plants are rascals and should be called "terrorist plants," and of course there should be sensible precautions to keep them out. He concludes by offering his advice for a small fee as to the worthiness of plants: "Remember, don't accept substitute opinions such as those from various botanic gardens or the USDA. My opinions are 'the real thing.'"

There are cycles in everything and Pierre believes that the gardening fever that spread across the United States in the late 1970s and 1980s has cooled. He thinks the decline is only partly due to the recession of 2008; it is generational. The Baby Boomers were deeply into gardening, but the current focus is on food. The passion is about eating locally produced and organic food, and eschewing all the "nots" – such as gluten, sugar, red meat, and dairy. That list never stops growing. It has become essential to ask any guests invited to dine if they have any food issues. One recent *New Yorker* cartoon showed two women at a restaurant looking at the menus; one complains to the other, "There is nothing I can eat here – everything on the menu is a food!"

Pierre in front of Gunnera in Patagonia

As a result, Pierre has been downsizing the Sunny Border inventory over the last five years. At its height, he sold 3 million plants a year and offered more than four thousand varieties as well as keeping track of a thousand more on trial. In the early days, his records were kept by hand, but with the development of computers and his revolutionary system of growing plants in pots, he could grow more than 100,000 plants in pots on a single acre while keeping track of the location of every pot within a very small margin of error. Now his total sales are down by about half, to 1.5 million plants sold each year. That's still an impressive number, but it represents a big change. He also closed down his only venture into retail sales. In 1991, he bought Comstock Ferre, in Wethersfield, Connecticut, the oldest continuously operating seed company in the Americas. It was in bankruptcy, and he ran it successfully for almost twenty years, adding plants to the seed offerings. He sold the business in 2009.

Just as with clothing, garden fashions also change,

and Pierre, the astute marketer, has been flexible and adaptive. Because the current interest resides in food, he began to grow and offer vegetables and herbs along with perennials. While expanding his offerings, Pierre's sharp eye spotted a variegated sport of the popular basil plant *Ocimum × citriodorum* and introduced *Ocimum* 'Pesto Perpetuo' that is columnar and nonflowering. When the Dutch perennial approach or prairie style of gardening became the rage, Pierre offered more grasses and sold more than 100,000 a year; it is now down to something closer to forty-five to fifty thousand. Now ferns have come into demand. Pierre believes that is in large part because so many homes built in the postwar building boom are now surrounded by trees planted decades ago. As the trees matured, they created shade everywhere. He has even coined a name for plants that are perennial in the milder climates of the south but only half-hardy in the north, plants like dahlias and cannas. He offers them as "Temperennials."

With the current focus on the environment, including climate change and energy conservation, Pierre has turned his attention to meeting the demand for creating and maintaining green roofs. Instead of the traditional black impervious roof surface that soaks up the heat of the sun and allows for excessive stormwater runoff, a green roof full of plants can absorb the sun's energy and save on air-conditioning costs. The plants take carbon dioxide out of the air and release oxygen, and they absorb pollutants and retain water instead of allowing excessive runoff. Pierre has developed a system for growing plants on material that is light enough not to strain the structure of the roof, yet suitable for sustaining plants. This material is porous, yet holds a lot of moisture for its weight; it can be rolled up fully planted for shipping and then unrolled and installed like an enormous carpet. Instead of a carpet of wool, it is a carpet of plants, almost always a mix of hardy succulents and perhaps some low grasses that can endure hot, dry conditions.

Plant patenting is also a relatively recent development. When Pierre's friend Darrell Probst, who had been the King of Epimediums, turned his focus to developing *Coreopsis*, Darrell started patenting his many introductions. Pierre agreed to not only include Darrell's expanding list of *Coreopsis* varieties in the Sunny Border catalogs, but to take on responsibility for administering the patents. They earned about $250,000 in 2015.

In 2007, Pierre's life took an especially happy turn. He married Cheryl Burkhead, who is herself an accomplished and knowledgeable plantsman. They live in the original Bennerup family home very near Sunny Border and, in fact, adjacent to one of the properties where the nursery grows plants. Both are engaged in maintaining the beautiful ornamental gardens surrounding their home as well as their extensive vegetable garden. Cheryl is a superb cook so everything grown is harvested and put to good use.

Pierre and one of his planted pot combinations

Pierre has begun to turn over more of the management of Sunny Border Nurseries to others, but his deep knowledge of plants continues to be an invaluable resource. He is loyal to his plant favorites, particularly his beloved alpines. His short list includes saxifrages and especially gentians – at one point he had more than fifty *Gentian* varieties and collected his own seeds that he traded for others. He even began manufacturing troughs that look convincingly like the original stone ones that he sells and uses to grow his alpines. He also admires plants in the Ranunculus family – *Trollius, Aconitum, Delphinium, Thalictrum,* and *Cimicifuga* (now *Actaea*), although admits he is annoyed that the botanists keep changing the names around. Every time something like the cimicifugas are suddenly decreed to now be actaeas, he knows he will have to throw away countless labels and order up new ones, never mind changing all the listings in the catalogs.

Pierre has been honored for his important role in American horticulture. In 2000 he received the Growers of the Year Award from the American Horticultural Society and the following year, the Gustav A. L. Mehlquist Award from the Connecticut Horticultural Society. In presenting him with its honorary medal, the Jackson Dawson Memorial Award in 2009, the Massachusetts Horticultural Society said that Pierre is "known around the world for being on the cutting edge of new plant development, an integral part of the global horticultural community, and has been instrumental in searching out new plants suitable for North American gardens."

With his usual self-deprecating sense of humor, Pierre asks, "So what is horticulture anyway? Horticulture is the art of cultivating gardens. Simple, isn't it? The key word here is 'art.' Look at it this way. The plants are the paint, the soil is the canvas." It is largely thanks to pioneers like Pierre that "gardening, like all art forms, is constantly redefining itself."

Coreopsis trial beds at Sunny Border Nurseries

Darrell Probst

*I called my nursery Garden Vision
because everyone was always telling me
I had a good eye for great plants.*

ARRELL PROBST'S GOOD EYE for great plants evolved when he was a
very young boy. It was an eye that began focusing on plants almost as
soon as he could walk. Over time, he would hone his eye on plant-finding expeditions that began in his early thirties; and this same eye would be
essential to his success in breeding and introducing new plants into horticulture. He is especially known for his work with *Epimedium,* a genus not widely
appreciated when he first began offering the results of his plant-finding and
breeding work through Garden Vision, with more than 150 different types for
sale. Now *Coreopsis* has taken over his life. He has trademarked and patented
many striking new plants that are sold under several trademarked series; the
first was his Big Bang series, followed by his Li'l Bang series. His impressive
plant breeding is ongoing. His focus and passion for these and other species
have helped to transform American gardens.

Darrell was born on September 23, 1962, in West Chester, Pennsylvania, to George and Beverly Probst, the second of their three children. One year
later, the family moved to nearby Kennett Square, where he grew up. His grandparents lived nearby and the entire family gardened. He says, "I was the trouble-
maker," always at risk of being grounded by his father. Part of the trouble was
caused by his early fascination with plants. While still a toddler, Darrell was
eager to understand how plants grew, why seeds germinated. The best way to
find out was to go into his father's vegetable garden and dig up the seeds his
father had just planted. How did those little dry seeds somehow produce green
sprouts above the ground? How logical to take a peek and see what was

happening underground. While his grandfather thought this was cute, it wasn't his vegetable garden that was being uprooted. Darrell's father was not amused.

His grandfather, an important influence, continued to encourage Darrell. Darrell recalls how he taught him to graft apple trees, sometimes grafting multiple varieties on a single stock so that a single tree could produce many varieties of apples. A neighboring farmer, Dr. David Stoddard, was also an important teacher. Stoddard owned an apple orchard in which Darrell's father had invested, and he taught a very young Darrell not only about plants, but about the interconnections of nature, about birds, insects, even weeds – what we would now call an ecosystem. Darrell's father's gardening was also influential, although he understandably lost patience when his son continued to rip up his seedlings. Darrell tried staying out of trouble by clearing other parts of his father's land and starting his own garden. But each time he established a new section, his father took over the nicely prepared ground to expand his own plot.

The solution arrived on farmland adjacent to his house, when one day Darrell noticed that alfalfa had been planted instead of the usual corn and a few rows had been missed. Well-plowed ground stood invitingly bare, ground that did not belong to his father. That field was part of a much-larger property called Hartefeld; it belonged to my husband's father, Charles Apel Robinson. Young Darrell bravely went to ask him if he could use that empty space to plant a garden. Charles Apel had a soft spot for children, especially one as enthusiastic and enterprising as Darrell. He and his wife, Josephine, were raising fourteen children of their own, half of whom had been adopted. Of course, Charles Apel said yes.

Darrell called it the Garden on the Hill. He quickly began planting, at first vegetables, but he soon added flowering annuals and then perennials. By the time he was eight years old, Darrell's neighbors had come to appreciate his gardening ability and asked him to work on their property. At first he earned fifty cents an hour in the vegetable and flower gardens of Dr. Stoddard. While he worked, he often spotted tiny volunteers, self-sown holly seedlings and other small trees that had begun growing under the existing bushes. He "rescued" these little saplings and planted them in the Garden on the Hill. Years later, long after Darrell had moved away to Massachusetts and his small saplings had grown into impressive trees, Charles Apel Robinson reaped his reward for his faith in Darrell. Many of these mature trees were dug up and transplanted to grace the main house at Hartefeld. A bamboo grove still grows in the Garden on the Hill in the spot where Darrell planted the first culm.

Other neighbors also noticed the young boy's skill. What a stroke of luck that two of those neighbors were Dr. Richard W. Lighty and his wife, Sally. Darrell's father did the winter snowplowing for Dick, and that is how Darrell came to work in Dick's garden. When Dick and Sally took off for the summer months

Darrell with Raz and Arisaema sikokianum

to go to the Adirondacks, Darrell mowed Dick's lawn and was exposed to Dick's plant-rich garden. Dick quickly recognized Darrell's horticultural talent and passion and allowed him to take divisions of any plant he found of interest, many of which Dick had collected on his plant-finding expeditions. From his own role as head of the Longwood Graduate Program at the University of Delaware and his prior work at Longwood Gardens, Dick thought the Longwood Professional Gardeners Program would be perfect for young Darrell.

After graduating from Kennett High School, Darrell took a year off to wait for another session of the Longwood program to begin. Because it is a two-year hands-on program, Longwood only accepts a new entry class every other year. Darrell began his studies there in 1982. As Dan Hinkley later observed of Darrell's decision, "Wise are those in their youth who understand that four years of impassionate edification at a four-year institution adds little foundation to a life already robust with discovered passion."

While studying at Longwood, Darrell met Karen Perkins, a student in the graduate program at the University of Delaware. In 1984, Karen moved to

Massachusetts to accept a job as education coordinator for the Worcester County Horticultural Society (WCHS), then in the process of searching for properties to buy in order to create a botanical garden. Darrell and Karen married a year later and he volunteered to photograph and map some of the properties under consideration. In 1986, WCHS acquired the property that would become the much-admired Tower Hill Botanic Garden. Darrell joined Karen in Massachusetts, and they both worked for WCHS, becoming involved in the development of a master plan for the new botanical garden. Darrell brought with him many of the perennials he had grown in the Garden on the Hill, offering to donate extra divisions to WCHS and suggesting they have a plant sale. He also used many of his plants to create a temporary perennial and vegetable garden he designed around the original house on the property. The plant sale became an annual event and Darrell's gardens still remain, now called the Cottage and Vegetable Gardens. Although some of the plants have changed, the fundamental design and structure are true to his original plan.

In 1989, Darrell opened Garden Vision to design gardens for private clients. He also taught at the Arnold Arboretum in Boston, designing a garden for the arboretum on a separate property called the Case Estates; it became a teaching garden. His focus was principally on perennials. Over time, although he continued to design gardens for clients, he became keenly interested in plant development and, in particular, in epimediums.

Epimediums were a status symbol among the cognoscenti. Those in the know prized this subtle but appealing genus that was not widely available or used in many gardens. Epimediums are hardy and grow in the most challenging spots, including dry shade, displaying lovely bell-like flowers in the early spring followed by beautiful leaves, some with mottled patterns. But they were not seen in gardens and certainly not readily available through regular nurseries. Sometimes called bishop's-caps and barrenworts, perhaps epimediums might have been more widely known and used if they had been called by their other and more enticing popular name of fairy wings.

A small coterie of enthusiasts had their own collections, many acquired on private trips to Japan and brought back from specialty nurseries there. The New York plantsman Harold Epstein, a force behind the creation of the American Rock Garden Society and a presence at the New York Botanical Garden, was a prime example of someone who liked to show off his treasures and invite visitors to his garden where they could *ooh* and *ahh*. But he was not likely to share any.

Darrell relishes a challenge, and the difficulty of obtaining epimediums, along with their aesthetic appeal, captured his interest. He realized that the only way he could manage to get a tiny piece of a longed-for epimedium from any of these collectors was to be able to offer them something in return, something they wanted but didn't have. He thought he could trade if he had a special plant to give in exchange for something he wanted himself. But he realized that to have anything special to tempt them, he would have to travel to find the plants and begin to breed them himself. He says, "I learn the most about a species by seeing it in its native haunts and/or exploring its hidden traits through breeding, so both have an equal pull."

When one of the collectors heard about Darrell's interest in developing an extensive collection of epimediums, he tried to discourage him from focusing so much energy on a single genus. As Darrell recalls, he said, "Everything to be known about *Epimedium* is already known!" But, Darrell says, "he didn't have a clue!" The gauntlet was thrown, and Darrell was ready.

In 1996, Darrell went on his first plant-finding expedition to China in the company of Dan Hinkley and a large group of about eighteen others. They went to Yunnan Province. Darrell had never been out of the United States before. After the rest of the group left, Darrell and one other intrepid soul stayed on with Dan for another two weeks to hunt for plants in Sichuan Province. Although Darrell was interested in other plants and, like many of his fellow travelers particularly keen to see plants growing in their native habitat, he concentrated on epimediums.

Darrell teaching Epimedium hybridizing to Aaron Kahn-Bork

The following year, he traveled with Dan Hinkley again, this time to South Korea and Japan. In addition to epimediums, he also focused on the genus *Tricyrtis*. When he returned, he admitted, "I raised so many *Tricyrtis* seedlings that I was feeding the thinned seedlings to young bantam chicks we were raising in the house." With patience and persistence, he eventually introduced *Tricyrtis* 'Taipei Silk' through a famous nursery based in the U.K., Blooms of Bressingham (a nursery also crucial to the development of Pierre Bennerup).

But it was epimediums that became the singular offering of the mail-order nursery Darrell began, also called Garden Vision. After several expeditions to western China, Darrell wisely hired Joanna Zhang to collect plants for him instead of going himself. She had served as his interpreter on his own trips to China, and he had trained her well. Joanna is Chinese; she lived there and could travel without the special permission required for foreigners. She had grown very interested in his work while guiding him, becoming so knowledgeable and experienced that she was eager to take this on.

This arrangement with Joanna is what Darrell believes "led to my becoming a night owl." Because of the time difference and the need to direct her to specific destinations, Darrell spent every night communicating with her via internet cafés. She would find a café and report where she had gone that day. In turn, with a map of China he had pieced together from several U.S. Aviation topographical maps covering his entire wall, Darrell would mark her locations as she worked and advise her where to go the next day. Then she would send the plants she had collected back to Darrell in Massachusetts, complying with the complex U.S. import regulations and filling out all the necessary paperwork. Darrell was kept busy potting up and caring for everything she sent back while carrying on his mail-order and plant-breeding business. In all, she was to go on twenty-three trips for Darrell.

After September 11, importing plants into the United States became far more onerous. Many USDA inspectors were sent to work for Homeland Security, providing extra staff to inspect all parcels entering the States. That left reduced staff to inspect incoming plants, and far too often the plants Joanna so painstakingly sent back would be stuck on a shelf for a month awaiting inspection, only to die in the process. Finally, Joanna had to stop. Although Darrell has not been back to China since, from these China expeditions alone he has introduced at least sixty-one new species into Western horticulture.

Darrell estimates that he has about ten thousand clones of *Epimedium,* close to a hundred different species, and that he has introduced at least thirty new ones to science. Some of these are still being studied and published. Several of the chemicals that occur in epimediums show promise for use in the treatment of cancer and heart disease. Darrell also advises the National

Arboretum with regard to their Asian collection and periodically goes there to identify plants. Recently, he reported, "I have a box of unidentified *Epimedium* specimens on my desk right now waiting for me to ID them. For obvious reasons, I love their China Valley installation and we've shared many plants with each other."

Beyond science, Darrell has also been interested in disseminating the wonderful plants he has so intensely studied to a broader gardening audience. To encourage nurseries to offer more species, he consulted with Dan Hinkley's Heronswood when it was operative and Tony Avent's Plant Delights Nursery to properly identify and increase the number of epimediums they offered. Tony Avent, one of Darrell's many admirers, says, "Darrell almost single-handedly revolutionized the genus *Epimedium* with his unparalleled focus, tireless research, and incredible understanding of this genus. The gardening world has yet to fully realize his impact in transforming *Epimedium* from a fringe-market plant to one destined to become mainstream."

Darrell did not let his intense engagement with epimediums stop him from working on other plants, especially the *Coreopsis* genus. He had admired the very popular *Coreopsis verticillata* 'Moonbeam,' which offered a paler yellow flower than the more common bright yellow. He liked the fact that the delicate foliage could weave in among other perennials and appreciated the plants' long-blooming qualities. Darrell thought it would be desirable to have threadleaf coreopsis in colors in addition to yellow.

Virtually all coreopsis then available to gardeners were yellow. Why did Darrell think that he could produce coreopsis in other colors? Nothing whetted his appetite more than a challenge even greater than epimediums. Coreopsis are self-fertile, which means that individual plants can pollinate themselves instead of having to rely on wind or insects to spread pollen from one plant to another. The good news is that this can make it easy for plant breeders to create seed strains that are uniform. Plants that don't require cross-pollination are more likely to stay true to their genetic makeup and avoid variation. The bad news is that this same trait makes it almost impossible to hybridize them to create dramatically different variations.

How could Darrell cross one *Coreopsis* plant with another in an effort to develop other colors? For a very long time Darrell couldn't figure this out, but he wasn't deterred. He was after a threadleaf coreopsis with a color that wasn't yellow. By 1999, he had his first cross that produced hybrid progeny between the diminutive pink-flowered *Coreopsis rosea* and the eight-foot tall *Coreopsis tripteris*. However, the resulting seedlings were entirely sterile and a dead end.

As he was starting down this unpromising path, someone happened to discover a coreopsis that mysteriously appeared with a maroon eye and called it 'Sweet Dreams.' Darrell thinks it was probably a self-created hybrid resulting from pollination that by chance took place between an annual and a perennial coreopsis. Its appearance suggested that Darrell might be able to get the color breaks he was seeking; it fueled his determination.

After many years without success, years that would have discouraged most mortals, he finally began to see results. By 2007, he had his first introduction. He called it 'Full Moon'; it was a deeper canary yellow, larger-flowered coreopsis with excellent foliage. It became the first in what is now his trademarked Big Bang series.

Because coreopsis are native throughout much of the United States, Darrell has taken extra steps to introduce only hybrids that are sterile, so they will neither self-sow and become invasive nor pollinate and contaminate wild populations. To obtain sterile varieties requires additional generations and many more years and expense, something

Darrell with Mark Laviana in Coreopsis trial beds

less scrupulous growers might not undertake. But sterile coreopsis do make popular garden plants since, in their ongoing but futile attempt to produce seed, they flower prodigiously.

Darrell sets very high standards for himself and for any plant he introduces. He has insisted on stringent trials for his developing coreopsis, working with nurseries across the country to test his plants and select those that are likely to do well in different climates nationwide. There is now an annual Coreopsis Summit; he invites nursery representatives to make the trek to his seedling fields, where they all spend two intense days inspecting possible choices. He offers the representatives between twenty to thirty thousand seedlings to consider before they select no more than a hundred. In an ingenious system, the participants each receive their own colored flag and proceed to spread out in the growing fields, planting a flag next to their favorites. When almost everyone chooses the same plant, that one is selected for further trials. Each year the group chooses from fifty to a hundred of the best seedlings, and Darrell then sends cuttings from their selections to each participant to grow in their own climate for a two-year period.

After all that, any plant that succeeds is a candidate for a patent application. Plant patents have been available for some time, but their use by the industry only began to take off about twenty years ago. The federal government grants plant patents to the person who invents or discovers a distinct and new variety of a plant, so long as it is not a tuber or plant discovered in an uncultivated place, such as those collected on plant-finding expeditions. The new plant might have appeared as a sport, a mutation discovered in a cultivated area, or a spontaneous or induced hybrid. It must be capable of being asexually reproduced. A patent runs for twenty years, giving the patent holder a monopoly on the production, and preventing anyone else from copying, reproducing, propagating, selling, or using the plant unless the patent holder grants permission. Permission is usually only granted on the condition the patent holder receives a royalty.

Predictably, some nurserymen resent selling patented plants that require royalty payments and prohibit their free propagation. Darrell believes this attitude helped fuel the nursery industry's promotion of the sale of native plants more widely. Since native plants cannot be patented, no royalty can be charged on their sales, providing a larger profit margin for the nurseries. Hence the push to have the public believe that only native plants are good for the environment and are the only politically correct plants to buy. While that argument has been forceful, enthusiastic gardeners have proved to still be eager to buy special plants like the coreopsis that Darrell breeds.

In 2010, Darrell and Karen divorced, and she took over the epimedium business, carrying it on under the amended name Garden Vision Epimediums. But Garden Vision had offered not only epimediums but also the other results of Darrell's plant breeding. Karen could manage the epimedium propagation and marketing but Darrell knew that "the plant breeding work is all in my head."

He still carries on his business as Garden Vision, along with an entity created for certain purposes, G-Viz Plants, LLC (DBA Garden Vision). Happily, he married Joanne Holtje in 2012, herself a garden designer who has become a full-time artist. They moved to western Massachusetts to a house on property that offers growing conditions in both shade and sun, so Darrell can continue to work with both epimediums and coreopsis, as well as other plants.

He continues to breed coreopsis, including a new series called Satin & Lace as well as new additions to the Big Bang series. But he is interested in many other genera, including *Podophyllum, Physostegia, Monarda, Lobelia, Geum, Lychnis, Gentiana, Liriope, Arisaema, Polygonatum*, and *Astilbe*, and he can probably be counted on to add a few others.

It was not until 2015 that the coreopsis project first broke even financially, finally covering his expenses. Plant breeding is seriously hard work, long-term and expensive, which is why it is usually only undertaken by very large companies. By insisting upon his rigorous demands for a long trial period, Darrell has only added to the length of time and the cost it takes for him to offer a new plant. Before the divorce, the epimedium business supported his plant breeding. Without that income, Darrell's plant breeding failed to produce any income for the first seven or eight years. Now Pierre Bennerup's Sunny Border Nurseries has taken on managing Darrell's patents and collecting the royalties from nurseries selling his patented plants. By the end of 2015, more than 8 million plants of the Big Bang series had been sold, finally covering costs.

Darrell has had many extraordinary friends and mentors, the likes of Dick Lighty, Dan Hinkley, Tony Avent, and Pierre Bennerup. In turn, he has mentored and inspired others, both by his example and through efforts to help others coming along. In one case, a young plantsman reminded Darrell of himself in his early days; they shared an interest in monardas. This young Ph.D. student was writing a description of a new species he had identified and intended to publish, without realizing that Darrell had found that same monarda ten years before; Sunny Border Nurseries had sold it as *Monarda* 'Snowbird' for several years. Despite having to disappoint him, Darrell connected with this young man who is someone Darrell sees as a kindred spirit. He has provided encouragement to the student and even supporting funds to underwrite his ongoing research and plant identification.

For the foreseeable future, without giving up his interests in other genera, Darrell expects to continue to work on *Coreopsis*. He uses the winter months to clean seed collected earlier in the fall, seeking to keep the plants sterile so they don't cross-pollinate. He is now attempting to produce larger flowers. Before this particular passion took hold, Darrell did not spend more than ten years on a single project, but he has already invested more than fifteen years in *Coreopsis*. Finally, he is getting the results for which he hoped. He works with a local Massachusetts farmer who reminds him of his own past in the Garden on the Hill at Hartefeld. This farmer takes Darrell's seeds, first sowing them into flats, then transplanting them to grow on in his fields. Once the plants are in the ground, Darrell takes over.

"Everyone told me, growing up, that I would never be able to make a living working with plants, so I thought it would always be a hobby … and I needed to have a real job. Coming out of school at Longwood at age twenty-one, I believed I could contribute more to the world of plants by focusing on specific genera no one else was working on, learning all I could about them and then sharing what I learned with others to disseminate the info." It is true that earning a living from plant breeding is still hazardous, but he is happy to say, "My sole income now is from plant breeding and frankly, I am pretty amazed that I can do that."

Andrew Bunting

*Part of me likes horticulture and part of me likes
the scientific evaluation side of things.*

His quiet, calm, boyish manner does not immediately reveal the intensity of Andrew Bunting's passion for plants. Tall and lanky, with a dazzling smile and prone to ducking his curly head, he has an almost shy manner that belies the strength and energy inside. Andrew is now the director of plant collections and assistant director of the Chicago Botanic Garden after a long and distinguished career as curator at the Scott Arboretum of Swarthmore College, Pennsylvania.

The Chicago Botanic Garden website states that Andrew "directs the content and curation of the Garden's permanent plant collection, including plant acquisition and collecting, accessioning, mapping, and labeling. He serves as a resource for the horticulture, education, and marketing and development staff, and assists the director of the Garden with special projects." Chicago Botanic Garden covers 385 acres and has an annual budget of $35 million with 240 full-time employees. More than a million visitors have come each year for the past two years.

In addition to managing all of the garden's plant collections, Andrew has been resurrecting and revitalizing a ten-year plan of plant-finding expeditions. Particularly expert in woody plants, Andrew loves all plants, and as a veteran of many plant-finding expeditions, he is certain to make this an exciting program.

Chicago is a homecoming of sorts for Andrew, since he was born in Hinsdale, a western suburb of the city, and lived on and off in Illinois for some years. He also had an early internship at the Chicago Botanic Garden in 1984 while still in college. Andrew was born on April 8, 1964, to Frank and Judith Bunting, their second son, followed by a daughter. Andrew believes that "middle kids are well balanced." All three siblings proved to be artistic, but Andrew was the only child to use plants as his medium.

His earliest garden experience was working in his mother's extensive gardens, where she grew mostly vegetables but also some flowers. She assigned Andrew the task of harvesting the vegetables. The family also drove each summer to Nebraska to stay on his grandfather's farm. He recalls, "Time on the farm was a great influence."

His family left Illinois to move to Santa Rosa, California, when Andrew was only three years old and lived there until he was twelve. Then his grandfather decided to retire from farming and gave the farm to Andrew's father, and the family moved there. After two years, Andrew's parents divorced and his mother returned to Illinois, taking Andrew and his brother with her. His sister stayed with his father in Nebraska.

Andrew went to high school and college in Illinois, attending Southern Illinois University at Carbondale. During the summers, he had a series of internships. His first was at the Morton Arboretum, on 1,700 acres in Lisle, Illinois, west of Chicago. That early experience helped nurture his lifelong deep interest in woody plants. In 1885, Joy Morton founded the Morton Salt Company in Chicago, and built an estate in Lisle. He enlisted the renowned Charles Sprague Sargent, director of the Arnold Arboretum, to consult on the development of the Morton Arboretum, formally established in 1922. As the oldest of J. Sterling Morton's four sons, he inherited an interest in trees along with the family motto – "Plant Trees." While serving as Secretary of Agriculture under President Cleveland, J. Sterling Morton established the national observation of Arbor Day. The idea for Arbor Day grew out of his background in Nebraska, where farming had virtually denuded the entire state of its trees. On the first Arbor Day, April 10, 1872, it is reported that one million trees were planted in Nebraska alone.

One of Andrew's most important mentors came from his time at the Morton Arboretum. Ray Schulenberg was the curator there when Andrew was an intern. Andrew says, "Ray was hard-core into woody plants." Though Ray's main interest was in woody plants, he is most remembered for his work recreating a prairie at the Morton Arboretum. It began on just eight acres but grew to a hundred acres over time. It is now named the Schulenberg Prairie in his memory. Not surprisingly, Ray also had a Nebraska connection; he grew up on a farm there.

Although Andrew interned at the Morton Arboretum for only one brief summer, it was a very formative time. Ray spotted something special in the young Andrew. Ray traveled frequently to look for plants, including plants for his evolving prairie, but also on cultural trips for pleasure, and he invited

Andrew plant hunting in Delhaas Woods, Silver Lake Co. Park, Bristol, Pennsylvania

Andrew to come along. Andrew accompanied Ray on a cultural trip to Mexico for about ten days in 1983, just the two of them. Ray spoke seven languages fluently and was at ease traveling anywhere. This was a budget trip. "We stayed in hole-in-the-wall places and took buses everywhere," recalls Andrew. It would set the standard for Andrew's plant-finding trips in later years.

Andrew interned at the Chicago Botanic Garden in 1984 and in 1985 at the Fairchild Tropical Botanic Garden in Coral Gables, Florida, a garden that features rare tropical plants. As a result of his time in Florida, Andrew's personal garden has always included some striking tropical plants even though it is in the temperate zone of Swarthmore, Pennsylvania.

He graduated from Southern Illinois in 1986 with a B.S. in Plant and Soil Science. The same year, he interned at the Scott Arboretum. When a full-time job opened in plant research and was posted in 1987, Andrew applied and was hired. He thought he would work there for one year. He stayed for more than twenty-five!

Located on more than 350 acres of the campus of Swarthmore College, the Scott Arboretum was created in 1929 in honor of Arthur Hoyt Scott, class of 1895, "for the purpose of enabling Swarthmore College to acquire, cultivate, and propagate the better kinds of living trees, shrubs, and herbaceous plants which are hardy in eastern Pennsylvania and which are suitable for planting by the average gardener." As part of an educational institution, the Scott Arboretum has always had an emphasis on public education and thinks of itself as a collection of "gardens of ideas."

Andrew was hired by Judith Zuk, then the director, who in 1990 went on to become the president of the Brooklyn Botanic Garden, following in Betty Scholtz's impressive footsteps. After almost two years, Andrew approached Judy Zuk to ask her to change his job title and promote him to curator; if she didn't, he would look for a position abroad. While she very much wanted to keep Andrew, Judy said she didn't have enough in her authorized budget to give him the salary increase the job title would require. But she agreed that working abroad was a fine idea, particularly if he could find a good position in England. She had worked there herself at one point and was then married to Christopher Woods, who was British and the director of nearby Chanticleer, at the time still a private estate that would later become a major public garden.

Andrew left the Scott Arboretum at the end of 1989 and went off to England for ten months to work for the legendary Penelope Hobhouse at Tintinhull, a National Trust Garden created by Phyllis Reiss in Somerset. Penelope's own gardens at Hadspen House were already internationally famous; she had written many books and was a leading garden designer and writer. After her divorce from Paul Hobhouse, she left Hadspen to live at and manage

Tintinhull with her second husband, Professor John Malins. Her gardens at Hadspen were carried on with great creativity by Sandra and Nori Pope, who became Andrew's close friends.

He recalls, "I had a great time working in the U.K. in 1990. I got to visit 120 gardens there." Managing to visit more than 120 gardens during the few days off from his full-time job each week in a period of less than ten months would not sound like fun to most of us. But when I personally visited seven English gardens in one exhausting, nonstop day trying to keep up with Andrew some years later, I could see it was all a pure joy for him.

It was an intimate experience. Andrew lived in the main house at Tintinhull and worked with Glyn Jones, the head gardener (still there when I arrived to work for Penelope a year later). Glyn went on to work at another National Trust Garden, Peckover House in Cambridgeshire. He then became head gardener for more than a decade at Hidcote Manor, the famous National Trust garden in Gloucestershire created by the American expat Lawrence Johnston. Now Glyn oversees all the Shakespeare heritage sites gardens of the Shakespeare Birthplace Trust.

What a time for Andrew to be in England in the leading gardening circles. He had an amazing experience with Penelope Hobhouse during his time at Tintinhull. Not only did he fit in visiting 120 other gardens throughout England, he met some of the horticultural greats – such as Rosemary Verey of Barnsley House and Beth Chatto, famous for her gravel garden in Essex and her principle of using the right plant in the right place, as well as the extraordinary Christopher Lloyd, whose important gardens at Great Dixter are being preserved for the public benefit.

After an intense ten months at Tintinhull, Andrew took off to New Zealand for another unique experience. His flight took him to Bangkok, Sydney, and finally to Auckland on the North Island of New Zealand. He then drove to Titoki Point, the extraordinary garden creation of Gordon Collier. This time, Andrew not only lived in the same house with Gordon and his wife, Annette – he took all his meals with them, even hanging out with them in the evenings watching *Jeopardy!* on TV. It quickly became a very close friendship. But it was the garden that was so amazing. The benign New Zealand climate can sustain an incredibly wide array of plant material – cold-hardy plants that survive in the American Northeast thrive alongside tender tropicals. Titoki Point was much more than a broad collection of plants; it was an artistic creation. Andrew was in plant heaven! He also managed to travel a bit on his way back home.

For anyone less upbeat than Andrew, his homecoming would have been an anticlimax. Andrew returned to Swarthmore without a job and with no prospects of one. He lived in one room of a family's house and took on odd jobs. He did some plant-records work for the Scott Arboretum and part-time work for several other organizations, including Chanticleer and the Tyler Arboretum in Media. He led garden tours for the continuing education courses at Longwood Gardens – just odds and ends to keep him going.

But in 1992, at last he was hired full time at Chanticleer with his desired title of curator. It was an interesting time because Chanticleer was in transition from private estate to public garden. While he enjoyed the challenge, at the end of that year Andrew decided to leave.

While working full time at Chanticleer, the ever-energetic Andrew started his own firm with a business partner, Tony Coia, who had earlier worked with Andrew on the horticultural crew at the Scott Arboretum. Andrew and Tony called their business Fine Garden Creations, Inc., and the partnership lasted for four years until Tony moved out to

Andrew with Tony Aiello of Morris Arboretum collecting cuttings of Magnolia virginiana

Aspen, Colorado, to manage property for one of his clients. Andrew carried on the business without him after that for another twenty-one years.

One of the most visible acts of Fine Garden Creations was the planting of magnificent compositions in large containers set out in public spaces around Philadelphia by the Pennsylvania Horticultural Society. These container creations were major statements, featuring strong foliage and bold color combinations. Andrew was one of the earliest to use dramatic tropical plants in these pots, making quite a show. He also did residential work for clients, which constituted about 80 percent of the business.

After Andrew left Chanticleer, things came full circle. He finally returned to the Scott Arboretum as curator, the title he had sought unsuccessfully before leaving for England. Happily, the position opened at the right moment, and Andrew quickly applied. Claire Sawyers, the director, wisely hired him. He began in January 1993 and stayed for twenty-two years.

During those years, Andrew not only worked brilliantly at the arboretum and carried on Fine Garden Creations, he became an important public figure and a highly regarded expert in woody plants. He took on leadership roles in major horticultural organizations, becoming active in the American Public

Gardens Association, chairing the Philadelphia Flower Show nomenclature committee, and serving as president of the Swarthmore Horticultural Society and on the Delaware Center for Horticulture's Rare Plant Auction committee. He also chaired the North American Plant Collections Consortium, was president of the Magnolia Society International, and more.

Magnolias are one of his special interests. He built a national collection of magnolias at Swarthmore that has been recognized by the North American Plant Collections Consortium. His book, *The Plant Lover's Guide to Magnolias,* was published by Timber Press in 2016. He notes, "One of my favorite cultivars is named in honor of one of my favorite people, 'Judy Zuk.' Back in the sixties and seventies, Brooklyn Botanic Garden had a breeding program, and it was their goal to create the first yellow magnolia, which they did – one called 'Elizabeth'." There were many other cultivars that had never been named, and one in particular was a fastigiate yellow magnolia. When Judy retired as president of BBG, they decided to name it in her honor. Andrew admires it because it "isn't a true yellow, but the flowers are like a suffusion of orange and pink. They're upright and chalice- or tulip-shaped. Some magnolias are fragrant, but this one doesn't have the fragrance of most magnolias. It's a fruity fragrance like the cereal Fruit Loops!"

He also has a keen interest in hydrangeas and many kinds of vines. Andrew has explored using combinations of many of the plants he loves in his own plant-rich garden at his home in Swarthmore. Even though he has now moved to Chicago, he continues to manage that garden, which draws wide acclaim, attracting eager visitors whenever it is open to the public.

Swarthmore is an educational institution and early on, Andrew worked on organizing what has become the highly popular annual Woody Plant Conference. It began in 1996 featuring lively speakers and appealing to a broad audience of professionals as well as amateur gardeners. Over time the conference attracted other sponsors in addition to the Scott Arboretum, including Chanticleer, the Pennsylvania Horticultural Society, Longwood Gardens, the Tyler Arboretum, and the Morris Arboretum of the University of Pennsylvania. One of the principal organizers, Andrew was often among the speakers, leading to invitations for him to lecture throughout the United States and abroad. He has also published more than two hundred articles in a wide range of journals and has even appeared on TV on *Martha Stewart Living.*

One of the best paybacks from all his work on the Woody Plant Conference was the chance to meet Dan Hinkley when Dan came to speak there. That led to Andrew's traveling west to visit Dan at Heronswood several times and, best of all, to receiving an invitation from Dan to join one of his plant-finding expeditions. Andrew jumped at the chance.

In 2012, Andrew went on his first trip with Dan and two other men to

Taiwan. He had been on a few plant-finding trips before. In 2010 he went on a plant-finding trip to Sichuan, China, when he was awarded a Chanticleer Scholarship in Professional Development.

His long-ago trip to Mexico would prove to be good training for the rigors of traveling with Dan Hinkley, a kindred spirit. One year after that first trip to Taiwan, Andrew went to Vietnam with Dan and then again to Hubei in South Central China in 2014. Dan Hinkley describes days "plagued by heavy rain and dense fog."

These conditions make the critical task of drying the seeds they collect almost impossible. It's hard enough if the seeds are contained inside relatively dry pods, but seeds contained inside fruit must first be extracted. That requires the fruit to be soaked in water, ideally soapy water, and massaged by hand in the water until the pulp comes off the seeds and floats to the top. The seeds fall to the bottom of the container and are very wet once the water and the pulp are drained off. After all that work, any seed that cannot be sufficiently dried will be likely to turn moldy or rot, and no longer be viable.

Undaunted by these difficult conditions, Andrew was ready to join Dan's next trip in 2015, but happy events precluded that. Andrew was wooed away from that expedition and his life as curator of the Scott Arboretum by the very special opportunity to become the assistant director of the Chicago Botanic Garden. Kris Jarantoski, the director who hired Andrew, was the same person who had hired Andrew for his internship job there in 1984! Kris retired in February 2017 after thirty-nine years.

Andrew describes his position as having two parts: "One is director of plant collections, and with that hat on, I oversee our curatorial staff. We have a woody plant curator and a curator of perennials, and that same department is

where all the labeling goes on, and where we keep the database for nearly ten thousand different kinds of plants." It is where they build the plant collections for the garden. "While we want to have ornamental gardens, we also want to have gardens that have as much diversity as we can within each garden." The second part is to develop a ten-year plan for plant-finding expeditions. Andrew's expects the plan to include at least one international and two or more domestic trips each year.

Andrew has already made some domestic plant-finding trips to the Northeast and the South. The fact that these trips are in the United States should not suggest that the conditions are any less challenging than those he faced in Asia and on his trips with Dan Hinkley. On one such trip in the North-east, after Andrew and his team collected cuttings from a group of magnolia trees and packed them into their bags, they faced murky waters standing between them and their way out. The waters were deep and dangerous, so wading out was not an option. They had no choice but to leap from hummock to hummock – floating islands of knotted vines, wild roses, and other invasive plants – in order to reach stable ground.

On the final leg of that journey, they explored the swamps of otherwise civilized Staten Island, part of New York City. They donned knee-high boots in what proved to be thigh-high waters, sinking in deeper with every step, while swatting away mosquitoes and dodging deer ticks. They pushed through sharp *Phragmites* and Japanese knotweed to make their escape. Worst of all, they found no evidence of any magnolias!

More trips are in the future plans for the Chicago Botanic Garden's pro-gram. Peter Zale of Longwood Gardens will lead a trip to Japan, and Andrew will attend an international meeting in Georgia in the Caucasus that is a collaboration

Andrew with Dan Hinkley, Ozzie Johnson, Scott McMahan and porters in Five Finger Mountains, Vietnam

with Armenia, Georgia, and Azerbaijan. He will also go to less exotic Kentucky.

"There are lots of parameters and variables that will evolve over time and also partnerships," he says, as these collecting trips will be done with a consortium of institutions from around the country. They will share and track results and store specimens at the herbarium at the U.S. National Arboretum in Washington, D.C. Of course, many specimens will also find a home at the Chicago Botanic Garden, where Andrew wants "to fill in the gaps in the garden's collections while also adding diversity."

Looking back to his role models and mentors, Andrew credits Judy Zuk as important early in his career, along with Ray Schulenberg. He in turn has become an important mentor to others. Several of his protégés have had year-long curatorial internships on his watch at the Scott Arboretum and gone on to great things. Jim Adams, who became the head gardener at the White House, worked at Scott with Andrew in 1993. Timothy Tilghman went on to work for Marco Polo Stufano at Wave Hill and is now head gardener at Untermyer Gardens. Chris Roddick has been head arborist at the Brooklyn Botanic Garden for twenty-two years; his wife, Rebecca McMackin, is head of horticulture at Brooklyn Bridge Park. Jody Lathwell, a superb horticulturist, is the only person I know who managed to get the rare turquoise-flowering jade vine, or *Strongylodon macrobotrys,* to bloom at Wave Hill; she now has her own garden business in Cleveland. And there are many others.

Andrew will have exciting challenges ahead as he grows into his leadership role at the Chicago Botanic Garden. He has already found living in Chicago a new delight. He continues to retain his Swarthmore home to return to from time to time while renting it to other horticultural friends. He was particularly pleased to have a group tour sponsored by the Chicago Botanic Garden include his garden in the itinerary.

Andrew has chosen to experience Chicago by living in the heart of the city. His apartment on the forty-second floor of the eighty-seven-story tall Aqua tower overlooks Chicago's beautiful Millennium Park, including the dramatic bandshell, now called the Jay Pritzker Pavilion, designed by Frank Gehry, and the impressive naturalistic gardens designed by Piet Oudolf and others. There is sure to be more news to come about Andrew Bunting and his important role in American horticulture.

Through his book, articles, and lectures, Andrew has been engaged in horticultural education directed to both experts and amateurs. As a hands-on gardener himself, he cares deeply about sharing his plant knowledge and delight in using great plants with broader audiences. In his role at the Chicago Botanic Garden, he is uniquely positioned to ensure that unlike too many other botanical gardens, Chicago continues to be both a major research center as well as a disseminator of worthy plants to the public.

Tony Avent

*What a great boon it would be to gardeners of the world if we could
somehow bridge the chasm between botany and horticulture.*

WIRED! TONY AVENT believes he was born with a brain wired to
plants. His high-level energy and his lifelong passion for plants
confirms his conviction. He says, "I was born with a fully func-
tional 7.0 horticultural operating system, along with some specialized apps like
an obsessive personality, an overactive imagination, an overly logical brain, and
a touch of ADD." Tony says that horticulture is why he was put on this earth and
he has been true to that vision.

Plantsman extraordinaire Tony selects the very best offerings to share
with the public through Plant Delights Nursery, Inc., the nursery he founded in
1988 in Raleigh, North Carolina. The nursery also supports Tony's Juniper
Level Botanic Garden, established at the same time and in the same place; it
now has more than 22,600 taxa, more than most long-established, much-
larger botanical gardens. While Tony is intensely serious and entirely professional in his knowledge, he is equally committed to disseminating great plants
to a broader public.

With his delicious and occasionally naughty sense of humor he also
wants everyone to understand that gardening is *fun*! When I first saw Tony
Avent in action, he was speaking to a group of garden enthusiasts in Charleston, South Carolina. His delivery was hilariously funny, loud, and intentionally
outrageous. Playing to the crowd, he used his broad Southern accent to the hilt
to deliver a talk full of jokes – jokes that played on plant names. The audience
roared with laughter while simultaneously madly taking notes. That comic,
hyperactive cover does little to hide the serious plantsman inside. With his joke-
filled, cartoon-adorned Plant Delights catalog, his writings, his countless talks,

*Plant Delights Nursery: View of one of the garden
borders toward the south*

and his elaborate website, Tony sees himself as an educator, determined to reach large and growing audiences. Where else but at Plant Delights is the price for ordering the catalog either "10 stamps or a box of chocolates"?

Tony was born on August 20, 1957, to Garland and Ann Avent in Raleigh, North Carolina, where he grew up with his younger sister, Marie. A horticultural child prodigy, he began shortly after he learned to walk: "Some folks fall into gardening, some are dragged into gardening, and a few others are born to garden. I fall into the last category." By three, he was already foraying out into the woods around his home hunting for plant treasures to grow in his terrariums. He has been hunting for and growing treasures ever since. Although his father was interested in gardening enough to breed iris as a hobby and grow a bit of everything, Tony didn't think his father was really very good at it. Tony seemed to sense instinctively when plants were suffering; he would come to their rescue and quickly learned how to nurture and save them.

By the age of six, he had taken to visiting local oddball nurseries growing interesting plants. Tony recalls it was during the "Green Revolution," and he found the places that "bought into that movement in the late sixties and early seventies. Save the planet, horticulture, going green, growing more plants were all part of that." He could not have endeared himself to the local nursery owners when, despite his youth, he presumed to "harass the employees about mis-named plants while peppering them with other plant-growing questions." By the time he was eight, his parents recognized this consuming passion and rewarded it by building him a greenhouse.

As he grew up, he did not go out of his way to ingratiate himself with his contemporaries either. For a young man in North Carolina, having a consuming interest in plants was seen as "weird"; it was "not something for a guy to admit in public." This consuming and peculiar passion, combined with his unusual sense of humor, was, he recalls, "definitely not cool." It may be that his perception of himself as a nonconformist outsider bolstered his refusal later in life to accept the gospel according to botanical authorities.

Although he didn't see himself as a very good student (no doubt because he was really *only* interested in plants), he did well enough to enter North Carolina State University in Raleigh, where he studied horticulture. He probably overstates when he says he never bought a textbook and that horticulture was the only class he could pass because he managed to graduate with a B.S. in Horticultural Science in 1978. While at college, he was fortunate enough to connect with and work for J. C. Taylor, head of the conservatory there, carrying on his early interest in houseplants and indoor growing from his childhood greenhouse. Before Tony graduated, he married his high school sweetheart, Michelle, who would become an important partner as he developed his nursery.

While still at college, Tony also joined the Men's Garden Club of Wake County, even though he describes the average age of the then members as "deceased!" The club was running the flower show at the North Carolina State Fairgrounds and needed someone to help out. Tony's father had been a member and one of the other members came to visit Tony at college, handing him an envelope with his membership dues prepaid. This older member knew they needed to attract younger people, and this is how he did it – just paid for them and invited them in for free. In Tony's case, the connection to the fairgrounds soon provided him with a job. The State of North Carolina, which ran the fairgrounds, had purchased shrubs from state surplus and needed someone to plant them. Tony arrived to help and discovered a mess, plants that had been bedded down in sawdust for more than a year. He spent two days untangling the roots from the sawdust and cleaning up, then showed the fairgrounds staff how to plant them. Those fateful two days stretched into the next sixteen years.

Tony's spectacular rescue prompted the assistant manager of the fairgrounds to ask if he would take a job while still in college. Tony accepted, working part time during his senior year and full time thereafter. The State Fairgrounds is almost a small city unto itself, functioning as a sprawling

The Alpine Garden

convention center with several buildings and covering more than 350 acres; events take place there year round. In his mind's eye, Tony envisioned how he would like the place to look. He also had set his mind on someday opening a small nursery. So Tony decided he would tackle the job of landscape manager as if he owned the fairgrounds; he would approach it as if he were already building and managing his own business, keeping track of costs and inventory, learning to manage people, and developing the skills he knew he'd need to run his own nursery. At the same time, he would be doing something to benefit the State of North Carolina, leaving as his legacy beautiful public grounds, full of unusual and wonderful plants. He anticipated it would take him about fifteen years to achieve his goals. Close. It took sixteen. He was there from 1978 until 1994.

Already thinking of himself as something of a maverick, he cleverly manipulated his masters to get his own way. Shortly after he came on full time at the fairgrounds, the assistant manager who had hired him quit. His new boss had no interest in improving the grounds and took an instant dislike to Tony and the entire horticultural program. In classic bureaucratic style, the new manager's only objective was to avoid any screwups. As Tony admits, when you undertake to do big, new things, you inevitably make mistakes. This boss refused to give Tony any budget for plants. Fortunately, North Carolina State University was right across the street, under the direction of the legendary J. C. Raulston, who had been one of Tony's college teachers. Tony crossed the street and began propagating plants from cuttings and seeds he gathered there. In turn, the arboretum, which had only eight acres of its own at the time, could spill over and plant on the 350 acres of fairgrounds. No surprise – rare and unusual plants began to appear.

Tony developed a clever strategy for expanding his budget and staff to handle the increased work. At the outset, he had only two part-time helpers, but by the time he left, he had built a full-time staff of twenty. How did he do it? He began to play mind games with his boss. He quickly perceived that the only thing his boss cared about was a crisply mown lawn. So Tony began to leave large areas of lawn unmown in highly visible spots. When the boss complained, Tony explained he didn't have enough staff to keep all the lawns cut at the same time. This strategy, repeated from time to time, yielded extra funds for additional staff. Odd that his boss never seemed to catch on!

Beyond additional staff, Tony also wanted more money for his ambitious plans to improve the fairgrounds. To raise the funds, he began an annual azalea sale with the Men's Garden Club, although the board was more than dubious. In North Carolina, azaleas are as commonplace as petunias, offered for sale at the time by every K-Mart, Walmart, and other big box stores. Tony decided to offer more varieties than anybody else. In the very first year of the azalea sale, the Men's Club sold twenty-three hundred plants in one weekend. Ten years later, total sales exceeded twenty thousand plants, raising close to $60,000. Tony then presented a list of projects he desired to his boss with the money in hand to pay for it.

In his spare time, Tony worked as a volunteer curator in the shade house at the adjacent arboretum from 1985 through 1994, finding a soul mate in J. C. Raulston. J. C., who had an important influence on a legion of gardeners, was the first "grown-up" on the same wavelength as Tony. Even though he was a professor, he shared Tony's belief that "you can't believe anything you read in books. You should try to grow as many different plants as possible. If the books say a plant can't grow in your climate, give it a try anyway. Very few books are written by real gardeners." J. C. validated Tony's own ideas, sharing his passion and commitment for getting great plants out to the public and increasing the diversity of the plant palette. Pressing for change, they both believed you have to break a few rules. As Tony learned so well at the fairgrounds, "it is easier to ask forgiveness than to ask permission."

Despite his view that very few real gardeners write, Tony began to write a newsletter for the Men's Garden Club and that led to writing a weekly garden column for the *News & Observer,* a Raleigh newspaper that reached the eastern half of North Carolina. Writing that column for twelve years helped Tony sell himself. He also initiated an open day program at the fairgrounds, drawing more than 250 people annually from all over the tri-state area for a day of tours and lectures, many of them starring Tony. At the same time, and just a mile away, Tony and Michelle opened to the public their own small home garden, where they grew more than eight hundred different plants on their tiny quarter acre. There, visitors could see just how much could be accomplished and grown on a small city plot. Tony also handed out enticing free plants, cuttings, and divisions. Each visitor was asked to sign a guest register. As a result, when Tony was finally ready to open his nursery, he already had an initial mailing list and potential customer base.

By 1988, the Avents were ready to move and start their nursery. They bought a small house on two and a quarter acres of what had been a tobacco field several miles outside Raleigh and, ambitiously and simultaneously, also started Juniper Level Botanic Garden. Here the word *level* means a flat area between creeks. Starting with one bed at a time, Tony began planting, slowly extending the garden farther out from the house, planting a little bit more and pressing on. Each year the plant sales grew, until he could add a greenhouse to accommodate ever-larger offerings. Finally, the nursery was sufficiently viable so that in 1994 the Avents could leave their day jobs to run their business full time. Tony resigned as landscape director of the North Carolina State Fairgrounds.

Despite his high regard for J. C. Raulston, Tony ignored him when he said, "Please tell me that you didn't quit your state job to do the nursery full time. There is no way you can make it as a mail-order nursery. You won't be able to support yourself without doing something illegal!" When J. C. later came for a visit, Tony greeted him with dollar bills suspended with clothes pins from a grapevine clothesline. J. C. didn't say anything at first but finally he asked, "All right. What is this?" Tony replied, "It's my money-laundering operation!"

Tony would probably describe his first plant-finding expeditions as starting with his early childhood forays into the neighboring woods. His first foreign trips to look for plants were relatively tame, taking him to England to visit gardens and comb through the rich offerings of their many small nurseries. Then, thanks to an introduction by J. C., who had been very impressed by Yucca Do Nursery founded by John Fairey and Carl Schoenfeld, Tony joined John, Carl, and Richard Hartlage on a plant-finding trip to Mexico in 1994. Tony expected the trip to be intense, but he was hardly prepared for the drama that ensued. John Fairey suffered a heart attack at eight thousand feet. Believing at first that John was just suffering from the usual Mexican stomach problems, the group left him at a local hospital for a few hours while they went off to continue searching for plants, only to return and learn the serious news. At John's urging, they continued on without him to more remote regions. During that time, Tony met his match as a clown in Carl. Recognizing Tony's fear of heights, Carl called his attention to a unique dahlia growing right below the edge of a cliff. As Tony came closer to peer over to see it, Carl jumped over the edge! Tony steeled himself to inch up to the very edge of the precipice, announcing as he did so, "Carl – if you are still alive and have the car keys with you, I will kill you!" With a dramatic flourish, Carl emerged from his perch on an invisible ledge below. Of course, he also had in hand the seed from that special dahlia.

Two years later, Tony joined Dan Hinkley on a trip to China. He had met Dan also thanks to J. C., who brought Dan to Tony's first open house right after Dan started his own mail-order business at Heronswood. Tony's invitation to the trip, though, came from Paul Jones at Duke Gardens. The impressive group included Pierre Bennerup; Darrell Probst; Kim Hawks of Niche Gardens; Mildred Pinnell Foeckle and Ozzie Johnson of Atlanta Botanical Garden; Roy Herold, a plant breeder from Boston; David DeRose of Denver Botanic Gardens; Elsa Liner, a volunteer from Chapel Hill; and Frank Bell, a plant collector–lawyer from Lexington, Kentucky. The following year Tony went on another trip to Korea for a month.

By 2016, Tony had completed eighty plant-finding trips, but contrarian as usual, he thought too many people were going to China – it had become "flavor of the month." Instead, Tony decided it was time to look in our own

The Rockery

backyard and began searching for great plants in the United States. So of his more than eighty trips, at least seventy have been within the United States, although he has also traveled to Argentina, South Africa, Thailand, Vietnam, Taiwan, Crete, Bosnia, Croatia, Montenegro, and Slovenia, in addition to China and Korea.

He began by exploring Texas systematically, a great gold mine of untapped plants and right next door to Mexico, where he began his trips. Half of Texas is Zone 6 or 7, perfect for plants that would grow in North Carolina. He focused on specific plants, particularly on baptisias. Inspired by an early monograph (written in 1940) describing species of *Baptisia* that were no longer available, Tony set out to see if any still existed in their native environment. The botanists writing about these plants were not gardeners, so none of them had collected living plants, just dried specimens for herbariums. Because baptisias don't grow true from seed, promiscuously interbreeding, Tony wanted to find the original source material and breed them true to type. He was rewarded when he found wonderful clumps of yellow, blue, white, and pink ornamental baptisias in full flower. Since baptisias are toxic, the cows won't eat them, although they eat everything else around them, leaving the baptisias to grow strongly and in full view. For Tony, this was the perfect substitute for lupins, which can't stand heat and don't grow well in the South. (Nor do they grow well in many other areas, including my own northern Connecticut garden where, thanks to Tony and Plant Delights, baptisias flourish instead.)

Baptisias happen to be native plants, although, not surprisingly, Tony is not a disciple of the native plant proselytizers. To the contrary, he is highly critical of those who seek to "purify" America, keeping out or, worse, destroying all plants that aren't American natives. He cites one example, a presidential order that created a new bureaucracy to monitor and eradicate nonnative plants, banning nonnative ornamental plants from all government properties, though nonnative edible plants are strangely excluded. Tony, like most great plantsmen, refuses to limit himself to native plants, much as he loves and grows them. He views every plant as native since once upon a time there was only one continent! The fact that the single continent divided with some plants going one way and some another should indicate that no plant is inherently guilty just because it survived on the wrong continent after the divide.

Political pressures have made importing plants into the United Sates harder than ever. While fully supportive of requiring permits and responsible monitoring to ensure that invasive and noxious species and pests are kept out, Tony is critical of decisions that declare certain plants invasive. At one point, a computer model was the predictor of invasiveness even though Tony claims that the model would have banned more than 40 percent of the plants we all now safely grow. He believes the model ignores the fact that plants invasive in one climate may behave perfectly reasonably in another. Conjure up a plant rampant in Florida, and you know it would behave demurely in Connecticut. According to Tony, of the roughly 275 worst plant invaders already on our shores, many were brought in by the federal government and planted by the millions by the U.S. Fish and Wildlife Service. He regrets that the government agencies focus on nurseries instead of regulating themselves. He believes it is often the nurseries that most effectively trial and test plants and that are the most knowledgeable about how they grow.

While searching for baptisias, Tony also found many other species likely to grow well in North Carolina. He has brought back specimens of *Verbena*, *Penstemon*, *Nolina*, *Dasylirion*, and many others. In 1998, he found a special new *Trillium* species when he happened to open his car door after stopping for a rest on the highway outside of Chattanooga, and *Trillium* has become his latest passion. His find is one of at least ten new *Trillium* species discovered by him and other like-minded explorers. One was discovered on Interstate 20 and another along the Savannah River, where only twelve plants remain in existence.

Tony is eager to get trilliums out into the trade so as to preserve them. Experimenting with propagation techniques, Plant Delights now has almost a full acre devoted to them, growing them both by seed and division. He is also working with other plantsmen who are experimenting with tissue culture. He had the first arisaemas ever propagated by tissue culture after he had been told that it was impossible. He loves a challenge. He worked with the same lab in Minnesota to tissue-culture variegated agaves after being told they too were impossible. Tony didn't think it could be that different from tissue-culturing hostas, where Tony is recognized as a renowned breeder. He has also encouraged tissue culture on cannas, plants that tend to be prone to virus. One lab tried tissue culture and managed to produce virus-free cannas, now one of Tony's best sellers. But he is amused to recall seeing a "variegated canna" offered in another nursery's catalog when he could tell it was just a canna that was heavily virused!

Tony cares deeply about plant conservation but disagrees with the politically correct plant conservationists who insist that plants should only be preserved in situ, on the very spot where they were first seen by European settlers. Tony maintains that those fragile twelve remaining trilliums, growing on a nuclear site and trampled by feral hogs, would be more likely to survive and thrive if they were propagated and grown on in other places, too. But he, like others in the nursery business, believe some authorities and academic conservationists disdain those engaged in commerce and too often interfere with serious nurserymen like Tony, who are eager to both conserve existing threatened plant populations and ensure that they could grow elsewhere to guarantee the survival of the species. Current laws prevent this. Under federal law, it is illegal to propagate and ship any plant that has been declared an endangered species. Tony thinks that "if you can grow it, why not? Preservation by propagation and sharing!" Gene flow between plant populations used to be the norm before highways and neighborhoods interfered.

Although a plant breeder, Tony is no big fan of people who improperly patent plants. Patents are intended to protect a creation, and they are also supposed to foster future introductions by others by sharing information about how the new plant was created. Tony thinks most applicants for plant patents don't really explain how they developed the plant in question. That important information about the successful breeding process would be helpful to others seeking to breed and improve other plants.

These days, Tony's own emphasis is on hybridizing, making seedling selections, and seeking to find and identify sports. He has long been active in developing different varieties of hostas, and he recently introduced several fast-growing miniatures, including a mini-form with yellow foliage he called *Hosta* 'Sun Mouse.' He also found a red floral mutation on *Dianthus* 'Firewitch' and propagated it, calling it *Dianthus* 'Wicked Witch.' He has developed and introduced *Baptisia* 'Blue Towers' and countless others.

In 2012, tragedy struck when Michelle, Tony's wife and business

Striking planting combinations featuring purple Canna

partner for thirty-four years, died much too young. Generous spirit that she was, she urged him to remarry after she was gone. A few years later, Tony married Anita, who has introduced a spirituality program to the garden. The Center for Mindfulness and Nonduality is now a featured part of the Juniper Level Botanic Garden. Recognizing how much Tony has always lived in the future, Anita has been insisting he get over it, teaching him about mindfulness and being more in the moment. Anita has also been influential in the design of the garden by encouraging more openness for better energy flow. Though they met online, they happily discovered that they had known each other as children.

Plant Delights Nursery continues to go from strength to strength, concentrating on offering rare and unusual perennials, though Tony is interested in all forms of plant material. In part, the emphasis on perennials reflects his history with J. C. Raulston. Because the J. C. Raulston Arboretum focuses on woody plants and functioned like a sister organization for him, first while Tony was at the fairgrounds and then continuing with Plant Delights Nursery, Tony's offerings focus on perennials instead. He uses a very limited amount of chemicals in his nursery, and then only to grow plants in pots, an artificial environment that puts plants under stress. But in the garden itself he uses no artificial fertilizers and virtually no chemicals, ensuring healthy plants by putting the right plant in the right place and providing adequate water and compost-enriched soil.

Juniper Level Botanic Garden allows Tony to grow a full range of plants, although he says he mostly plants here in "drifts of one!" For twenty-five years, it has been an accredited botanical garden, a member of the American Public Gardens Association, and it is now recognized as a qualified charitable organization. More than 22,600 taxa grow on his twenty-eight acres, substantially expanded from the original two and a quarter. He adds roughly two thousand more plants each year but also loses many along the way. His plan is to close the mail-order division of Plant Delights Nursery when he has built up enough of an endowment to allow the botanic garden to support itself.

Critical of other botanical gardens for their failure, or unwillingness, to distribute plants they collect to the public, Tony tests and identifies plants that will do well in North Carolina's climate, pushing those plants out into public use. New plants found on expeditions are set out in trial beds, and worthy ones are then fast-tracked to the public. With very limited funds, Tony is doing by example what he believes other botanical gardens and arboreta *should* be doing. He regrets that these major public institutions with far greater financial resources, though they support important plant expeditions, don't seem to feel any responsibility for getting new plants out into the horticultural mainstream.

When Tony began his nursery, he felt that there was a shortage of good perennials for an awakening public interest. In his Plant Delights catalog, he attempts to offer the most garden-worthy of any particular genus, although he grows many more varieties than he lists. The catalog lists the very best of the lot, a gratis preselection system for customers. Total listings in the catalog are approximately five hundred, although there are an additional six hundred plus on offer on his website, which also includes complete and detailed encyclopedic descriptions of roughly 4,500 different plants.

Tony continues to write, including numerous articles and a monthly blog. His book, *So You Want to Start a Nursery,* was published by Timber Press in 2003, and he wrote a chapter in *The Roots of My Obsession: Thirty Great Gardeners Reveal Why They Garden,* edited by Thomas C. Cooper, in 2012. He frequents the lecture circuit (more than 790 since 1987) in far-flung geographical locations. A recent tour had him in Germany en route to a talk in Virginia, demonstrating his commitment to public education.

For all he has done and continues to do in the field of horticulture, he has been recognized and honored. He generously gives of his time and knowledge by serving on numerous committees and boards, including the Woody Plant Advisory Committee for the J. C. Raulston Arboretum, the advisory committee of the USDA-ARS Hardiness Zone Map Revision, the North Carolina

Department of Agriculture Rare Plant Conservation Scientific Committee, and others. He received the Award of Merit from the Perennial Plant Association in 2013, the Certificate of Recognition from the Garden Writers of America, the Outstanding Commercial Award for an Individual from the American Horticultural Society, and perhaps most fitting of all, the J. C. Raulston Distinguished Leadership Award from North Carolina State University. Often featured in the media and television, he has appeared on *Martha Stewart Living*.

Tony's own offbeat sense of humor continues to infuse his catalogs, talks, and everything about Plant Delights without in any way minimizing the serious nature of its offerings. Tony insists gardening should be fun and he makes sure it is. My most recent order from Plant Delights arrived with the address label on the outside of the box reading in big letters: LIVE PLANTS!!! OPEN IMMEDIATELY!! HELP!!! LET US OUTTA HERE! WE NEED AIR, LIGHT, WATER, AND TENDER LOVING CARE! The instructions inside contained big headings: "Yes! My plants are here ... life is complete!" And "Stress Counseling" as well as "I ordered a plant and all I got was a pot of dirt ... you dirty rat!" However, beneath each memorable heading was detailed information about how to successfully grow the plants.

The catalog covers are always in cartoon form – topical, timely, and hilarious. The one for Spring 2016 read, "It's Alive ... the Soil Is Alive!" and showed all forms of life above- and belowground, as well as an awakening Frankenstein of a tree with caricatures and quips about Hillary Clinton and Donald Trump. An earlier cover showed a basketball scene; the players were stylized arisaemas in action (*Arisaema* being the Latin name for what is popularly known as jack-in-the-pulpit). The joke played off Nike's Air sneakers. Often, the plant names in the catalog contain puns and jokes of a distinctly political nature, which results, as Tony recounts with some pride, in a huge amount of hate mail from both sides of the political aisle. It means people are paying attention and that he is an equal opportunity offender!

Once Tony achieves his goal of making Juniper Level Botanic Garden self-sustaining, there will no longer be a Plant Delights Nursery catalog to make us all laugh while offering the best and most exciting perennials. But there is no doubt his passion will continue to inspire his ongoing work in plant development and public education and will continue to spread the message that gardening is fun!

Tony Avent

Barry Yinger

I tend to love the unloved. I tend to be most fond of those plants
that don't get much respect in the greater world of horticulture.

PIPHANY IS A WORD Barry Yinger uses to describe special moments of
his life. The first he recalls occurred when he was a teenager not far
from his family's Pennsylvania farm. Still in junior high school, he was
helping in a nearby garden that had been designed by a landscape architect,
something unheard of at the time in Central Pennsylvania. When he asked
what a particular tree was, he was told it was a holly. But how could it be a holly
without spiny leaves? he asked. He learned this was a Japanese holly, totally
unlike the American holly he knew and one of many Asian plants that, though
related to native Pennsylvanians, look completely different. He recalls, "There
was this great flash of light – I really need to know about this!" And come to
know he certainly did, becoming proficient in several Asian languages and an
authority on the many unusual plants he collected on the other side of the world,
all of which culminated in the opening of his extraordinary specialty nursery,
Asiatica, located on that very same family farm. Although Asiatica is no longer
operating, Barry continues to be a force in the introduction, identification, and
dissemination of underappreciated, or what he prefers to call unloved, plants.

Early on, Barry became convinced that he could only find accurate information about Asian plants from original sources written in the relevant Asian
language. The English translations didn't make sense to him. His intense drive
to understand these plants and find accurate information about them sustained
him through the enormous challenge of learning first Japanese and later Korean.
Not only mastering the languages but coming to understand the cultures were
essential to Barry's success in introducing very special plants to American horticulture. His plants included the rare and unusual as well as those with such

broad appeal that eight have been declared Gold Medal winners by the Pennsylvania Horticultural Society over the years, more Gold Medal winners than any other single plantsman has introduced.

It was not predictable that Barry would be drawn to Asia, since he has lived almost all of his life on the family farm in Lewisberry, where he was born on November 9, 1948, to Richard and Betty Lucille Mummert Yinger. He was the middle child, the only boy of three children in the family. His maternal grandmother (who had a magnificent garden around her large Edwardian house in Altoona, Pennsylvania) was a strong early influence. She managed this despite the opposition of a strict husband who thought she should spend all her time caring for her children and their house. In quiet rebellion, she used to hide the dirty dishes under the sink so she could "goof off" – which was her husband's view of her gardening. The garden was where she could escape and decompress, and where she introduced Barry to the exceptional plants she grew there.

For her generation, Barry's grandmother was unusual. She graduated from college in the first class of women admitted to Millersville University. She became a schoolteacher, riding the milk train to the school where she taught while living at home with her parents. When she married Barry's grandfather, she knew that married women weren't allowed to keep their jobs. It was understood that their husbands should support them and they shouldn't occupy a job that might be filled by a man. So she kept her marriage a secret and continued working. Her garden is Barry's first memory of "a real garden, a composed, ornamental garden." She used grasses and tropicals that she wintered over indoors; instead of the usual petunias and marigolds, she used castor beans (*Ricinus communis*), *Amaranthus*, and the like. And she gave Barry small bouquets with flowers he had never seen before. His conventional grandfather had no interest in the ornamental; he worked for an insurance company and Barry describes him as a "hardworking, hard-charging man who grew some vegetables."

In high school, Barry was a member of the debate team, a prizewinning group ranked number two in the state. His teachers sensibly advised him that he'd be unlikely to earn a living working with plants, and, given his debating skill, they encouraged him to become a lawyer. Following their advice was "the biggest mistake of my life!" After enrolling in American University, he soon gave up his full scholarship and dropped out. Though his family considered it a "disgrace," he retrospectively advises others to "ignore what everyone says and do what you really want to do."

Barry's grandmother, Elsie Meyers Mummert

After dropping out of the university, Barry began working in horticulture at a garden center in Washington, D.C., where he had attended college. Growing up a farm boy, he knew how to run equipment, so he soon became foreman, staying at the garden center for more than two years. He began to take a few courses at the University of Maryland and finally enrolled full time. This time, it took. He worked two nights a week and every weekend to support himself while benefitting from the lower tuition rate for residents and a modest five-hundred-dollar-a-year scholarship.

While in college, Barry had a part-time job as a mail delivery boy in the Tokyo Broadcasting System offices. Confessing to a Japanese receptionist that he was interested in learning the language, she told him firmly that it was impossible, an assertion that set his resolve to prove her wrong.

Barry's interest in learning Japanese arose from his conviction that most English-language sources about Asian plants were derivative and incorrect. Fortunately, the University of Maryland allowed him to study horticulture and botany along with Japanese and Chinese. At the time, the U.S. Department of Agriculture, concerned that too few students were learning Asian languages, set up a program allowing students who signed up for Asian language courses while studying plant science to have some general course requirements waived. His language proficiency would allow Barry to read original source material about the Asian plants that fascinated him.

In 1974, Barry went to Japan for a semester of independent study, his first trip outside the United States and his first time on an airplane. His professor at the University of Maryland, Dr. Robert Baker, made sure he would get academic credit for this semester abroad.

When he arrived in Japan, Barry quickly discovered the challenge involved in learning to speak the language. The actual everyday speech was so very different from his university classes. His Japanese teacher in Maryland knew an American student living in Japan who was going to be away traveling, and Barry was able to sublet his room. It proved to be very basic quarters indeed. There was no heat and no private bathroom, only a communal toilet and access to the public bathhouse down the street. Public bathhouses were common on almost every block since most people did not have bathrooms in their homes.

The experience provided full immersion in the Japanese language and culture. Barry intentionally avoided any Japanese people who wanted to practice their English on him. But his contacts at the two universities important in horticulture, Kyoto and Chiba, all spoke English and insisted on speaking English to him. Luckily, early on, Barry went out to the Japanese nursery district and made contact with a relatively young nurseryman, Akira Shibamichi, whom Barry recognized as a "real plant guy, the most knowledgeable Japanese person

still living that knows the ornamental woody plants of Japan in depth." Akira adopted Barry; he was endlessly cheerful and good-natured, certain that if he spoke Japanese nonstop Barry would catch on. At first, Barry didn't understand a word but Akira persisted, convinced he would learn. By the time Barry left, "I could understand a lot. He really helped drag me inside the culture."

While he was in Tokyo, Barry came to understand that horticulture was a Japanese passion when he saw men in a bathhouse changing room admiring a display of bonsai forms of *Prunus mume*. One particularly dirty laborer was taking his four-year-old son around the table, painstakingly instructing him in the nuances of each plant. Barry thought, "Back home, any boy who loved plants was a geek. But here, and at every level of society, the minutiae of the plant world is part of who they are, as much as their blood or skin. I felt I had come home." Describing the culture shock of this trip, Barry says, "That was the epiphany of my life."

He also became fascinated with the Japanese horticultural tradition *koten engei*, in which gardeners select mutated forms (variegated, twisted, weeping, or dwarfed) of otherwise plain, ordinary plants, such as wild gingers and whisk ferns – bits of green that to a Western eye might seem insignificant or even unattractive. These odd forms are displayed like jewels, in special decorative pots. Over the years, the aficionados often create a fervor for particularly favored specimens, resulting in ferocious bidding wars, much akin to the European tulip craze.

After Japan moved to liberalize trade with the United States and Europe,
Barry helped many Japanese nurserymen develop their international business.
He earned an award from the local government of the Angyo region, where the
nurseries flourished, for his role in advancing horticulture in that area. Rarely
did the Japanese confer honors on an American.

Returning to the United States, Barry graduated from the University of
Maryland in 1975 and was encouraged to continue his studies for a Ph.D. He
was torn, but he had no money and needed work. He found a job working for
Gustin Gardens, a garden center outside of Washington, D.C., where he was put
in charge of the nursery. He enjoyed it, especially being sent around to auctions
to buy plants, sometimes at nurseries going out of business. Wayside Gardens
held a weeklong auction in Ohio, where he went in 1976 to buy old stock plants.
He remembers a gnarled *Cornus kousa* 'Milky Way' still in the ground that was
on offer for 50 cents so long as he could dig it out. He had it hand-dug and hand-
wired, and sold it for fifteen hundred dollars, a huge price at the time, to be
planted in a circle at Amory Firestone's private gardens in Centreville, Maryland.
When he brought ten smaller *Cornus* back to Gustin Gardens, they thought he
was crazy and that the trees would surely die, but they sold out in a week.

One nursery auction proved to have a major impact on his life. He went to the final auction at Millcreek Nursery, owned by William H. Frederick Jr., in the Brandywine Valley just outside of Wilmington. Bill Frederick was then the chairman of the board of Longwood Gardens, and when he met Barry at the sale, he encouraged him to look at the Longwood Graduate Program in Ornamental Horticulture. Barry had also heard about the program from Professor Baker. He had recently grown disillusioned at Gustin Gardens, where he felt his best employee, a strapping black man six feet four inches tall and a great guy, was being treated unfairly. Sufficiently upset, Barry left his full-time position and applied to the Longwood program at the University of Delaware. There, he earned his master's in ornamental horticulture from the program started by Dick Lighty.

When he began his studies at Longwood, Barry intentionally sought out the few Japanese students to maintain his proficiency in Japanese. Longwood also helped with a grant partially supporting one of his trips to Japan. On one of these trips, he discovered the stunning vine *Schizophragma hydrangeoides* 'Moonlight.' It lights up the woodland as it clambers up trees, displaying its silvery variegated leaves. Barry was the first to find it growing wild in Japan. "I literally stumbled over it when I was walking in the mountains in Nara Prefecture," he recalls, "and it's one of the finest flowering vines for shade there is."

While at Longwood, Barry also worked for Brookside Gardens, part of the Montgomery County Parks System, located in Wheaton, Maryland, near Bethesda. Barry worked part time recording their collections in the very early days of computers. It was a good time to work for Brookside Gardens, then led by Carl Hahn, who wanted to increase the plant diversity in the public park system by growing plants that were unavailable commercially.

Barry received his degree from Longwood in 1979 upon completing his thesis on Japanese *Asarum*. He is told that at the University of Delaware it is still the most requested student thesis in horticulture in the English language.

A lucky break then took Barry to Korea. Bill Thomas, who is now executive director of Chanticleer, the outstanding public garden in Wayne, Pennsylvania, knew Ferris Miller, the American who had created his own Chollipo Arboretum in Korea. Ferris Miller and his arboretum were important sources for many Americans in horticulture. Miller happened to be in the United States, and Bill Thomas arranged for Barry to meet him. A friend of Barry's had worked in Korea, and, although it wasn't Japan, Barry was excited about the possibility of going there even though he couldn't speak the language. However, he knew that Korean was structurally similar and at least in the same language family as Japanese, and he looked forward to the challenge of adding Korean to his language competency.

For the next two years, Barry worked at Chollipo Arboretum on Korea's west coast, living in a remote village without modern amenities. Despite his proficiency in Japanese, mastering the Korean language proved to be more difficult than he expected. Fortunately, he made friends with soldiers in the Korean Army, as well as older Koreans who spoke Japanese, a language they had learned during the Japanese occupation of Korea that began in the early 1900s and ended at the conclusion of World War II. These older Koreans could communicate with him in both languages.

While at Chollipo, Barry read a scholarly Japanese paper and became convinced that there were wild cold-hardy camellias unknown to Western science growing on the northern Korean islands. Always determined and resourceful when plants were concerned, Barry applied repeatedly to one government office after another for permission to visit the island, which was occupied by the military and closed to visitors. Despite continual refusals, he didn't give up and went to the nearby port to see if he could find any way onto the island. He came prepared, carrying a bottle of whiskey bought at the U.S. Army commissary. And once there, he saw "a sleazy strip of bars like any waterfront in the world" so, equipped with "some bottles of good Scotch whiskey, I went looking for the weak link." A sailor gladly accepted the bottles in exchange for getting Barry on a ferry headed for the island.

Once he was on the island, the guards thought he was crazy but harmless, so they accompanied him on his search. Then on the north side of a mountain, "there they were, twenty feet tall, their glossy leaves standing out against all that brown winter vegetation." Just as he had hoped. Huge camellias, magnificent and flourishing, grew there, even though he describes it as "very cold and bleak there, with these awful winds that come down from Mongolia." The seeds Barry collected led to the introduction of the hardier *Camellia japonica* species now grown in the West. Barry credits his success on this and his subsequent Korean collection trips to having his friend Yong June Chang with him.

After returning from Korea, Barry went to work for the U.S. National Arboretum as curator of Asian plants. While there, he developed a three-year strategic plan for trips to different parts of Korea when few others were traveling there to collect plants. He led the first two years of trips, spending at least three months each time. The legendary J. C. Raulston, along with Dr. Ted Dudley of the National Arboretum, joined Barry traveling through unexplored regions. During his repeated visits, Barry had become an important mentor to many younger Koreans, several of whom came to study in Longwood's graduate program or foreign student program. Many returned to work in Korea while others remained in the United States.

The wonderful plants Barry brought back from his plant-finding trips to Korea and elsewhere did not fare as he hoped. He was upset when plants were neglected and many failed to survive. But worse, he recalls with lingering frustration that "we introduced a lot of wonderful material, but the plants were not getting into commerce. The whole point was to see these plants growing in people's gardens." This refrain is so often repeated by many other plant finders who have brought back fine plants only to see them fail to be spread to the public, causing some of these plant finders, eventually including Barry, to open specialty nurseries as a remedy.

After working at the U.S. Arboretum for approximately four years, Barry was recruited by the University of Missouri to come as the first director of a new botanical garden being established on the western side of the state about thirty miles east of Kansas City, a counterbalance to the well-established Missouri Botanical Garden to the east in St. Louis. A wealthy family had given a large parcel of land and some funding to the university to create the new botanical garden, and Barry was offered full control of its development. Two years later, Powell Gardens separated from the university to become an independent charitable organization with many of the donor family members on the board. Clearly the intention was to sustain an impressive ornamental display garden, not a research institution. Barry bailed out.

Another opportunity beckoned. Barry received a call from Michael Bartlett, who had been part of the landscape crew Barry had supervised in his role as foreman at the university. Michael had become a landscape architect in the intervening years. His grandfather, Leonard J. Buck, had been a trustee of the New York Botanical Garden and in the 1930s had developed his own garden in New Jersey, a rich collection of alpine and woodland plants beautifully displayed in a naturalistic setting. After Buck's death in 1974, his wife gave the garden to Somerset County to be a public park, although subject to family control. Somerset County was looking for a director of horticulture for the entire county, and Michael wanted to be sure the position would go to one who would take proper care of the Buck Garden. He approached Barry and made him an offer with good pay, and Barry accepted a five-year contract that allowed his travels to Japan to continue during his vacations.

After fulfilling his five-year contract, Barry declined Somerset County's offer to renew. He was not well suited to navigating the complexities of New Jersey politics, but during his five years with Somerset, he had also been working as a part-time consultant to Hines Growers with the county's permission. He decided to leave New Jersey and work full time for Hines.

In 1993, Barry moved back to the family farm in Lewisberry, Pennsylvania, buying the seventy-three acres and buildings from his parents. Hines was interested in offering more sophisticated plants than the usual offerings from commercial nurseries, but they were based in California. Since Barry had just

Cypripedium japonicum in Barry's Pennsylvania garden

Hosta yingeri at Cholippo Arboretum, Korea

bought the family farm, moving west was not an option. But the management at Hines, also hoping to identify plants that would grow well on the East Coast and enhance their market there, were happy to have Barry remain in the east to do this. With his parents living in the house he had grown up in, he took over a large barn on the property, carefully retaining and restoring the best of the original beam structure while creating work and living space for himself. He also built a greenhouse, renting part of it to Hines, whose mandate was to grow and identify the best new plants. This was something he loved to do, and Hines also committed to help support his ongoing plant-finding trips. In addition to Korea and Japan, which he visited repeatedly, Barry has been on plant-finding trips to Taiwan, Singapore, Pakistan, Indonesia, India, South Africa, China, and Thailand.

Simultaneously, Barry started his own nursery and called it Asiatica. Like so many of his fellow plantsmen, Barry had been disappointed in his hopes and expectations that botanical gardens would somehow disseminate the many wonderful plants he and others had brought back. A specialty nursery seemed the best solution. Continually introducing new plants, Asiatica was part of the growth of small specialty nurseries intent on expanding plants used by American gardeners.

The first Asiatica catalog came out a year later in 1994. Andy Wong, who also worked for Hines and took care of the Hines plants growing at Barry's farm, became Barry's business partner. Andy is Chinese but grew up in Malaysia so between them, Barry says, "We had most of the Asian languages covered!" While Barry resumed his plant-finding trips several times each year, he also made frequent trips to meet with Hines in California. Andy kept the nursery going in his absence.

It is not easy to start a nursery, but Barry's association with Hines helped financially, and Asiatica grew and became known as a unique source for unusual plants, especially shade plants for the woodland. Shade plantings had been widely seen as limited to pachysandra and ivy. Asiatica countered that simplistic view with a long list of woodland treasures, such as Asian arisaemas, far more interesting than the native jack-in-the-pulpit, and also photteas, woodland plants unfamiliar to Western horticulture. Barry loves asarums, of course, from his Longwood Gardens days, but also hydrangeas, climbing vines (including Barry's famous find Schizophragma hydrangeoides 'Moonlight' and Aristolochia, sometimes called Dutchman's pipe), hostas, and even hardy orchids.

He is particularly proud that one of his Hosta species, found in Korea, has been named for him, Hosta yingeri. It has handsome thick, glossy foliage. He also introduced the golden foliaged woodland treasure Aralia cordata 'Sun King' that he discovered in Japan. As his interest expanded to tropical plants, he came to admire hoyas and many other more tender delights.

View of the Yinger farmhouse (left) in Lewisburg, Pennsylvania, and the farm in spring (right)

Things were progressing nicely until disaster struck in 2003. A fire totally destroyed Barry's home, wiping out his office and his extraordinary library. Although the insurance company treated him badly, he struggled to carry on, but found "expenses kept going up and sales kept going down." Propane prices, three times what they had been, badly impacted operating costs, and a plummeting dollar made his imports more expensive.

In 2005, soon after the fire, Barry's work for Hines also ceased. The company had been acquired by a venture capital firm that resulted in Hines declaring bankruptcy and ultimately ending up in reorganization. Ever resilient, Barry turned to doing some consulting for the Conard-Pyle Nursery, based in West Grove, Pennsylvania, and known for Star Roses. Eventually, Conard-Pyle was bought by Ball Horticultural Company, and Barry was no longer needed. The demand for unusual plants was on a downward trajectory and many other specialty nurseries went out of business. Finally, Barry couldn't continue to subsidize his nursery. Sadly for its devoted fans, Asiatica closed in 2010.

The fire also caused Barry to give up his dream of writing a book on asarums, based on his earlier thesis, but he carried on with his developing passion for tropical plants. Despite only a modest competence in the Thai language, he opened a small nursery in Thailand. But management long distance proved to be just as difficult as running Asiatica, and he transferred his interest in that nursery to his partner in Thailand.

He went on to lead a strategic planning process for the Henry Foundation for Botanical Research, located in Gladwyne, Pennsylvania. The Henry Foundation garden dates back to 1948, and the board decided it was time to move the garden to a higher level and retained Barry to advise them.

In November 2016, Barry finally sold his farm in Pennsylvania to a neighbor and returned to Thailand, where he will be spending much of his time. He has re-engaged with his partner and their nursery there and will be working hard to expand and strengthen it. So there is more news to come. He also plans to continue to take consulting projects from time to time.

Barry is glad that Tony Avent's Plant Delights Nursery, a specialty nursery Barry particularly admires, carries on. However, he knows that Tony will close the mail-order nursery as soon as there have been sufficient donations to support the related Juniper Level Botanic Garden. Barry thinks that it is the best botanical garden in the United States. Not only does it have an extraordinary plant collection, but he appreciates the fact that Tony not only knows each and every one of them, but employs someone full time to correctly identify and document the growing database. Many of the plants at Juniper Level have never been grown in the United States before and some are not grown anywhere else. Barry sees Tony Avent as the most important person in contemporary horticulture. In turn, Tony deeply respects Barry for his depth of knowledge and for their shared passion for properly identifying and disseminating great plants.

Barry maintains his interest in the plants he featured and grew at Asiatica Nursery. His Thai experience has expanded his interest in tropical plants, beyond the many hardy, unusual woodland plants he loved and offered through Asiatica. Even though he has introduced many popular Gold Medal winners over the years, including his beautiful *Schizophragma hydrangeoides* 'Moonlight,' he continues to appreciate plants with less popular appeal. From the *koten engei* tradition of Japan, Barry still "loves the unloved. I tend to be most fond of those plants that don't get much respect in the greater world of horticulture."

Barry Yinger

GARDEN CREATORS

Parterre at Hollister House in spring

George Schoellkopf

I love formal structure; it is so liberating. The plants
can be freer and don't have to do it all by themselves.

THE GARDENS George Schoellkopf has created at Hollister House in Washington, Connecticut, may have been inspired by the great English garden at Sissinghurst, but they are definitely his original and very American creation. When George first saw Sissinghurt, he recalls, "I immediately wanted a garden just like it! I didn't have a castle but I did have an eighteenth-century house, an ancient structure around which to create a garden." An imposing brick wall was an early and major project, patterned on the ones at Sissinghurst. George favors geometric lines and formal structures, but within those crisply outlined spaces he lets his plants rip! There is an artist's eye at work, enhanced by a collector's zeal for the rare and unusual. Best of all, George has decided to give his garden to the public so that it will be preserved to enchant and inspire all who are lucky enough to visit.

Coming from a prominent Texas family, George never anticipated that he would settle in New England. He was born in Dallas to J. Fred Schoellkopf Jr. and his wife, Anne Craddock, both of whom were natives of that city. Both of George's parents had been sent "back east" to prominent boarding schools as teenagers, his father to Hotchkiss in Connecticut and then to college at Princeton, his mother to the Baldwin School in Bryn Mawr, Pennsylvania, and then to the Finch School in Manhattan. They both returned to Dallas to live. After only two years at Princeton, his father went into the family business that had originally sold saddles but had turned to selling wholesale appliances; he eventually abandoned that business and proved to be a very astute investor.

George was the baby of the family. Arriving in 1942, eleven years after his older brother and nine years after his sister, he began to garden as a small child in the very hostile Texas climate, following his mother's example. She tried to grow phlox in Dallas! It was an impossible challenge, for the Texas climate is far too hot to grow northern plants and much too cold for semitropicals. Evergreens and azaleas proved a better bet, but his mother was always willing to experiment. George recalls choosing his first plant order as a very young boy. He selected *Lilium speciosum,* despite his mother's warning that the plant wouldn't survive. In fact he managed to get two of the bulbs to bloom, although the others failed, and the foliage of the two survivors quickly burned out. Although no one else was impressed with the lilies, George was thrilled! His first garden triumph.

Following his father's example, George went east to attend boarding school at Hotchkiss, where he fell in love with the beauty of New England, especially the glorious fall colors. Instead of Princeton, he attended Yale. It was the tumultuous sixties, and George became a participant in the civil rights movement.

Although he was a product of the sixties and engaged in political protests with only modest success, his desire to serve a worthy cause remained, and while at Yale, he converted to Catholicism. During college breaks, he volunteered to work in Church programs in Mexico and other venues. The High Church service spoke to George – he loved its ceremony and beauty. Catholics were just beginning to adopt the Protestant custom of singing hymns during services, and George decided to step in to help move the idea along. Since there had never been a tradition of hymn singing, there were no Catholic hymnals

Hollister House and barn complex viewed from across the stream looking west

readily available, so enterprising George went out and found some old Anglican hymnals for fifty cents apiece which the Yale chaplain agreed to purchase. Ultimately, a furious bishop banned any further use of Protestant hymnals, but George still takes perverse delight in remembering the congregation loudly belting out Luther's "A Mighty Fortress Is Our God" when the bishop arrived.

Passionate about anything he undertakes, after graduating from Yale in 1965 with a degree in medieval art history, George decided to become a monk and joined a Benedictine monastery in St. Louis. Benedictine rules require a novice to be trained in an abbey, but the St. Louis monks were only a priory; they had not yet qualified as an independent abbey. Therefore, even though George would have liked to stay in St. Louis, they sent him to an abbey in Yorkshire in the United Kingdom to be properly trained. Although he still admires the monks, it took only three months for George to realize he wasn't really well suited for that life. He now believes he made his decision based on his feelings about being gay when he thought it would be best to choose a celibate life.

After returning to Yale as a Special Student, George eventually went on to Columbia University, where he earned his master's in medieval art history. Living in New York, he decided to start an antiques shop. A friend of his had just closed her shop, so he bought all her stock and opened his store in Greenwich Village, offering American antiques. Within three years, he had built this into a sufficiently serious business to justify moving uptown to more upscale quarters on Madison Avenue and 81st Street. On weekends, he went hunting for antiques in his Volkswagen bus, searching throughout Pennsylvania and New England.

The Cutting Garden

On one of these forays, he found and soon bought a house in Massachu-setts, the perfect location for his antiquing and a lovely place to spend the sum-mer. The house came with a garden, including a wonderful lawn made up entirely of violets, so he began to garden a bit. He loved the look of that violet lawn and has since tried repeatedly – and unsuccessfully – to replicate it.

Around the same time, George went to visit his friend Gregory Long at his country house and admired Gregory's garden. Gregory gave him what proved to be a momentous book about Vita Sackville-West and her husband, Harold Nicolson, and the famous English garden they created in the 1930s at Sissinghurst Castle in Kent. That book prompted George's first visit to Sissing-hurst that same summer. In Britain he also saw and admired Hidcote, the gar-den created by the American Lawrence Johnston in the English Cotswolds that had influenced Sissinghurst, as well as Christopher Lloyd's oustanding garden nearby at Great Dixter. But it was Sissinghurst that spoke to George. He loved its formal structure, its high hedges and brick walls creating separate garden rooms, one room leading into another, all with glorious plantings and special color themes and situated around a tall Elizabethan tower. He knew he would have to create something like it.

Not too long after his trip to England, George's aunt Celie (Lucille) died, leaving him the then handsome sum of $150,000. In 1978, he used that bequest to buy Hollister House, an eighteenth-century farmhouse with twen-ty-five acres on Nettleton Hollow Road in Washington, Connecticut. The house itself is an American antique, originally the homestead of Gideon Hollister, among the town's prominent early settlers. Situated not far off the main road on the side of a steeply sloping hill that ran down to a stream below with no signs of any garden in sight and no flat ground to create one, it seemed an unlikely site for George to create an ambitious vision of an English garden.

Fortunately, George had some expert horticultural friends. He had just met Ron Johnson, who was to become his partner for the next fourteen years. Ron had studied horticulture at Cornell with Hitch Lyman. Hitch claimed he had flunked a course because he liked to design with right angles when the politically correct approach at the time was to insist on more naturalistic curves. No straight lines allowed. Both Ron and Hitch knew a great deal about plants and garden design. Hitch now manages his own garden in the Finger Lakes region of New York, as well as his Temple Nursery, specializing in countless varieties of snowdrops.

Despite the challenges of restoring the house and trying to plan and site a garden, George was thrilled with his new home. He recalls hosting his first cocktail party as an early housewarming. One particular grande dame from the neighborhood came and pronounced, "You bought the thermal sieve!" Although

The reflecting pool within yew hedges

tactless, she was right. George learned the house lacked any insulation; interior heating quickly escaped through the loosely fitted clapboard siding. When George later created a small garden in an L-shaped nook right outside the walls of the house, he dubbed it the "furnace garden" since it was so effectively warmed by the furnace through the exterior walls. There he could grow semi-tropical plants despite the frigid New England winters.

With his vision of Sissinghurst firmly in place, he was determined to establish a formal English garden that would also relate to the house, with proper brick walls and yew hedges providing the structure and enclosing his own garden rooms. Ron wisely suggested that they first try to level the steep hillside by creating a series of terraces, but George rejected that idea in favor of more dramatic changes.

When George first arrived in Nettleton Hollow, it was just eight years after my husband and I bought our own wreck of another pre-Revolutionary farmhouse just two miles north on the same road. We had never gardened before and found our house surrounded by overgrown fields reverting to woods. Those first years were what I call our era of the "Clearances." Eventually, as we worked to clear the land, my husband introduced me to vegetable gardening, and it wasn't long before my rows of vegetables began to yield to flowers. How lucky to have George arrive to become my gardening role model and treasured friend.

Unlike my own timid initial efforts, George had the big picture in mind from the start. I watched in amazement as major earthworks began changing the landscape at Hollister House – an entire hillside was excavated to create level planting areas, a small bow to Ron's terracing idea. Major steel beams with enormous cement anchors were driven into the excavated hillside to provide support for what became the elegant brick wall George envisioned.

Those invisible steel underpinnings could have probably supported something as major as the George Washington Bridge. But without them, any brick wall in the harsh New England climate would soon crumble and collapse from the severe winter frost heaves. As proof, just consider the ancient stone walls snaking through the Connecticut woods, and you realize what frost can do to stone, let alone more delicate and water-absorbent brick.

Much of the wall is a retaining wall, holding back the excavated hillside. On the flat ground on top, George planted a formal parterre garden, with low clipped boxwood hedges creating geometric shapes, filled with white and gray plants – shades of Sissinghurst's famous white garden, but uniquely George's style.

At right angles to the retaining wall is another freestanding brick wall, with an arch leading into another part of the garden beyond. From the parterre garden looking down to the base of the brick walls below, there is a lovely twenty-eight-foot-long reflecting pool with subtle gurgling sounds emanating from its small fountain. The right angles of the brick wall on two sides and tall yew hedges frame the space and its thickly planted herbaceous borders.

The brick wall is anchored more than eight feet deep belowground and sits on a platform of a six-foot-wide cement slab. Reinforced concrete inside the wall further strengthens it. The side of the wall that appears freestanding is independent of its interior support; the bricks enclose air space on either side of the reinforced concrete so any water that manages to sneak in and freeze won't push the bricks out.

As an art historian, George understands perspective and tricking the eye. To make what might otherwise appear to be a very thick, heavy brick wall look thinner, he designed a feathered edge around the arch, making it much narrower than the rest of the wall. When the visitor passes through the narrow area of the arch it initially seems that the entire wall is that width, but it is only an illusion. It appears an elegant slim creation rather than the heavily engineered structure that it had to be. It has withstood the test of time. Now, more than twenty-five years later, the wall stands straight and firm, providing a dramatic backdrop at the heart of the gardens.

When the brick walls were installed, George was away, unable to supervise the construction. On his return, he was dismayed to discover the two walls had been built at an acute angle, rather than at a true ninety degrees. That made it difficult to have the interior reflecting pool actually line up with the walls. Thanks to George's skill and the lush plantings, one would never notice anything askew. But George acknowledges, "If seen from the air, every bit of the garden is really crooked!"

George's early focus for his garden was on the design of strong structures to support the plantings. The brick walls were only the beginning. He soon developed a love of stone, especially the heavy stones once used as curbstones in nearby Hartford. He cornered that market, adding strong stone steps linking areas of the garden. "Walls, rooms, hedges, divisions, and paths that meet at right angles. Straight lines. The whole impact of this garden is its tightly formal framework, across which you see the landscape. You look out from the man-made into nature, and then back again. Your eye is always drawn on. It's the transition from one space to the next that I find exciting," he says.

He also wanted the garden to relate well to the house while not being too obvious. "The house is the star of the garden – the entire garden was planted to accompany it. There is never a straight-on view of the house – you always see it from an angle."

When George first began, he didn't know anything about plants, but that has certainly changed over time. He laughingly recalls, "I killed a lot of plants!" His hearty chuckle is infectious as he goes on to remember weeding in Gregory Long's garden and mistakenly ripping out rare treasures. While he had firm ideas about design and structure, he was happy to have Hitch and Ron contribute their expertise about the challenge of gardening in the Northeast. Hitch was a big help with the early plantings and with his eye for what was interesting. As they waited for the perennial plantings to mature, growing larger in size and impact, they put in great temporary fillers, like the annual white cleomes – adding instant showy interest.

Now mature, the borders are profuse and exuberant. The strong structure supports an amazing array of plants, ordinary and rare, hardy and tender, all constantly edited and improved by George's artistry. He claims, "I'm very big on having tightly packed, very planned, very structured, condensed plantings that I try to keep looking good all year long."

George generously credits many others for helping him in his beginnings, for encouraging and appreciating what he was trying to do. In the nearby town of Southbury, Wesley Rouse quickly became what George calls his "first

The Rill Garden

gardening friend," his first "big connection." A professional landscape designer with a background in plant science, Wes Rouse taught extension courses for many years and supervised both his own wonderful gardens and his firm, Pine Meadow Gardens, Inc., which provided landscaping design and services to a wide range of sophisticated clients.

George thinks it was Wes who invited a group from the Perennial Plant Association to visit George's garden. During that visit, George first met Pierre Bennerup, who became and remains a valued source of the best, newest, and most interesting perennials, through his Sunny Border Nurseries in nearby Kensington. The fact that this group and Pierre were enthusiastic was validating, what George calls "a big shot in the arm – that they liked the garden."

Wave Hill was also an important influence. Marco Polo Stufano and John Nally arrived at Hollister House early on to offer important advice. They were a major force in introducing perennials not yet in common use in the United States, generating tremendous excitement as they brought back and made known wonderful plants from England.

By the late 1980s, the Hollister House gardens were well established although George continued to expand and plant new areas. Rosemary Verey had already written a book called *The American Woman's Garden* and had begun to work on *The American Man's Garden*. An American woman, Ellen Samuels, volunteered to help identify gardens to feature in the book and was looking for candidates. She happened to be visiting me in Connecticut, and I arranged to have her visit George's garden. She had expressed some doubts, but when she saw the garden, she quickly realized it had to be included, and after publication it was recognized as one of the book's stars.

George and his garden continued to grow up together, and then he turned fifty years old in 1992. That is often a sobering moment in anyone's life and can be an important turning point. Having earlier parted ways with Ron Johnson, George was fortunate to meet Gerald Incandela, an accomplished and recognized photographer of visually compelling and beautiful works of art, with work included in many museum collections. Although Gerald was not a gardener, his visual talent and sense of composition quickly became an important asset. George and Gerald married in 2015.

Then California beckoned. George's mother and father began to go to the San Ysidro Ranch before it became a fancy place. They also spent time in Jamaica, but his father had a friend from boarding school in Santa Barbara, so they bought the lease of a small cottage at a local country club. George went to visit one winter while he was participating in an antiques show in Los Angeles. He hadn't realized how pleasant the winters could be in California. Not long after, he bought his first house there. His father liked it. His strong-minded

View from the parterre down through the yew hedge

mother, having been forewarned by George that the house was not beautiful, refused to comment, except to declare, "Well, you said the house was ugly!"

Some years later, after enjoying the escape from the cold winters in Connecticut, George sold that house and bought an amazing parcel of land high up in the hills of Montecito with spectacular views out to the Pacific Ocean. It was a lucky find, for the bank had just foreclosed on it. George and Gerald, delighted to get it, built a wonderful house there along with a magnificent barn that Gerald designed for their horses. Naturally, George has planted an extensive garden and spends most of his winters there. He says, "It helps me to avoid having competitive feelings about English gardens and the things they can grow there and we can't in Connecticut."

One example of a plant he relishes is his ten-foot-tall *Plumeria*, a fragrant tropical native of Central and South America sometimes called frangipani. It is doubtful whether even the English can grow *Plumeria*! It is in full and glorious bloom for George in California, as are other strange and wonderful rarities in his Santa Barbara garden. The site, high on a hill, helps keep the garden even warmer than land at lower elevations. One winter morning, George awoke to an unusual frost, finding the water completely frozen in an outside trough. He was terrified all his plants would die! None were hurt in the least bit thanks to the higher microclimate.

Hollister House remains George's principal passion. He began to write a gardening column for a local newspaper, the *Newtown Bee*. Although a regular newspaper, it features a locally read and respected weekly antiques section that is a free handout. The owner, Scudder Smith, was, like George, in the antiques business himself so they were acquainted. Invited to write a column, George continued for more than four years. People loved it because he wrote with both a deep knowledge of plants and in a chatty, personal, and accessible style. He is now writing a book about gardens, plants, and garden history, especially the American fascination with English gardens and garden history that have had such a profound influence on himself and others.

George Schoellkopf

While George is not in the business of garden design, he has occasionally agreed to advise special friends. He worked with Susan Burke, a fortunate beneficiary and a member of the board of the Garden Conservancy, on the design of her Nantucket garden that is often open to the public during the Garden Conservancy Open Days. George is particularly pleased with the ha-ha there, an element taken from the English, and intended to create a recessed, vertical barrier to prevent access to the garden by livestock or other animals in the fields. A trench is created and at the bottom a fence or retaining wall is built. Looking out from a distance, the trench is invisible, creating the illusion of a seamless, uninterrupted landscape. It is thought that the name ha-ha originated when an early walker suddenly came upon the trench, eliciting the exclamation "ah ha!" In Susan Burke's case, the ha-ha links the view from the house to the sea beyond.

George loves his garden and is delighted it will be preserved for the public after he is gone. Thanks to the Garden Conservancy taking it on as one of its projects, Hollister House Garden is now an incorporated charitable organization with its own board. George has been transferring fractional interests to it and will continue to do so in his lifetime and through his will. He has also committed to providing an endowment, although additional public support will always be important.

Hollister House is open to the public on Fridays and Saturdays as well as by appointment. It organizes an annual seminar weekend with prominent speakers, participating plant vendors, and social gatherings that attract hundreds of people from near and far. George has recently rebuilt a major barn complex to host future public events. These will include workshops, lectures, and other educational programs. He also continues to expand and improve the gardens for increased public use. Throughout the growing season, there are other special events in the garden. Nothing could be more magical than to sit in that glorious verdant place in the warmth of the setting summer sun, a glass of wine in hand with the transporting sound of performing musicians wafting on the air.

The Garden Conservancy chose wisely in naming Hollister House as one of the exceptional American gardens worthy of becoming one of its preservation projects. George's design blends some of the best of the great English gardening traditions with his uniquely American style. The gardens will continue to inspire those who come to visit and there are already in place important educational programs to teach the skills needed for aspiring gardeners.

George continues to be the head gardener at Hollister House, constantly editing plantings and modifying the structure to improve movement through the garden rooms. He feels content with what he has created: "a permanent framework in which all kinds of things can happen. The structure is here to work with for those who will follow me."

Hollister House in fall

Peckerwood: The drama of the dry garden with blue wall

John G. Fairey

Painting came to seem so limiting. The garden was three-dimensional.

OHN GASTON FAIREY's artistry has been channeled into the creation of his garden masterpiece, Peckerwood. Located near Hempstead, Texas, Peckerwood is about halfway between Houston and College Station, where John came to teach design to the "Aggies" of Texas A&M University in the early 1960s. Originally a painter, he was in his colorist-minimalist phase when he moved to Texas from the East Coast and eventually began his garden. He recalls, "Painting came to seem so limiting. The garden was three-dimensional." Imagine a silvery blue sphere of spikes atop a tall plinth – no, not a modern sculpture (although there are many in the garden), but a dasylirion, one of the many astonishing rare plants John has brought back from his plant-finding trips to Mexico and brilliantly placed in the garden. Peckerwood, named for the Georgia plantation in *Auntie Mame* as well as its many woodpeckers, has been open to the public since 1988 and will carry on as the Peckerwood Garden Conservation Foundation for the benefit of future generations.

It is hard to adequately describe a visit to Peckerwood. The different areas of the garden all relate to the house, a precept John strongly endorses. Near the house forceful, strong shapes of the dasylirions, agaves, and yuccas he has collected are enhanced by striking sculptures created by artist friends as well as by a gallery displaying his collection of Mexican folk art. Architectural features add stong impact, such as the cobalt blue wall that sets off one area of the dry garden much as a frame sets off a painting. Farther away from the house paths meander through more informal woodland conditions that include the many unusual trees, shrubs, and groundcovers John has planted over the years, among them a rare *Styrax* he spotted on his first plant-finding trip to Mexico. John terms these special experiences "garden events." Although John no longer paints on canvas, his painterly sensibilities are evident everywhere in this, his lasting masterpiece.

John was born in South Carolina, and his soft, mellifluous voice and gentlemanly manner still reveal his Southern roots. He grew up on a farm, but like many farmers' sons, he hated the garden chores, especially when the weather was hot and humid: "All I wanted to do was be in the nearby pool." He was born November 17, 1930, in St. Matthews, a small town in the middle of the state's hill country, arriving after an eight-year gap between him and his three older brothers. His father, Philip Fairey, had a chain of Chevrolet-Oldsmobile car dealerships; he made a decent living, supplemented by the work of John's mother on their farm. She grew cash crops, such as cotton, corn, wheat, and pecans, and raised pigs and chickens, and with her husband they earned enough to put all four sons through college and send two of them through medical school. John's grandparents lived there too, and both were medical doctors.

The family had a cottage on the coast where they spent summers. On these trips, one of John's favorite pastimes was to spot and identify wildflowers, with his parents and brothers all participating enthusiastically. His parents also liked to take guests to visit Brookgreen Gardens near Murrells Inlet and close to their coastal cottage. John usually went too, and he remembers, "It had a big impact on me." Created by Archer and Anna Hyatt Huntington, Brookgreen Gardens combined what had been four separate rice plantations to be their winter home in 1929. Anna Hyatt Huntington decided it was the perfect site to show off her sculpture, and indeed it became the first public sculpture garden in America, featuring more than 1,445 works by Anna and others scattered over nine thousand acres.

Although John didn't enjoy anything pertaining to gardening as a young boy, he did enjoy the company of his great-uncle and -aunt, who lived just sixteen miles from the family farm. Uncle Jake Fairey and Aunt Kitty were passionate about camellias and had a great collection. John would tag along with them on their plant-finding excursions, visiting local nurseries and specialty growers where they hunted for special camellias. These early forays helped train John's eye to spot the unusual, a talent he used to great advantage later on his own plant-finding expeditions.

John began high school in St. Matthews but finished by boarding at Episcopal High School in Alexandria, Virginia. Before he went off to boarding school, John's mother, concerned about his isolated life on the farm and realizing all his older brothers moving out had left John without any young company, enrolled him in after-school art classes at South Carolina University. He loved them. He went on to attend Erskine College, in Due West, South Carolina, about a two-hour drive northwest of St. Matthews. Erskine, a small private

Christian college, offered undergraduate liberal arts and a graduate theological seminary.

As a young man, John wanted to become an architect but his parents discouraged him, convinced he lacked sufficient proficiency in mathematics. Instead, he majored in history, minored in business, and continued to study art. After graduating from Erskine in 1952, during the Korean War, he was drafted into the army, where he spent two years as a corporal as the war wound down.

After the army, John pursued his interest in art, heading to Philadelphia to study first at the Academy of Fine Arts, and then at the University of Pennsylvania, where he was awarded a scholarship. He spent a year studying in Europe, but, having no particular interest in gardens, he failed to visit any while there. He spent most of his time in Italy looking at art.

While in graduate school, John had a very formative experience working collaboratively with people from many disciplines. He and urban planners, architects, landscape architects, other painters, and sculptors mounted a special exhibition connecting all the arts to the discipline of city planning.

John continued his studies but was barely self-supporting. His parents subsidized him as he worked at various odd jobs, teaching painting to local ladies and working with institutionalized mental patients among other things. He earned his master's in fine arts in 1964. That degree "was a good thing since it got me my first – and only – job."

One of the participants in that formative special exhibit had been a student at Texas A&M University, and he suggested that John might find a job there, teaching design. Following up, John wrote the dean and sent some pictures of his artwork that had been in the exhibit. Initially, he was told he should try again the next year, but serendipitously, a position opened up at the last minute, and John accepted the job over the phone without an interview. He had no idea what he was getting into.

Texas A&M University, or TAMU, was the first public institution of higher education in the state; it was formed in 1871 pursuant to the Morrill Act as one of the land-grant colleges, and originally named the Agricultural and Mechanical College of Texas. It admitted only white males and required every student to participate in military training. By the time John arrived, the college had changed its name to Texas A&M University, the letters a symbolic link to its history. During John's first years there, it began to accept African Americans and eventually even women. It also made participation in the Corps of Cadets voluntary, although it still boasts of having the largest uniformed body outside of the country's national military academies. With more than 59,000 students, or "Aggies" as they like to be called, and filling 5,200 acres on the College Station campus, it is among the largest universities in America.

When John first arrived, he must have seemed quite the alien and in turn, he found TAMU "a culture shock." He laughingly admits, "In fact, it still is." He thought he would teach there for one year and then move on, but they asked him to stay for another year and then another; he stayed for just shy of fifty years, leaving in 2013. His teaching career was very successful. Highly regarded, he finished at TAMU as a Regents Professor, a title that honors outstanding work, especially international work, which in John's case took place in Mexico.

It was instantly clear that College Station, where TAMU is located, was no place for John to live. He was a foreigner come to teach design to the all-white male cadets of TAMU. At first, he found an apartment there, but he soon wanted to put some distance between his work and where he lived. John observed that College Station "was not a good place for single people, men or women," and particularly not good for an artist among all those military men. The first six months were made bearable by his weekend escape to a studio he found in Houston, ninety miles away. Thanks to a sympathetic dean, who liked him and gave him a lot of leeway, John soon received permission to live off campus, and in 1965, he moved to Houston.

In 1971, after six years of his grueling commute between Houston and his three-hour studio sessions, John bought property in Hempstead, and that was the beginning of Peckerwood. Located about halfway between College Station and Houston, it wasn't much, only seven acres and a "falling-down house" abandoned by the prior owners and covered in vines and thorns. There were also a few small outbuildings and some bits of fencing. There were no trees in the front of the property but there were some huge ones behind. Erosion had done major damage to the land. Mostly, the property consisted of overgrown pastures and scrubby woods with a small creek rambling among oaks and cypress. For John, "The site with its clear, spring-fed brook reminded me of magical places in South Carolina where I grew up. What began innocently, as a pursuit of a sense of place, fast evolved into a passion." Renting nearby, he began the slow, arduous process of designing, rebuilding, and renovating the original house.

His first initiative was to work on the land and to plant. The garden came about almost by accident when his mother sent him a box of *Lycoris* bulbs she had dug up in her garden in South Carolina, carefully separated, packaged, and mailed to John. She told him that he must plant them out, so he did. It was August and very hot, bringing back memories of why he had never liked working in gardens in the first place. But it was a beginning. By now, sadly, all those original bulbs are gone, shaded out by other plants, but other *Lycoris* continue to thrive elsewhere, a reminder of the beginning.

Peckerwood: Woodland walk with collection of oaks

In addition to his mother's *Lycoris,* John's first planting efforts looked as if he were trying to replicate the gardens of South Carolina. He planted azaleas, camellias, and magnolias, but most died, unhappy in the Texas heat and drought. Eventually, he learned that some could survive if protected by dappled shade. He concluded that "people who don't do anything don't make mistakes, and they don't get criticized. Criticism is an honor."

Two years later, John was able to move into the renovated house. He later built an addition. Several years after that, he demolished the old house, used the addition as gallery space for his Mexican folk art collection, and built a new house, attaching it to the gallery by a handsome porch.

Soon after he began planting, John stopped painting. He had been in his minimalist phase, creating two-dimensional color studies, but the lure of creating three-dimensional art using plants with strong shapes and textures proved irresistible. He began to scour local nurseries, and other people who shared his enthusiasm gave him plants. The garden became his art medium.

The garden was all about light and shade – "the light in the summer is very white. It glitters like Impressionist paintings" – foliage and bark, rock and water, shape, color, and texture. John used to tell his students, "Light is a free commodity and should be used all the time."

When asked to indicate the best time to visit the garden, John replies, "It's all about space. This garden is not about bright colors. I tell people when they ask 'When are things going to be in bloom?' to go to Walmart!" Instead of focusing on colorful blooms, John wants the visitor to experience the garden "as an aesthetic experience involving all the senses. You are forced in this garden to touch and feel and smell, whether you want to or not."

Just as the garden was coming into its own, disaster struck. In 1983, a tornado ripped through the property, demolishing nearly all the trees. Many of John's students came to help and pitch in with the cleanup of the felled trees, a process that would require five years. Carl Schoenfeld, the roommate of one of John's students, came along. Carl became so engaged in the project that he stayed to buy land next door, and, with financing from his father and John as his partner, he started the nursery Yucca Do in 1987 to share the promising new plants they were discovering and selecting. John recalls that the idea for a nursery first began with Carl growing seeds in a plastic hoop house in Peckerwood's driveway.

What had been a major calamity also proved an opportunity. John had to address the newly blank canvas surrounding the house. Where once a huge live oak had stood providing shade there was now earth exposed to dry, searing heat. That led to the creation of John's dramatic dry garden with its stunning combinations of palms, yuccas, dasylirions, and agaves. As he restored the garden, John sought new plant material from many sources. He began his plant-finding trips; the first was to New Zealand with Carl for six weeks. They visited many impressive gardens there and admired the extraordinary range of plant diversity that thrives in that benign climate. John was profoundly influenced by the many gardens he saw in New Zealand, especially by the textures and drama of the plants. His countless plant expeditions to Mexico began after New Zealand.

Lynn Lowrey owned a local nursery and had been going to Mexico to collect plants for more than thirty years. Among Lowrey's many credentials was a botanizing expedition he led for the great British plantsman Sir Harold Hillier of Hillier Nurseries. They collected Mexican oaks, many of which continue to grow in Great Britain in what has now become the Sir Harold Hillier Gardens. Carrying on the tradition of Lynn Lowrey's trip with Hillier, John also sent seed of Mexican oaks to Hillier Nurseries for many years.

John became a frequent customer of Lynn Lowrey's nursery, buying plants for Peckerwood, but he says, "Lynn gave me more plants than I bought. It was almost embarrassing." He thought Lynn was "very knowledgeable and very humble." Lynn, for his part, clearly recognized a fellow spirit and invited John and Carl to join him on his next botanizing trip to Mexico.

On that first trip in 1988, the group consisted of Lynn, John, Carl, and one other botanist, Charles Peterson. They drove to Laredo in the desert and then on to Monterrey and up into the Sierra Madre. John quickly put his old plant-spotting abilities from his childhood camellia forays with his great-aunt and -uncle to good use when he noted an unusual *Styrax* from the moving car. When John first saw that tree, he didn't even know it was a *Styrax,* but he knew it was different, that it didn't fit in with the plants around it. John went back to the same tree the following August to collect seed, which he sent on to the renowned J. C. Raulston in North Carolina to grow and identify. It proved to be not *Styrax youngiae* as originally thought, but the far rarer *Styrax platanifolius* var. *mollis.* An offspring still grows at Peckerwood.

That trip to Mexico was just the first of more than eighty subsequent plant-finding trips. On many of these later expeditions, Eduardo Estrada, a young Mexican botanist from the School of Forestry at the Autonomous University of Nuevo Léon at Linares, accompanied them. Often Eduardo took more than 150 herbarium pressings on these trips that greatly helped identify many of their new and unusual finds.

John credits Lynn Lowrey with teaching him everything about these expeditions – how to get permits, how to clean seeds, how to name plants, how to get them into the United States legally. All the trips were arduous, the work continuing for long hours, often carrying on into the dark. Lunch rarely occurred before 4:00 P.M. with only a brief interlude for eating. They rarely camped in tents, finding them too hard to dismantle and dry out. Besides, the seeds collected needed a dry floor on which to be spread out and turned over several times to dry. Lynn never liked camping out anyway – wise man. In later years, John and Carl rarely camped out; most of the places they traveled had become too dangerous.

Instead of tents, they found "fleabag motels," and over time learned which motels were relatively clean, safe, and not too risky for their food. The trips usually lasted from one to three weeks. On the go all day long and cleaning seeds most of the night, John and his traveling companions were pretty oblivious to where they slept anyway. At the end of most trips, the group often rewarded themselves with a stay at a favored lovely hacienda.

John particularly liked that these trips were not competitive. Everyone in the group shared what they collected. John describes the effort as "collaborative," a word he likes, and one that recalls his early work on the special art exhibit in Philadelphia.

The group members were also extraordinarily resourceful. On one trip when they could find no fallen seed because the squirrels or the birds had gotten it all, they collected the scat instead: "It germinated on the way home in plastic bags!"

"When you are collecting, your adrenaline goes sky-high," says John. In fact, his own once spiked a bit too high – he suffered a heart attack during a collecting trip, and despite having to stay in a Mexican hospital, he insisted the others (including Tony Avent) press ahead without him. And they did, leaving him behind as they carried on their obsessive hunt for great plants.

One plant-finding trip was focused on medical research rather than garden plants. In 1991, John and Carl led a Harvard University group looking for a rare form of yew native to Mexico (*Taxus globosa*). The scientists hoped that paclitaxel, a compound that could be extracted from this particular species of yew, would prove effective in the treatment of cancer, especially ovarian cancer. Research continues using drugs such as Taxol, derived from paclitaxel, to destroy cancer cells.

On every trip, John has always kept a handwritten journal, a precise record of everything he collects, each item assigned its own number. Computers were not in wide use when John first started collecting. Not overly fond of digital electronics, he points out that in Mexico's mountainous terrain, satellite navigation doesn't generally work well anyway. Instead, he made do with an altimeter and the mileage gauge on his car, along with basic road maps, to record where the seed was collected. By now high tech seems to have prevailed at Peckerwood, as the entire collection is being systematically cataloged by computer.

A wide variety of plant material can be found in the parts of Mexico that John explores because growing conditions are excellent. In the mountains, the

Peckerwood: Plants as sculpture

JOHN G. FAIREY ✱ 253

climate is cooler, particularly at night, but there are often much warmer temperatures during the day. Plants that grow on the south-facing side of the mountains are completely different from those that grow on the sides facing north, east, or west. Just outside of Monterrey, a road runs through a valley between mountains, with one side of the road dry and the other wet. Each side of the valley supports very different plant life. The dry side supports wonderful forms of cactus.

John doesn't collect cactus, though. They don't grow at Peckerwood and collecting cactus is prohibited by the CITES treaty (the Convention on International Trade in Endangered Species of Wild Fauna and Flora) that seeks to protect wild plants and animals from exploitation and extinction. Instead, John focuses on dry-loving dasylirions, yuccas, beschornerias, palms, and agaves, strong bold plants that add so much to the sculptural quality of Peckerwood. He also continues his early interest in oaks, with 170 of the total 250 known species of oaks represented. When John first began his plant-finding trips, he collected trees and shrubs while others focused on tiny treasures, but he has branched out, collecting a broader range of plant material, choosing selectively and looking for plants with good potential for his garden.

John always subjects any plant he collects to at least three trials and, if a rare plant, four or five before using it in the garden or sharing it with others. "Vital to our mission is a trial garden for plants from areas that share similarly demanding conditions." This effort clearly requires patience. When a tree grown from the seed of one particular magnolia took nineteen years to flower, John quietly observed, "Creating significant beauty takes time, but it was well worth the wait." But like any gardener, John knows that "gardening is about discovery. It's the act of doing and making, not the end product, that's important."

Encompassing three different growing regions, namely Piney Woods, Coastal Plains, and Post Oak Savannah, Peckerwood sustains a wide diversity of plant life that thrives in different parts of the garden. It is almost like a horticultural laboratory, with areas of moisture, drought, heat, and cold as well as shade and baking sun. Over the years, the original seven acres have grown to close to forty and Peckerwood now contains several thousand different plant species.

John and Carl created a seed bank that evolved into an extensive exchange program, sending seed to many other important institutions, including the Arnold Arboretum in Massachusetts, the J. C. Raulston Arboretum in Raleigh, the University of California at Berkeley and at Santa Cruz, the Chollipo Arboretum in Korea, and the Royal Botanic Gardens at Kew in England.

Years ago, John began to worry about what would happen to his garden. If anything happened to him, he feared the "garden would fall apart." In 1998,

John Fairey

inspired by the example of the Ruth Bancroft Garden in California, he decided to preserve it through the Peckerwood Garden Conservation Foundation, which he established when his garden was selected as one of the Garden Conservancy's preservation projects.

Among his mentors, John would certainly first name Lynn Lowrey, and, like so many others, he'd add J. C. Raulston. After John sent seed from that first rare *Styrax* for identification, he continued to send J.C. seeds he collected from his later plant-finding expeditions. In one year, J.C. grew and distributed nine thousand plants from seed John and Carl collected in Mexico, and he also accompanied John on two of his Mexican trips, putting him in touch with important people at the University of California at Berkeley and with Ferris Miller, the American who had the outstanding Chollipo Arboretum in Korea, as well as with Bill Funk at Mereweather Arboretum in Australia, which holds its own extensive collection of oaks, including Mexican oaks. They all returned the favor, sending him special seeds and sharing information. Marco Polo Stufano, who headed the committee for the Garden Conservancy that selected exceptional gardens to be sponsored projects, was also an important influence.

Tony Avent, creator of Plant Delights Nursery and Juniper Level Botanic Garden in Raleigh, North Carolina, also traveled to Mexico with John. Tony says, "John has truly been a pioneer in finding and popularizing plants from Mexico. While John certainly wasn't the first American to botanize Mexico, his broad interest in plants other than cacti, the sheer number of trips, and his mail-order nursery outlet allowed a huge array of John's finds to be distributed far and wide – something that many prior collectors failed to do."

John has been widely recognized for his work and contributions to horticulture. His honors include the Liberty Hyde Bailey Award, the highest award from the American Horticultural Society (2015); the Foundation for Landscape Studies Place Maker Award (2016); the Scott Medal from the Scott Arboretum at Swarthmore College for "his national contribution to the science and art of gardening" (2013); the Commercial Award from the American Horticultural Society, shared with Yucca Do (1996); and the National Teacher's Honors Award from the American Institute of Architects.

Peckerwood will carry on "as a garden with a mission to encourage other

gardeners to see beauty in landscape that is consistent with our plants and climate. It is a garden that looks to the future, not to the past."

Beyond its evident beauty, Peckerwood is committed to ongoing research
and education. John's work in plant exploration, conservation, garden design,
and the introduction of new plants to enrich American gardens and the public
landscape will continue, along with his important message about preserving
fragile ecosystems threatened by overgrazing, development, and other pressures. As a teacher, John understands the importance of reaching young people:
"We've got to excite people about gardens when they're young to inspire them
about the preciousness of what they see, and what we could lose if we don't
protect it."

Peckerwood: The dry garden with the blue wall

Selected Bibliography

Tom Armstrong, *A Singular Vision: Architecture, Art, Landscape* (Quantuck Lane Press: 2011)

Tom Armstrong, *An American Odyssey: The Warner Collection of Fine and Decorative Arts* (The Monacelli Press: 2002)

Tony Avent, *So You Want to Start a Nursery* (Timber Press: 2003)

Andrew Bunting, *The Plant Lover's Guide to Magnolias* (Timber Press: 2016)

Francis H. Cabot, *The Greater Perfection: The Story of the Gardens at Les Quatre Vents* (W. W. Norton & Company: 2001)

Thomas C. Cooper (ed.), *The Roots of My Obsession* (Timber Press: 2012)

Daniel J. Hinkley, *The Explorer's Garden: Rare and Unusual Perennials* (Timber Press: 1999)

Daniel J. Hinkley, *The Explorer's Garden: Shrubs and Vines from the Four Corners of the World* (Timber Press: 2009)

Daniel J. Hinkley, *Winter Ornamentals* (Sasquatch Press: 1993)

Gregory Long, *Historic Houses of the Hudson River Valley 1663–1915* (Rizzoli: 2004)

Lynden B. Miller, *Parks, Plants and People: Beautifying the Urban Landscape* (W. W. Norton & Company: 2009)

Elizabeth Barlow Rogers, *The Forest and the Wetlands of New York City* (Little, Brown: 1971)

Elizabeth Barlow Rogers, *Frederick Law Olmsted's New York* (Praeger/WhitneyMuseum: 1972)

Elizabeth Barlow Rogers, *The Central Park Book* (Central Park Task Force: 1978)

Elizabeth Barlow Rogers, *Rebuilding Central Park: A Management and Restoration Plan* (MIT Press: 1987)

Elizabeth Barlow Rogers, *Landscape Design: a Cultural and Architectural History* (Harry N. Abrams, Inc.: 2001)

Elizabeth Barlow Rogers, *Romantic Gardens: Nature, Art and Landscape Design* (David R. Godine: 2010)

Elizabeth Barlow Rogers, *Writing the Garden: A Literary Conversation Across Two Centuries* (David. R. Godine: 2011)

Elizabeth Barlow Rogers, *Green Metropolis: The Extraordinary Landscapes of New York City as Nature, History, and Design* (Alfred A. Knopf: 2016)

Elizabeth Scholtz (Preface) & Rae Spencer Jones (ed.), *1001 Gardens You Must See Before You Die* (Barron's Educational Series: 2007)

Acknowledgments

THIS BOOK IS entirely thanks to the eighteen people featured in it – they have each given me endless hours of their time with grace and generosity. Although Frank Cabot and Tom Armstrong are no longer living, their stories reflect my many happy hours in their good company as well as told by their own writings. Frank and Tom's families and the Garden Conservancy team stepped in to help me with their chapters. All the others in this book endured my countless follow up questions, kindly read early drafts and offered important comments and corrections. And all have responded to my requests for photographs. Beyond their help on this book, they have been treasured friends and role models for many years. I look forward to following the next chapters in their stories.

Once again, I am grateful to Olga Tarnowski Seham who edited my early drafts with her usual skill and tact. Along the way, she kept me going with her enthusiasm and encouragement. Kathleen Fridelia agreed to copyedit the manuscript but did so much more. In addition to relentlessly tracking down and correcting names, facts, dates, punctuation and grammar, she added valuable stylistic and editorial suggestions.

David Godine accepted the book for publication without having seen anything other than my very brief description. As was true for my first book, he undertakes to edit any book he agrees to publish, and once again he has improved the writing. His team at David R. Godine Publisher, provided the necessary support. Many thanks to Chelsea Bingham, who maintained her sense of humor despite my constant pressure to move this along, and to Heather Tamarkin who helped me understand what I had to do to collect and prepare everything to be print ready. Carl W. Scarbrough, once part of the Godine team but now working independently, provided his usual impressive creativity in designing the book and its beautiful cover.

For her wise counsel and ongoing help over too many years to count,

I have been sustained by my dear friend, the renowned editor, Kate Medina. Not only did Kate connect me to great talent, such as Olga Seham and Kathleen Fridelia, she has provided ongoing insights into the very nature of producing a book and the world of publishing while cheering me on. With her own leadership at Random House, and her willingness to unfailingly respond to my many cries of despair along the way, she has been invaluable beyond words.

My husband Charlie has constantly nudged me throughout. Having produced his own outstanding online documentary, *The Naval War of 1812*, as well as the book version, and more recently his book *Lake Waramaug Observed*, featuring his 39 paintings of the Lake along with its history and geology, he understands the power of persistence. He is not only my live-in conscience, he is and has been the love of my life.

Index

A NOTE ON THE TYPE

Heroes of Horticulture has been set in Scala, a family of types originally designed in the 1990s by Martin Majoor. A distinctly contemporary face, Scala roman marries the proportions of old-style types to the monoline strokes of geometric sans-serifs and the slab serifs of so-called Egyptian faces. The harmony between roman and italic reveals the designer's attention to detail. Although its ancestry can be traced to no single family of types, Scala succeeds in a wide range of uses by virtue of its clean drawing, its vertical emphasis, and its personable, somewhat casual letterforms. ⚔ The display type is Rudolf Koch's Eva Antiqua, and the initials have been redrawn from an ornamental alphabet created by Maria Ballé for the Bauersche Gießerei.

DESIGN & COMPOSITION BY CARL W. SCARBROUGH